A Short Guide to Writing
about Science

THE SHORT GUIDE SERIES
Under the Editorship of
Sylvan Barnet
Marcia Stubbs

A Short Guide to Writing about Literature by Sylvan Barnet

A Short Guide to Writing about Art by Sylvan Barnet

A Short Guide to Writing about Biology by Jan A. Pechenik

A Short Guide to Writing about Social Science by Lee J. Cuba

A Short Guide to Writing about Film by Timothy Corrigan

A Short Guide to Writing about History by Richard Marius

A Short Guide to Writing about Science by David Porush

A Short Guide to Writing about Science

DAVID PORUSH
Rensselaer Polytechnic Institute

HarperCollins*CollegePublishers*

Senior Editor: Patricia Rossi
Project Coordination: Ruttle, Shaw & Wetherill, Inc.
Design Manager/Cover Designer: Wendy Ann Fredericks
Cover Photo: C. J. Pickerell/FPG International
Text Designer: Alice Fernandes Brown
Electronic Production Manager: Valerie A. Sawyer
Desktop Administrator: Hilda Koparanian
Manufacturing Manager: Helene G. Landers
Electronic Page Makeup: RR Donnelley Barbados
Printer and Binder: RR Donnelley and Sons Company
Cover Printer: RR Donnelley and Sons Company

A Short Guide to Writing about Science

Library of Congress Cataloging-in-Publication Data

Porush, David
    A short guide to writing about science / David Porush.
      p. cm.—(The Short guide series)
    Includes bibliographical references and index.
    ISBN 0-06-500754-9
    1. Technical writing. 2. Communication in science. I. Title.
T11.P67 1995
808´.0666—dc20   94-3119
                                             CIP

95 96 97   9 8 7 6 5 4 3

To the memory of my father,
Abraham

Brief Contents

DETAILED CONTENTS   ix

CHECKLISTS   xix

PREFACE   xxi

1—INTRODUCTION: SCIENCE WRITING
    AND THE IMAGINATION   1

2—WHY GOOD SCIENTIFIC THINKING
    CAN LEAD TO BAD SCIENCE WRITING   10

3—WRITING FROM THE MOMENT OF OBSERVATION:
    LAB AND FIELD NOTEBOOKS   21

4—FROM LAB NOTEBOOK TO LAB REPORT   48

5—PREPARING TO WRITE THE RESEARCH PAPER   63

6—HOW TO WRITE TITLES   71

7—HOW TO WRITE ABSTRACTS   75

8—HOW TO WRITE THE INTRODUCTORY SECTION   85

9—HOW TO WRITE ABOUT HYPOTHESES, MODELS,
    AND THEORIES (HMT)   98

10—HOW TO CITE AND LIST REFERENCES   112

11—HOW TO WRITE THE MATERIALS AND METHODS
    SECTION   121

12—HOW TO PRESENT RESULTS   131

13—HOW TO COMPOSE AND USE VISUAL MATERIAL   136

14—HOW TO WRITE ABOUT YOUR INTERPRETATION
       OF RESULTS   150

15—HOW TO WRITE CONCLUSIONS   164

16—HOW TO WRITE ABOUT SCIENCE IN ESSAYS
       AND TERM PAPERS OR REPORTS   174

17—REVISING AND EDITING   200

18—A SCIENTIFIC APPROACH TO STYLE   209

19—HOW AND WHEN TO DEFINE YOUR TERMS   228

20—HOW TO USE NUMBERS, SYMBOLS, UNITS,
       FORMULAS, AND EQUATIONS   235

21—CONCLUSION: ONE WORLD—
       SCIENCE AND WRITING   240

APPENDIX A: AVOIDING SEXIST LANGUAGE   250

APPENDIX B: STYLE GUIDES, ARTICLES, MANUALS,
       AND BOOKS ON WRITING ABOUT SCIENCE   256

APPENDIX C: SCIENCE AND ENGINEERING
       DICTIONARIES AND ENCYCLOPEDIAS   259

ENDNOTES   263

INDEX   269

Detailed Contents

CHECKLISTS   xix

PREFACE   xxi

**1 — INTRODUCTION: SCIENCE WRITING
AND THE IMAGINATION**   1

   Science Is Communication   1

   Writing as a Creative Opportunity in Science   3

   Finding Your Real Audience   5

      Define the Goals of Your Writing   6

      Imagine Your Audience's Needs   6

      Practice for Real-World Writing   8

**2 — WHY GOOD SCIENTIFIC THINKING
CAN LEAD TO BAD SCIENCE WRITING**   10

   Why Science Writing Tends to Be So Complex   11

   **Why Science Writing Contains So Much
Passive Voice**   12

   Why Scientists Are Wary of Descriptiveness   13

   **Why Science Writing Is Plagued by Overly
Conditional Language**   14

   Why the Style of Scientific Prose Is Conservative   18

   A Simple Cure   19

3 — WRITING FROM THE MOMENT OF OBSERVATION:
LAB AND FIELD NOTEBOOKS   21

Writing Begins in the Lab and the Field   21

What Is a Lab Notebook For?   23

What Must Go in the Lab Notebook?   24

Prepare the Notebook   25

Introduce the Experiment   27

Describe the Materials Completely   27

Describe the Assembly of Your Apparatus   29

   Sample Setup Description   31

Describe the Method or Procedure of Your
Experiment   32

Prepare Data Sheets   33

Follow Guidelines for Recording Data   34

Should You Substitute the Computer for a Handwritten
Lab Notebook?   35

Analyze the Data Briefly   37

Draw Basic Tables and Graphs   39

Interpret the Data Briefly   43

Define and Calculate the Precision, Error, or Standard
Deviation in Your Observations   46

Draw Conclusions Briefly   47

Some Final Words about the Lab Notebook   47

4 — FROM LAB NOTEBOOK TO LAB REPORT   48

Lab Notebook Versus Lab Report   49

   Letter of Transmittal   50

   Title/Cover Page   51

Abstract or Summary 54

Table of Contents 54

Introduction 55

Hypothesis or Expected Outcome 56

Literature Review 57

Methods Section 57

Interpretations of Data/Conclusions 57

Sketches of Apparatus and Other Illustrations 58

Conclusion 58

Bibliography or Literature Cited 59

Nomenclature/Glossary 60

Appendices 61

Final Words about the Lab Report 62

5—PREPARING TO WRITE THE RESEARCH PAPER 63

Preparing to Write 65

From Lab Report to Research Article 65

6—HOW TO WRITE TITLES 71

7—HOW TO WRITE ABSTRACTS 75

What Is an Abstract? 75

When Do You Write an Abstract? 75

Where Does an Abstract Appear? 76

Why Do Readers Need Abstracts? 76

Rules of Thumb for Writing the Abstract 77

What You Can Leave Out 79

Types of Abstracts 79

Informative Abstracts 79

Indicative Abstracts 81

Descriptive Abstracts (Executive Summary) 83

Some Final Words about Abstracts 84

8 — HOW TO WRITE THE INTRODUCTORY SECTION 85

Taking Too Broad an Approach 85

Taking Too Narrow an Approach 86

Finding the Middle Ground 87

Finding the Proper "Pitch" 87

A Digression on the Question of Where Problems Come From 90

Define the Problem Using "Prewriting" Exercises 91

What Am I Trying to Discover or Prove? 92

Which Kind of Problem Am I Working On? 92

Relate the Problem to Theory 93

Why Is This Problem New or Distinctive? 95

9 — HOW TO WRITE ABOUT HYPOTHESES, MODELS, AND THEORIES (HMT) 98

Theories 99

Models 100

Hypotheses 101

Formulate the Hypothesis with the Help of Prewriting 101

How to Evaluate and Compare Different Hypotheses, Models, or Theories 104

Discussions of HMT Require Especially Careful Wording 105

Where to Put Your Discussion of Hypotheses, Theories, and Models 109

10—HOW TO CITE AND LIST REFERENCES   112

    Why Cite the Literature?   112

    Where to Cite the Literature   113

    How to Cite a Reference from the Text   113

    How to List References: The Bibliography   115

    Final Words about Citations   120

11—HOW TO WRITE THE MATERIALS AND METHODS SECTION   121

    Parts of the M & M   121

    What Is Method?   122

    Points to Consider in the M&M   123

12—HOW TO PRESENT RESULTS   131

    Final Words   135

13—HOW TO COMPOSE AND USE VISUAL MATERIAL   136

    Visual Presentations Should Simplify Information   139

    Tables   142

    General Guidelines for Using Figures   144

        Graphs   144

        Charts/Computer Flowcharts   145

        Illustrations, Schematic Diagrams, and Line Drawings   147

    Final Words About Pictures   148

14—HOW TO WRITE ABOUT YOUR INTERPRETATION OF RESULTS   150

    Make a Convincing Case   151

        Order Your Presentation of the Data Logically   152

Logical Language   156

Biased Language   157

How to Coordinate Your Presentation of Data   158

15—HOW TO WRITE CONCLUSIONS   164

State Your Conclusions   164

Restrict or Expand Your Results   165

Compare Your Conclusions with Those of Others in the Field   167

Define Unanswered Questions   169

Don't Be Afraid to Express Uncertainties   169

Recommend Directions for Future Research   170

Express a Broader Vision   171

Final Words about the Research Report and Article   172

16—HOW TO WRITE ABOUT SCIENCE IN ESSAYS AND TERM PAPERS OR REPORTS   174

Formal Scientific Reports Versus Term Papers and Essays on Science   175

Steps In Writing the Essay, Report, or Term Paper   178

Choose a Topic   178

Begin Researching the Topic   178

Narrow Your Topic and Refine Your Thesis   179

Adopt an "Angle" or Point of View 179

Write the Paper   180

Kinds of Science Essays   180

Leads or Introductory Sentences   181

Exits or Closings   186

Themes and Topics for Science Essays and Term Papers   189

The Style of Science Essays   194

Establish a Point of View   195

Use Analogies   196

Use Metaphors, But Exercise Caution   197

Some Cautionary Words about Telling Science as a Story   198

17—REVISING AND EDITING   200

The Real Writing Is in the Rewriting   200

An Exercise in Editing   201

Editing Means More than Fixing Errors   204

Six Steps to Deep Editing   206

18—A SCIENTIFIC APPROACH TO STYLE   209

How Do Sentences Work?   210

Avoid Orphaned Verbs   211

Links, Contexts, and/or the Subject of a Sentence Should Come First   213

Use Transitional Words to Help the Flow of Ideas   213

New and/or Important Information Should Be Placed in the Last Part of the Sentence   215

Using Forms of the Verb "to be" Makes Weak Links   216

Use Active Voice and Avoid Passive Voice   216

Use Verbs; Avoid Nominalization and Noun Strings   222

Getting Cheap With Words Is Inefficient   223

Don't Bury Important Points in Subordinate Clauses or Sub-Subordinate Clauses   225

Final Words about Scientific Style   227

19—HOW AND WHEN TO DEFINE YOUR TERMS   228

How to Define Terms   229

A Note on Jargon   233

*The Perils of Assuming Your Audience
Is "In the Know"   234*

**20—HOW TO USE NUMBERS, SYMBOLS, UNITS,
FORMULAS, AND EQUATIONS   235**

Numbers   235

Measures and Dimensions   237

Numbering Lists and Items   238

Equations and Formulas   238

Final Words about Mathematics and Science
Writing   239

**21—CONCLUSION: ONE WORLD—
SCIENCE AND WRITING   240**

Science Is Not Only a Rational Activity   241

Science Always Involves a Point Of View   242

There Is No Science Without Someone Telling
Its Story   244

The History and Future of Science Writing   246

Science Tells Many Different Stories   247

The Scientist Coauthors the Script of Science   249

APPENDIX A: AVOIDING SEXIST LANGUAGE   250

Less Desirable Solutions to Sexist Language   253

**APPENDIX B: STYLE GUIDES, ARTICLES, MANUALS,
AND BOOKS ON WRITING ABOUT SCIENCE   256**

Disciplinary Style Guides   256

American National Standards Institute Publications   256

General Style Guides   257

Research about Science Writing   258

APPENDIX C: SCIENCE AND ENGINEERING
  DICTIONARIES AND ENCYCLOPEDIAS   259

ENDNOTES   263

INDEX   269

Checklists

1—PARTS OF A LAB NOTEBOOK   25

2—STYLE FOR THE NOTEBOOK   26

3—GUIDELINES FOR RECORDING DATA   35

4—USING THE COMPUTER AS A LAB NOTEBOOK   38

5—STEPS IN INTERPRETING DATA   45

6—PARTS OF THE LAB REPORT DEVELOPED
   FROM THE LAB NOTEBOOK   49

7—PARTS OF THE LAB REPORT NOT FOUND
   IN THE LAB NOTEBOOK   50

8—QUESTIONS TO ASK YOURSELP BEFORE WRITING
   THE ARTICLE   66

9—PARTS OF THE RESEARCH PAPER   67

10—PREPARING TO WRITE THE ABSTRACT   77

11—RULES OF THUMB FOR WRITING ABSTRACTS   78

12—WRITING THE INTRODUCTION   97

13—WHAT TO INCLUDE IN THE HMT DISCUSSION AND
   WHERE TO PUT IT   111

14—THE METHODS AND MATERIALS DESCRIPTION   129

15—PRESENTING RESULTS   134

16—PROTOCOLS FOR ALL VISUALS   137

17—A QUESTIONNAIRE FOR VISUAL PRESENTATIONS
     141

18—COMPARISONS OF TYPES OF VISUAL
     PRESENTATIONS   141

19—COMPOSING TABLES   142

20—COMPOSING FIGURES   144

21—DISCUSSION/INTERPRETATION OF RESULTS   163

22—WRITING THE CONCLUSION   172

23—GENERAL GUIDELINES FOR WRITING ESSAYS
     ABOUT SCIENCE   199

24—SIMPLE GUIDELINES FOR STRUCTURING
     SENTENCES   211

Preface

"Every great advance in science has issued from a new audacity of imagination."

—*John Dewey*, Democracy in Education (1903)

Science has always been an encouragement to dream and imagine. Physics promises to decipher the fundamental laws governing the waltz of energy, matter, and space-time. Biology beckons us with the promise of uncovering the secrets of life. Astronomy takes our imagination across the galaxy, hunting for new species in the bestiary of the sky and giving us a glimpse of the origins of time. Geology, chemistry, computer science, fluid dynamics, mathematics, meteorology, materials science, ecoscience, and all the other science and engineering disciplines tantalize us with the promise of discovering the new or telling a fascinating story about an old corner of the universe.

Just what was it that first captured your imagination? What made you embark on a career of science? During your education, your own answer to these questions may be forgotten in the maze of details—in memorizing terms and formulas, in wrestling with lab equipment and experimental machinery, in using difficult computer software, in taking tests, in learning new concepts, and perhaps in writing an occasional research paper within very strict guidelines mandated by your instructor. As you become a practicing scientist, the higher ideals of science may become obscured by the even more complex details of practicing your profession, finding support for your research program, and fulfilling your responsibilities to colleagues, research assistants, and students.

I have written this text in the belief that writing can be the means for you to continually reinvigorate your career as a scientist. In all aspects of science, writing plays an essential role. You will write to report your research. You will write to communicate with colleagues at other institutions. You will write to request financial support for your work. You will write to colleagues, managers, and subordinates in your own institutional setting. You will write instructions and memos, and keep lab notebooks. You might even write to explore your own ideas, theories, and speculations. In each of these writing tasks, you have an opportunity to connect your imagination with your work, because each time you write about your work, you must refine and redefine what is most important. Essentially, writing is not only communication, it is a form of self-interrogation. How can I convince my audience of the importance of my work? By defining and refining that importance for myself. This is a constant throughout the career of a scientist, from his or her earliest days as a student in a lab course through the time he or she is sending articles out for publication on a regular basis. That's why this book is designed for scientists who write at all levels.

Unfortunately, for many students writing becomes a distasteful and difficult part of fulfilling degree requirements. Many of my students in the sciences and engineering even seek to minimize the amount of writing they do by avoiding courses which require lots of it. In many cases, they just don't like to write. I have often conjectured that this is because no one has explained to them the intimate connection between success as a scientist and success as a writer. Yet, as Sir Francis Darwin said, "In science the credit goes to the man who convinces the world, not to the man to whom the idea first occurs." And for the scientist, the best way to convince the world has always been through the written word.

I hope this book not only shows you *how* to write but also *why* you should make writing one of the most important parts of your career as a student and scientist. This book is founded on the idea that writing presents opportunities, not obstacles. Writing presents an opportunity to reconnect your work in science with your imagination. Writing gives you a chance—one that is often missed—to find a new perspective on your work, to become more precise about and to understand the importance of what you are doing by writing it to others. Writing is both communicative and creative, expressive and exploratory.

A Short Guide to Writing about Science should help you learn not only how to write about science, but how to express your ideas in the clearest and most vigorous way so that they will yield the largest benefit both for your work and for science itself. The sooner you learn how to write as a scientist, and the better you do it, the more fully you will be able to share your discoveries and knowledge with the larger community of scientists and with the culture in general.

My goal throughout has been to try to show you how the writing you do is directly connected to the professional practices of a scientist and the nature of science itself. Rather than encouraging the sort of "make believe" quality of many writing assignments, I have shown how the actual forms, styles, and elements of good science writing flow directly from and are integrated with the way science really operates in the world. As a result, I have explained these important practices: how scientists use titles and abstracts to research new problems; how scientists set new problems; what the relationship is between the scientist-author and the audience he or she is trying to reach; how journal editors decide to publish a paper; what goes on in the lab that makes a lab notebook so important; how lab notes grow into research articles; and finally, why certain habits of mind that make good scientists can make poor authors and how to correct those habits.

If you are a student, throughout this book I encourage you to imagine that the writing you are doing for the artificial circumstances of a course is practice for the writing you will eventually do when you become a professional. I show you mental exercises that will help you accomplish this. Even if you are a student in a writing course with no intention of being a scientist, you should find the advice about how writing works in science and how to write the general essay about science (Chapter 16) useful; in many instances this advice can be generalized to other disciplines.

If you are already a practicing scientist, then you will probably find the first few chapters a bit elementary, and you certainly don't need me to lecture on the importance of writing. You are immersed in a profession that depends on writing and reading for its life's blood. However, I believe much of the advice in the later chapters, from Chapter 6 on, will be useful to you, and you will be able to put that advice here into practice in your next research article.

About the Mechanics of This Book

This *Short Guide* is intended to be used as a stand-alone guide or text for students in the sciences, students who write about science in non-science courses, and for practicing scientists. It does grow in sophistication as the chapters progress. However, it can also be used as a handbook or reference guide to refresh your memory on points of style and usage. Much of the material is incorporated in the form of checklists that you can use to remember important points [indicated with a box, (□)] about specific aspects of science writing.

The book also contains numerous reference sections, including chapters and appendices on how to use numbers, formulas, symbols, abbreviations, and units. Information on where to find additional sources as included at the back of this book.

Excerpts of actual science writing are set in typewriter font. For example,

```
In early December, if all goes according to
schedule, two airlock doors will close, and the
new world will be locked up tight inside a
giant greenhouse as long as two football
fields. For better or worse, 3,800 species of
plants and animals—as well as eight repre-
sentatives of Homo sapiens—will be shut in
together on 2.5 lush acres, to share and swap
the same air, water, and nutrients for two
years.¹
```

Many of these are excerpts from actual journal papers, essays, and magazine articles. In some cases, I have altered them to make them more readable or to demonstrate a point. My apologies to the authors. In all instances, the originals are noted with a superscript number corresponding to the list of references at the end of this book.

I have used a warning mark (**X:**) before each example that illustrates a poor practice.

Although this book makes most sense if it is read front to back, it can also be used as a guidebook or reference. For this purpose, there is a complete index at the back of this book that will help you locate specific items.

Acknowledgments

I would like to thank the many people who helped me evolve my own thinking about writing and who gave specific advice about ways to improve this book. Many of my colleagues at Rensselaer Polytechnic Institute gave me advice and encouragement. Dr. David Carson in the

Department of Language, Literature & Communication initiated me into the rigors and pleasures of teaching writing in nonliterary ways. Much of the wisdom about writing in the real world is due to him. Dr. Karen LeFevre helped me refine my notion of what a writing textbook should do and also gave me access to the resources of the Writing Center at Rensselaer, which she directs. Dr. Steven Cramer in the Department of Chemical Engineering shared his view of writing about science, and his enthusiasm. Dr. Tom "Doc" Shannon in the Department of Physics provided actual examples of course writing and laboratory assignments. Linda Blackwell was my extraordinarily patient and able research assistant; she also gave me good advice about the style of my own writing. Polly Pettingell, research librarian at Rensselaer Polytechnic Institute, rose to the challenge of my most arcane requests.

I also want to thank the editors and former editors at HarperCollins, Anne Smith and Constance A. Rajala, who initiated this project and helped guide me through it, even when I felt the challenges were formidable. Jennifer Lonoff, formerly of HarperCollins, in particular, was very patient with me and the manuscript when it was still in its most woeful state. She also assembled a team of reviewers whose collective care, rigorous criticisms, and collegiality evolved this book into something presentable. My thanks to Frank Andrews, University of California–Santa Cruz; Philippa J. Benson, Carnegie Mellon University; W. Murray Black, George Mason University, Va.; Rebecca E. Burnett, Iowa State University; John de Cuevas, Lesley College, Mass.; Carol Freeman, University of California – Santa Cruz; Lucille B. Garmon, West Georgia College; Jared Haynes, University of California – Davis; John J. Ruszkiewicz, University of Texas – Austin; Charles Schuster, University of Wisconsin – Milwaukee; Christopher Thaiss, George Mason University, Va.; and Lili Fox Velez, Carnegie Mellon University. I am very grateful to them for their unblinking honesty. I am indebted to Patricia Rossi, who always kept her humor about my deadlines and her faith in this project long after others would have despaired.

Finally, I would like to thank my wife, Sally, and my children, Valerie, Dana, and Ben, who tolerated my absenteeism, even when I was in the next room with my computer.

DAVID PORUSH

1

Introduction

Science Writing and the Imagination

"[We] love to wonder and that is the seed of science."

—*Ralph Waldo Emerson,* Society and Solitude *(1870)*

SCIENCE *IS* COMMUNICATION

You are probably reading this book because you are facing some assignments in a course in science or writing, or because you want to improve your writing practices. Perhaps you are tackling one of your first research papers, lab reports, or essays about science and you need some guidance. This book is written to help you.

Your writing assignments are practice for one of the most important aspects of your future career: communicating and explaining your work to others, especially if you are planning to be a scientist. It may at first be difficult to see the importance or understand the necessity of writing about science. But science writing communicates what you know to a specific audience. By publishing a discovery, an insight, a new theory, or results of an experiment, you will have contributed to science and advanced your career. The dissemination of scientific ideas is crucial and inseparable from science itself. What good is an incredible breakthrough or discovery if nobody hears about it outside your lab? How will your colleagues interpret your data unless they read about them? How will new theories get tested, proven, or disproved unless they are first broadcast in rigorous, formal, and convincing terms in a proper journal?

Furthermore, it is difficult to get ahead in science without writing. Writing is a visible token of your continuing activity as a professional. It gains prestige for you and your work. It helps you correspond with colleagues in the field, and helps you obtain the funding, resources, equipment, and superior colleagues, research assistants, and collaborators necessary to implement a successful research program and to further your broader vision of important research. Every application for research funding, no matter to what agency, involves a detailed written description of your proposed research project. This is not simply a bland presentation of neutral facts, but an attempt to persuade. Without the crucial ability to write clearly and forcefully, you will find the process of getting support for your work more difficult.

Science could not survive as anything but an interested attitude toward the universe if nobody wrote about their discoveries. Even in the most pragmatic terms, scientists know they cannot survive in the marketplace—of ideas, of careers, of financial support for their projects—without getting their story out. It establishes their "bragging rights" to being the first to arrive at new facts, conclusions, or theories; publishing new findings also advertises their work. Pride of accomplishment underlies even the most sober scientific report.

If you look at the careers of famous scientists who changed the way we saw the world—Galileo, Newton, Darwin, Freud, Watson, Einstein—one trend is clear: most of them had a knack not only for seeing over the edge of the horizon but also for telling others what they saw. They all wrote eloquently. They knew how to tell the story and explain the *meaning* of their discoveries. Sometimes scientists have help: In the nineteenth century, T. H. Huxley made a career out of "bulldogging" for the stage-frightened and often sickly Sir Charles Darwin. Huxley debated all comers on the broad points of Darwin's theory of evolution and its implications for religion.

Even today, it is hard to imagine that the new science of chaos, for instance, would be as successful were it not for the popularization it received in the press. James Gleick's nontechnical book *Chaos* has had as much to do with the success of the science as any journal publication. Many important scientific breakthroughs are reported in newspapers and popular science magazines. These reports publicize important new work not only to the general public, but to other professional scientists, thereby cross-pollinating science itself.

A recent study conducted by David R. Phillips of the University of California at San Diego examined articles in the *New England Journal of Medicine* that were later reported in *The New York Times*. He discovered that these articles received 73 percent more citations in subsequent medical reports than their counterparts that were *not* mentioned in *The New York Times*. It is obvious that even popularizations of science are part of science, that scientists read newspapers and magazines and watch television just like everyone else—maybe even more so. Scientists are part of this culture that popularizes science, and they cannot help but be influenced by it.

Unfortunately, many of your science courses will probably not spend enough time teaching you how to *express* science. Nor will they teach you how to use writing as a tool of science. Yet learning how to write about science in a disciplined way is as important as learning how to understand theories, formulate hypotheses, perform experiments, and analyze data in a disciplined way. Learning to write persuasively, with fervor, vigor, imagination, and precision, is one of the keys to success in your practice of science.

WRITING AS A CREATIVE OPPORTUNITY IN SCIENCE

Short of taking a writing course especially tailored to the sciences, if you are lucky enough to find one at your college or university, how will you acquire the real skills needed to write about science? Most of you will write under extreme pressure, tackling an assignment too late and rushing to hand it in on time. No wonder so many science and engineering students feel that the act of writing is the worst part of their academic lives.

There is no doubt that writing can be hard work, hard work that may at first seem to be disconnected from the glamorous and interesting part of science itself. So your first job is to reconnect your writing to your vision of science. To do this, there are four ideas you can rehearse.

First, try to view every communication as a means of making your scientific work more successful rather than as an obstacle or as something irrelevant to the primary work you do.

Second, think of your writing, even when it is most technical, as an act of self-expression. Take personal pride in your writing as an extension of your work and your ideas.

Third, think of writing as intrinsically *creative*. This is an aspect of writing which is often underemphasized or even totally ignored in most discussions of writing about science because the emphasis on science writing is accuracy, and the word *creativity* is too uncomfortably close to the notion of *making something up*. Yet, sometimes the very act of composing your thoughts in an orderly fashion forces you to think about your subject in a new way. You can use writing to create and explore. This is no less true for the student producing a lab report for a course assignment than it is for the senior scientist describing the shape of her new theory for a professional journal.

Finally, think of the advantages you will have as a scientist-writer writing about your own research:

- As a student in the sciences, and even later as a professional scientist, when it comes time for you to write about your work, you already know your work intimately.

- You won't have to agonize much over how to present your work since research articles follow a fairly regular format.

- You won't have to worry about where to publish your work, since the journals that mark your discipline are well-defined.

- For the most part, you don't even need to agonize over matters such as format, style, use of technical terms, length, tone, and so on. The profession, your discipline, has already made these decisions for you.

You may not be thoroughly familiar with all these rules. This book will help you become familiar with the existing conventions as they have been gleaned from the advice of professional journal editors, from scientists, and from actual practices found in the journals.

The need to produce a formal report or a summary of a proposed research project for a grant application is part of the familiar routine of any successful scientist. While these occasions may seem burdensome, involving deadlines and following the strict rules of a granting agency or a journal's conventions, they are also invitations to reevaluate your work, to put things in context, to reconsider the imaginative resources of your research project and its connection to larger theories and the work of others. Writing represents an invitation to imagine, to place ideas and data in context, to see the larger picture. In return, writing that reflects imagination, contexts, and connections tends to be better, more communicative, more inviting, and more stimulating for the reader, and thus more successful as science.

FINDING YOUR REAL AUDIENCE

Have you already had an opportunity to define important scientific questions *you* wanted to answer and devised the experimental means for getting that answer? In other words, have you been able to set the goals of your own research? If so, then you probably have also struggled with questions about how to reach a wider professional audience by publishing the results of your work.

However, as a student you are usually writing papers as a command performance for an audience of one: your instructor. Sometimes, your audience may expand to include your fellow students in a lab or group project or in a class where you have been asked to give a presentation. Yet, in your professional careers, you will be communicating to a much wider and more complex audience. Writing for that single professor under the artificial circumstances of a course assignment, and with the added burden of a grade, hardly seems anything like the communication situations you will eventually face. Even the way your instructor will judge your writing is likely to be different than the way a professional audience will, simply by virtue of the fact that your instructor must grade it.

Many students never even realize how *unnatural* such writing can be. There you are, supposedly in training to be a professional scientist, and you are practicing writing skills in the wrong way, learning to write procedurally, as if you were filling out a long bureaucratic form. It is no wonder students complain about their "plug-and-chug," fill-in-the-blanks sort of lab reports. These assignments can make you feel like you are filling out long bureaucratic forms rather than expressing your intellectual accomplishment or recording the fruits of your original labor. It is as if you are being trained to dance by following painted footsteps on a floor, instead of by listening to the music and moving in rhythm with a partner.

How, then, do you get practice for the real writing you will do as a professional scientist? How are you to figure out who your real audience will be and what their expectations are? The place where students learn the skill of defining an audience is normally in composition courses. However, though writing and composition courses are virtually a universal part of education today, very rarely do these general composition courses address the special aspects of writing a scientific article, essay, or lab report. And few science textbooks address the role of writing when they explain the concepts and formulas that define the science.

In order to make course writing practice for a real communication situation, you have to do three things: (1) Define the reasons you are writing; (2) define your audience; and (3) define which parts of your writing assignment give you practice for real-world writing.

Define the Goals of Your Writing

First, even as your grade in a course looms large as both motivation and terms of judgment, you have to look beyond the grade and think of other motivations for your writing besides merely satisfying the course requirements. What is your goal?

To explain a new concept?

To demonstrate the efficiency of a method that you executed?

To lay out in a clear and logical way the data you measured or captured with an experiment?

To describe the existing research or thinking about a problem?

These are just a few of the possible writing tasks in science. But in any case, you should define what it is you are trying to accomplish besides getting a good grade. Have your purpose clearly in mind when you begin to write. I would suggest that you answer the question in a single sentence and write it out at the head of your paper or in your folder, or tack it up over your desk or near your computer screen. If you remember your goal, chances are the whole paper will be more coherent.

Imagine Your Audience's Needs

Without a consideration of your audience, your writing runs the risk of seeming overly procedural or mechanical. Many poorly written research reports seem like lists of data rather than explanations of relationships among meaningful pieces of information. And even professional journals publish reports that seem like they've been written in a vacuum, or sound like reports written by computers for computers. The exercise below will give you a strategy for adapting words to your human audience in ways that make your communications successful.

Your challenge as a student is to pretend that your professor, who is obviously the real—and often the *only*—audience for your work, is *not* the only audience. You have to imagine another audience, one made up of scientific colleagues. However, if you imagine your audience as smarter than you or very critical of your work, then it is likely you will contort your writing into unnatural postures. It is best to begin by imagining that your audience consists of people very much like you. Like you, they are curious and are reading in order to find out the answers to specific questions. Like you, they are interested, but maybe a little impatient. The only major difference between you and your audience is that they do not know specifically what you know, and they are hearing it (reading it) *for the first time* in your report. What would *you* like to see in the report under those circumstances? Probably,

- a concise statement of the goal of the paper,

- clear language,

- precise descriptions of procedures,

- good graphs and charts,

- definitions of all the technical terms, and

- a summary of findings.

Perhaps even more importantly, what *wouldn't* you like to see? Probably,

- obscure language and terms,

- long, difficult-to-read sentences,

- consideration of subjects which cloud the issue or take you off the main track, and

- poor contexts for understanding new ideas.

The basic advice you can now give to yourself based on this thought experiment is obvious: write clearly; define your terms; make sure your graphs, tables, and charts are clear; and give contexts for understanding new information. We will discuss ways of doing all these throughout this book.

Practice for Real-World Writing

Finally, you must practice writing reports that will prepare you for the professional writing you will do. In order to do that, you must have a clear idea of what the scientific report will require. When doing other kinds of writing, or even when doing your research or lab work, it is helpful to *anticipate* what the eventual report will require. Generally, the basic outline of the scientific report has changed little in over a century:

I. Front Material

    A. Write an abstract, summarizing the experiment or research in 100–300 words.

    B. Write a title that describes the major intent of your work.

II. Introductory Material

    A. Define the problem, explaining the importance of the problem wherever possible and necessary.

    B. Specify your hypothesis.

    C. Describe what others have said and done in attacking a similar problem (Literature review).

III. Body

    A. Describe the methods and materials you used in the lab set-up (experimental apparatus) and for data collection.

    B. Describe the data you collected.

    C. Analyze the data.

    D. Interpret the data.

IV. Conclusions

    A. Draw generalizations from your analysis of the data.

    B. Draw conclusions from your generalizations in a summary section.

V. List of Citations

This looks like a straightforward pattern, a sort of algorithm or program you can generally follow in virtually every formal scientific report. Yet it also tells a story; it has a certain kind of plot:

In general terms, this is what I'm going to tell you about. But before I do, let me tell you what others have said about the same subject. My view is the same as (or is different from) theirs in the following way. . . . Here's how I discovered what I did. Here are the specifics of what I found, and what I think they mean. Here's the basis on which I interpreted the specifics. And here's what I've concluded from these activities.

Each of these sections listed above requires a different strategy, and each relates to different aspects of scientific procedure and thinking. If you have not had a chance in your undergraduate career to write a report that follows a format like this—and you would be in the majority if that is the case—then this book is meant to fill the gap. It will take you step by step through these parts of the scientific report and show how the styles and strategies they require connect to what you actually do in scientific practice.

In the meantime, remember the general advice in this chapter: think of the positive aspects of writing, the opportunities it gives you to create and broadcast your work. Try to envision the needs of your audience. Be clear about the goals of your writing. And anticipate the shape of the report you will eventually write, even before you put pen to paper or finger to keyboard.

2

Why Good Scientific Thinking Can Lead to Bad Science Writing

"It is impossible to dissociate language from science. . . . To call forth a concept, a word is needed."

—*Antoine Lavoisier,* Elementary Treatise on Chemistry *(1789)*

Much of scientific writing is unnecessarily dry, difficult to read, obscure, or ambiguous. Even many scientists themselves think so. F. Peter Woodford, an editor of *Science,* described the situation this way:

> All are agreed that the articles in our journals—even the journals with the highest standards—are, by and large, poorly written. Some of the worst are produced by the kind of author who consciously pretends to a 'scientific scholarly' style. He takes what should be lively, inspiring, and beautiful, and in an attempt to make it seem dignified, chokes it to death with stately abstract nouns; next, in the name of scientific impartiality, he fits it with a complete set of passive constructions to drain away any remaining life's blood or excitement; then he embalms the remains in molasses of polysyllables, wraps the corpse in an impenetrable veil of vogue words, and buries the stiff old mummy with much pomp and circumstance in the most distinguished journal that will take it.[3]

These bad writing habits, and others, are so prevalent that they have become confused for the conventions of proper scientific writing. Younger scientists who want to play it safe often imitate the styles they find already in the journals, although there are no especially good reasons for the persistent use of passive voice, nor for the phobia of writing in the first person. As a result, generation after generation of scientists learn poor writing habits by imitation. However, the relationship between science and language is a little like a good marriage:

it is inevitable, intimate, and enduring, though it sometimes suffers from a failure to communicate.

Besides confusing him for the real author of Shakespeare's plays, many people remember Francis Bacon as one of the fathers of modern science. In his book *The New Organon* (1620) he describes several "idols" or false gods. The idol of the mind, the idol of the marketplace, the idol of the theater, and the idol of the cave were metaphors for tendencies in thinking and culture that lead philosophers (the word "scientist" hadn't been invented yet!) away from the truth.

There are similar idols in writing about science that tend to lead scientists away from good writing. These come from habits of mind in science that carry over into writing about science:

The Idols of Science Writing

X: Complex sentences are more precise and intelligent than simple ones.

X: Passive voice is more objective than active voice because active voice involves stating the agent, who is often a human, and humans introduce subjectivity.

X: Descriptive prose is imprecise and unscientific because descriptions rely on adjectives which are often unquantifiable.

X: Claims about scientific fact must always be cautious; thus, using very cautious language—squirrel language—in scientific prose is always prudent.

X: Be as wary of innovation or taking chances in language as you are in the lab.

X: Revision is unnecessary because language is transparent.

WHY SCIENCE WRITING TENDS TO BE SO COMPLEX

Many students, and even professional scientists, realize at some level that how they are perceived on some "authority scale" might influence how the audience receives their experimental report or theoretical argument. They know they have to sound "expert." However, they haven't really figured out which features of language work to create the sense of authority they seek or how to write that way.

As a result, many writers learn to mimic or parody the style of the experts without really managing the content or distinguishing between the side-effects of the game and the real skills. Like a young baseball player who feels that chewing tobacco is as important as swinging a bat, you might intuitively grasp certain positive features of scientific prose that add complexity to sentences, but then apply it in sentences where complexity is unnecessary. In short, it is easy to confuse pompous phrasings for precision of language, complicated grammatical structures for careful reasoning, and jargon for technical terminologies.

In your defense, the same learned editor who gave such a harsh indictment of science writing at the beginning of this chapter says that if you end up writing this way, it isn't really your fault. Left to your own natural style, the one you brought with you to college as freshmen, he feels you would write pretty well—"with admirable directness and clarity of purpose." Yet, he complains,

> Two years later, these same students' writing is verbose, pompous, full of fashionable circumlocutions . . . The student can no longer write, he pontificates. What has brought about the change? Clearly the students have copied these dreary and pretentious phrases from the scientific literature. They have been dutifully studying it as they are urged to do, and it has warped their style to the point that they can no longer walk to the door without "utilizing a pedestrian relocation," or sip their coffee without "prior elevation of the containing vessel to facilitate imbibation."[3]

Again, it is easy to believe that pretentious writing is important to how your message will be received. Yet the real basis of your authority as a writer is the work you've performed as a scientist; the research you've done in collecting data, analyzing it, interpreting it, and matching it to current theories or knowledge; and how well your writing explains this work to your audience. Gaining your audience's trust depends on your knowledge about language and their expectations. By the same token, you can quickly lose your authority as a scientist by undermining your audience's confidence in you as a writer. This is true whether you are writing for the most specialized journal in your field or for your classmates. So the first victim of scientific writing is often simplicity.

WHY SCIENCE WRITING CONTAINS SO MUCH PASSIVE VOICE

People generally read an article about science with a slightly different standard of judgment from the one they apply to other kinds of communication. In simplest terms, this perception is as follows:

Science is a very human activity, and the science report is primarily an act of reportage. Authors should strive to present their work with pure objectivity and thereby leave their own views out of it.

The author is unquestionably qualified to make the report because he or she witnessed the gathering of data or invented a theory or hypothesis.

How can the science writer meet these expectations? It is true that the core activity of science is the objective application of the scientific method to observations of nature. The scientist isolates a portion of nature—either by looking at it exclusively through a measuring instrument, or by setting up experimental conditions that will permit the observer to measure, study, and compare aspects of that piece or niche of nature. But how do you get from objective activities as a scientist to writing that communicates your objectivity?

Unfortunately, striving to apply these scientific ideals of complete logic or objectivity often leads to poor writing. In general, many science students begin with the right idea: they strive for utter objectivity and impersonality in their writing. But they confuse subjectivity with having a point of view, so they end up controlling their language to avoid describing their own actions or those of any other humans. They eliminate the words *I, we, he, she,* and *they.* When they describe procedures, or discuss speculations or theorizing based on data, they use the passive voice ("The experiment was conducted . . . The titrations were measured . . . The data were analyzed . . ."). Such language often confuses the reader as to who or what is performing an action or where an idea or abstraction came from. So the second victim of scientific prose tends to be *the active first person voice.*

WHY SCIENTISTS ARE WARY OF DESCRIPTIVENESS

In the same vein, many science students believe that the process of writing has to mirror the nature of scientific experimentation itself by being methodical, bland, and repetitive.

We know that a science report is supposed to represent the scientist's most rigorous and precise communication of the facts of a story as he or she knows it. And we know that the scientist gets at the story in one or more controlled, formal ways, following strict rules: via experiments, mathematics, modeling, logic, or formal reasoning. So it is easy to confuse qualitative description with bias. As a result, your tendency may be to shy away from making generalizations that can't be reported mathematically, even when those generalizations are firmly supported by the data. Similarly, you might be tempted to avoid descriptive prose, even when description or the choice of the proper concrete adjective may be important to understanding an observation. Conversely, many students—and professional scientists, too—use too many large words and elaborate constructions where simple ones will do, because they mistakenly believe that larger words are more precise and communicate more information than smaller ones (or because they believe it sounds smarter).

But the application of the scientific method is not the whole story of science. If it were, then science would be a very narrow enterprise indeed. Thankfully, science also requires imagination: wrestling speculations into formal hypotheses, interpreting data, hunting for clues, synthesizing a massive amount of data and a number of varying ideas into a cohesive theory. And thus, writing about science, even within the fairly narrow confines of writing a science report for a course or a journal, requires writing styles that reflect these imaginative activities. It is all too easy to let the third victim of scientific prose be *descriptiveness*.

WHY SCIENCE WRITING IS PLAGUED BY OVERLY CONDITIONAL LANGUAGE

Scientists are as careful about their language as poets are; unfortunately, the results are less pleasing to the ear because the motives are different. The poet strives for music, the scientist for precision and accuracy. The poet seeks to strike the emotions of his readers, the scientist to appeal to reason and defend a position.

Because scientists value precision and are imaginative, many statements they make may seem to deserve extra context-setting or conditionals. In many instances, such conditionals are justified. However, in some instances, the same habits of mind that enable you to be a good scientist can undermine your writing:

- Attention to detail
- Imagination of alternatives
- Care about strict statement of the truth
- Caution about making claims

It is because of this necessary caution that the language of scientific argument and exposition seems so "squirrelly," not just in theory sections but also in the sections concerning the formulations of hypotheses and interpretation of data. *Squirrel language sets in when the author writes cautiously without a good reason.* The result is weak and vague prose.

Such unnecessarily conditional writing may sound like "squirrel language": timid-seeming phrases that accumulate to sound like nervous chittering. Squirrel language is a way to hedge your bets in case some future disaster or new data falsifies a claim.

You can see why squirrel language occurs so frequently in scientific writing. Different abstract points of view, incomplete or contradictory models, or ambiguous data call for language that reflects these ambiguities. But it is easy to go overboard:

```
In order to resolve such issues in superstring
theory it is presumably necessary to understand
the deep principles on which the theory is based.
In a sense the development of superstring theories
is in sharp contrast to the development of general
relativity.⁴
```

The word "presumably" and the phrase "in a sense" are vague and unnecessary. Rather than makes things better, they make them fuzzier. Why is it *presumably* necessary? The phrase "is in sharp contrast to" tries to be bold, but the author undermines its courage with "In a sense. . . ." In what *sense,* precisely, is the development of superstring theories in sharp contrast to the development of general relativity?

If you look closely at squirrel language you'll often see why the language is justified in the author's mind. For instance, this author probably felt that without these phrases he would be saying that it is *absolutely* necessary to understand the deep principles on which the theory is based, and it is *absolutely* true that the development of superstring theory contrasts with that of general relativity. Because he is intelligent, he probably thought of alternatives and counterexamples even as he phrased the sentence. This led him to include the offending phrases "in a sense" and "presumably." Yet it sounds as if the author is being overcautious and hedging his bets because he doesn't explain further.

With a little work, the author could have dispensed with trouble-some conditionals. Why might it *not* be necessary to understand the deep principles? In *what* sense is the development of superstring theories in sharp contrast to the development of general relativity? Had the author answered these questions, he could have made his point. And with a little attention to simple stylistic maneuvers—eliminating forms of the verb "to be," which create weak sentences—he could have made it vigorously:

```
In order to resolve such issues [in superstring
theory] scientists must understand the deep prin-
ciples on which the theory is based because . . .
[explanation]. Since it . . . [explanation], the
development of superstring theories contrasts
sharply with the development of general relativ-
ity.
```

However, in many instances you *want* to hedge your bets. Indeed, scientific procedure and ethics often demand that you stay cautious about claims. Therefore, *none of the following phrases are unacceptable in themselves.* You must decide actively whether a claim deserves more forceful treatment—and so should be stripped of these conditional phrasings:

Under these circumstances

Under certain circumstances

It appears that

From these _____ we can conclude that

. . . to some extent . . .

Based on this, one might expect that

From these we can infer that

Until now it has been assumed that

As might be seen

It is possibly the case that

Although the results of the experiment were unclear, it might be inferred that

It is generally the case that

It has been apparently (seemingly) (possibly) shown that

It might be tempting to suggest that

The results suggest (imply) that

The results cannot be explained simply by referring to

It may be the case that

We are tempted to suggest that

could

would

might

may

We believe that these observations are compatible with the suggestion that

In spite of the foregoing, we tend to agree that

These results are by no means inconsistent with

Despite these

Nonetheless

In some situations

In some cases

In some subjects

From this point of view, the rather modest case treated here is merely representative but not definitive (conclusive).

If you do use conditionals, make sure it is clear why and under what circumstances the conditionals apply. Do not use conditional language unnecessarily.

WHY THE STYLE OF SCIENTIFIC PROSE IS CONSERVATIVE

Even as science asks you to stretch your imaginative wings and appreciate daring new ideas, the day-to-day practice of science teaches you to be intellectually cautious, wary of new results and procedures, leery of making sudden changes.

When this attitude carries over into other realms like the use of language or politics, the result can be unpleasant. Scientific prose tends to be unnecessarily stiff and unnatural. Many science and engineering students handle language as if it were a rattlesnake on the end of a long stick. They fear getting bitten by the unexpected.

At one point in your career someone in authority has probably told you, "If it isn't in the dictionary, don't use it." And it *is* hard to deny that certain new expressions sound barbaric, especially those that arise from bureaucracies. The military bureaucracy seems to be the worst in this regard. I shuddered when I first heard the term "prioritize." A feeling of nausea overtook me when I heard a colleague in a Department of English, of all places, say, "That notion has been problematized."

However, language continually evolves. As Eric Partridge, a very proper English grammarian noted, "Journalists, authors, and the public whim—sometimes, also, the force of great events, the compulsion of irresistible movements—have raised lowly words to a high estate or invested humdrum terms with a picturesque and individual life or brought to the most depressing jargon a . . . general currency. Such words gain a momentum of their own. . . ."[5] The mechanisms for this evolution, like those in biological evolution, are the *mutation* and *adaptation* of words—the spontaneous emergence of new words and the application of old words to new senses: a sort of linguistic natural selection.

Furthermore, the rules about proper expressions themselves change, although some conventions last longer than others and therefore take on the force of law. But the play between proper usage and innovation keeps a language alive and healthy. The greatest resources of new terms are from cultural specialties, the fringes and edges or the most technical and arcane: rock and roll and astrophysics, the fashion world and psychiatry, the ghetto and artificial intelligence, sports and microbiology. When street argot, vernacularisms, slang, jargon, and technical languages stop influencing the mother tongue, a language is doomed, like Latin, which was frozen by the Church and accidents of history.

A short list of words and expressions that have infused the popular idiom from computer science in the last couple of decades make a fascinating list: *input, output, feedback, interface, program, generate, expert system, kludge, knowledge engineering, software, chips,* and so on.

Language is both a resource and a playground. Don't be afraid to build a few sand castles and swing on the bars. Don't be so afraid of getting it right that you spoil the fun of words. Your specialty is very likely to be a source of linguistic innovation. Use new terms freely, but of course always remember your audience and define them carefully.

A SIMPLE CURE

My general advice for curing many of the problems that tend to recur in science writing is really quite simple: *Think of yourself as a reporter, as well as a scientist.*

You can learn something from journalists when you write the formal science report. Scientists and journalists share an absolute commitment to objective gathering and reporting of facts. But the similarity does not end there. What is more obvious, perhaps so obvious that it is sometimes easy to forget, is this:

Having something to say is only half of the communication equation.
Call it EXPRESSION.
Having someone to say it to is the other half.
Call it RECEPTION.

Reception is something journalists can never forget, but scientists often do. Journalists must make their audiences receptive to the message.

Communication = Expression + Reception

Science writing is not as procedural as the scientific method itself. There are other parts to doing science: drawing conclusions, analyzing the data, speculating about hypotheses, synthesizing all you know to arrive at a theory. In all of these, there is a role for *persuasion;* for advocating one view or interpretation over another. There is certainly a need for clarity, for an absolute commitment to being understood by your audience without ambiguity. The writer interested in communication—and this is especially true for the scientist-writer—must make sure the audience receives the message.

There is one other important aspect of journalism that might seem strange to the science writer, but whose value will emerge: the journalist writes a narrative—a coherent story that has a definite message, a flow, and even a certain dramatic element. Even in the most straightforward science report there is a coherent narrative, often one with quite a bit of drama. The heroes of this drama are not people: they are ideas and information and procedures for investigating phenomena, but they are no less dramatic for all that. David Spangler and William Irwin Thompson, in their book about science, *Reimagining the World,* describe this storytelling quality of science:

> Our society is structured around the telling of stories. Religion tells stories, politicians tell stories, business is in a large way a storytelling profession, and science is a telling of stories . . . Science is also a community of storytellers. I remember years ago talking with a friend of mine who was a practicing scientist. He said, "You know, you talk about the emergence of a planetary language—it is the community and language of science, of scientists." . . . The mythic side of science is often as important, and in fact may have a much more profound impact on a society, than the technological side of science. It engenders images for us, and these images then become the metaphors and language by which we think about and describe our world.[6]

Even in the most procedural kinds of science writing—a lab report, for instance—it is helpful to keep sight of the larger, imaginative contexts for your work. Why are you conducting this experiment? What is the laboratory exercise meant to show? Why is that demonstration important? How does this connect to the larger picture? By keeping the answers to these questions at least in the back of your mind as you write, you will find the act of writing about your work more cohesive and satisfying. By bringing them to the forefront, you will give your readers—experts and nonexperts alike—a sense of the place and salience of your work while reconfirming it in your own mind.

3

Writing from the Moment of Observation

Lab and Field Notebooks

"When you've hit a really tough one, tried everything, racked your brain and nothing works, and you know that this time Nature has really decided to be difficult, you say, 'Okay, Nature, that's the end of the nice guy,' and you crank up the formal scientific method.

"For this you keep a lab notebook. Everything gets written down, formally, so that you know at all times where you are, where you've been, where you're going and where you want to get. In scientific work and electronics technology this is necessary because the problems get so complex you get lost in them and confused and forget what you know and what you don't know and have to give up. . . . Sometimes just the act of writing down the problems straightens out your head as to what they really are."

—*Robert M. Pirsig*, Zen and the Art of Motorcycle Maintenance

WRITING BEGINS IN THE LAB AND THE FIELD

The advice in this book on how to write a paper or article about scientific research is based on the idea that *writing begins with and is inseparable from your scientific research.* Writing begins in the laboratory or in the field of observation, where you conduct your experiment or gather your empirical data. The moment you record your data or observations, you have begun composing your research report. And the success of your eventual scientific article or report is founded on developing good writing practices in the beginning.

The following chapters take you through a step-by-step process showing how the science paper evolves directly from the records the scientist keeps at the moment of observation. Throughout this book, I refer to the "laboratory," meaning not only the lab, but also the "field," as well as any other context in which a scientist makes empirical observations or conducts experiments.

If you are simply interested in writing a second-hand report about science, as in an essay, a library research report, or a journalistic piece about other researchers' work, you will still find much of the discussion in the next chapters of how science and writing work together quite relevant. Writing the science essay or term paper is covered later in Chapter 16.

Let's explore the typical ways information flows through science. A scientist chooses a scientific problem after being immersed in the literature of a scientific domain. Or perhaps a scientist begins with curiosity about a problem and then goes to the literature to discover to what extent the problem has been answered or solved. After understanding fully what work has been performed in the field, the researcher defines the problem more narrowly and devises an experiment or series of experiments for obtaining more information.

The experiment yields both quantitative and qualitative observations. The scientist records these observations in the *lab notebook* or *field notebook* in a disciplined fashion. Work recorded in the lab notebook becomes the basis for a *lab report* or even a published *research article* directly. In turn, this journal article helps other researchers define their research interests and narrow their own target problem in a sort of feedback loop between problem-setting and the journal literature.

While this is not the only way information flows through science, it is a typical scenario. When we put it all together, we see the feedback process by which the scientific literature promotes more research, which in the end promotes more literature, beginning the cycle again (see Figure 3.1).

In the following sections, we will look in turn at each of these writing tasks that are so important to the scientific process.

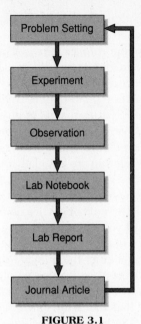

FIGURE 3.1
Communication Flow in Science

WHAT IS A LAB NOTEBOOK FOR?

The primary function of the lab notebook is to serve as a record of experimentation and observation, whether or not you are working in a lab. Indeed, for every mention of the word "lab" in this book, you could easily substitute the term "field" as in "field notebook."

In a strict sense—from the point of view of the scientific method itself—the lab notebook carries legal weight. It is an eyewitness account recorded at the scene during the action, a foundation of the practice of science that is as important as experimentation and observation. It is the bedrock testimony on which all future theorizings and extrapolations are built. Indeed, in most labs, witnesses regularly sign and date the lab notebook for legal purposes such as patents and ethical purposes such as establishing the priority of discovery.

The secondary function of a lab notebook is that in the normal course of scientific practice, it will become the basis for a more formal report, perhaps as a lab report to a supervisor or professor, or eventually as a research article in a professional journal.

The lab notebook's true grandparents are both the bookkeeper's ledger sheet and the "natural philosopher's" diary. Scientists since the seventeenth century kept diaries that were often given over to ruminations, speculations, theorizings, freehand sketches, more general (if not irrelevant) observations, anecdotal evidence, flowcharts, brainstorms, and doodles. While you are not likely to find many of these in the professional scientist's lab notebook today, there's no reason why you can't also keep a lab notebook that doubles as a sort of intellectual diary as long as these other sorts of entries don't obscure or interfere with the primary data. If you are unsure, you may want to reserve a section of your notebook at the rear for such "doodlings."

It is important to remember the ultimate significance of your lab records and reports. A recent and widely publicized case involved a conflict in the way data were reported in a genetics research lab. It resulted in a controversy that shook the entire scientific community to its foundations. Some scientists accused others of a cover-up, of trying to minimize the ambiguities and conflicts in recording and reporting data. This incident eventually harmed the careers of at least one research professor and one laboratory worker. It contributed to the decision by a Nobel prize-winning biologist, president of a prestigious research university, to resign his post because he had been directly involved in the laboratory research and his name appeared on an article based on those data. It set in motion congressional hearings on scientific accuracy and threatened to provide the Congress of the United States with sufficient motivation to establish an oversight committee to monitor science. Perhaps most importantly, the entire affair cast a long shadow of doubt on a large body of data and interrupted an important line of research.

Remarkably, the case hinged around inconsistencies in a lab notebook.

WHAT MUST GO IN THE LAB NOTEBOOK?

The primary function of the notebook is to explain and record the data from an experiment. It is helpful, though, to think of it in several ways at once: as a legal document; as a record of raw data; as a diary or

CHECKLIST #1

PARTS OF A LAB NOTEBOOK

☐ Clear identifications of time, place, and personnel who were directly involved in conducting the experiment.

☐ Brief statement of the problem and purpose of the experiment; the hypothesis or theory it is designed to test.

☐ Brief statement of predicted results (optional).

☐ Detailed descriptions of the apparatus.

☐ Detailed instructions for setting up the apparatus.

☐ Detailed instructions for conducting the experiment.

☐ Description of the method for collecting data.

☐ Complete records of data on prepared data sheets as well as other observations.

☐ Description of method for analyzing data.

☐ Brief analysis and interpretations of data, including graphs and charts.

☐ Brief statement of conclusions.

chronological account of events; and as a rough draft for a more formal presentation of research results in a lab report or journal article.

PREPARE THE NOTEBOOK

Most of the problems with lab notebooks stem from the fact that the author composed the notebook for his or her own use. As a result, many notes may be cryptic and the writing difficult to decipher. Terms may go undefined, procedures are described by sketchy remarks, and the handwriting may be quirky.

Since so much of a lab notebook involves recording data or listing regular bits of information, most lab notebooks are made of bound graph paper. Graph paper encourages neatness and allows for quick preparation of tables, charts and graphs. A bound notebook also

---

CHECKLIST #2

STYLE FOR THE NOTEBOOK

☐ Will other researchers be able to understand everything in it?

☐ Is my handwriting legible?

☐ Did I number all the pages in the notebook before I began?

☐ Does every entry have a date and time.

☐ Is every entry signed?

☐ Is every new experiment clearly demarcated and identified?

☐ Have I eliminated blank spaces by cross-hatching or filling them in?

☐ Did I state things simply and unambiguously?

☐ Have I defined my technical terms?

☐ Will other researchers be able to reconstruct the experimental apparatus based on my description alone?

☐ Will other researchers be able to perform the experiment based on my description of it alone?

☐ Will other researchers be able to understand the reasons the experiment was performed?

☐ Will other researchers be able to understand the results?

☐ Will other researchers understand the conclusions I drew about the experiment?

---

makes it difficult to remove pages, and very difficult to do so without leaving a trace of the deletion, a helpful feature when you understand the protocol of lab notebooks. Furthermore, because the notebook carries legal weight, everything must be written in ink.

To put yourself in the proper frame of mind to make entries into a notebook, it is most important to remember that you are not writing notes to yourself but to a much more public audience, beginning with a supervisor or colleague. Imagine that ten years from now, laboratory scientists who know as much about your discipline as you do but who are thoroughly unfamiliar with this particular experiment will read your lab notebook. In keeping your lab notebook, ask yourself the questions in Checklist #2.

In a major research project, a single lab notebook would ordinarily be devoted to one or two experiments at most, simply because experiments tend to be complex and require numerous repetitions. But in college courses, experiments tend to be simpler and require fewer repetitions, so a lab notebook might include several experiments.

INTRODUCE THE EXPERIMENT

- **State the purpose/goals of the experiment in a few sentences**.

   The purpose of this experiment is to measure the effects of an unbalanced force—gravity—on an unimpeded object—a ball bearing rolling down an inclined plane or ramp in a straight line. The goal of the experiment is to prove that the force acting on an unimpeded body will cause the body to accelerate.

- **Refer to the textbook or reference that provided you with the theory or inspired your apparatus and method, or gave you the assignment, in the first place. Write this as a regular bibliographic entry.**

   Waytey, V. "New considerations of the theory of unbalanced forces acting on unimpeded bodies," *Journal of Experimental Physics* vol. 700, no. 2: 112–15.

- **At your own discretion, state the expected outcomes of your experiment.**

   This experiment should demonstrate that the velocity v increases positively and regularly over time as a result of gravity acting on the ball.

DESCRIBE THE MATERIALS COMPLETELY

Remember, your description of the apparatus must be complete enough that someone who has never seen it can reproduce it.

• Describe, in order,

the parts of the apparatus and their function;

the setup; and

the method for operating it (conducting the experiment).

For instance, the following description of the parts of the apparatus in a simple physics experiment might serve to jog the memory of the researcher, but it would be insufficient for someone who wanted to try to replicate the experiment.

```
1. Ramp
2. Ball
3. Ladder
4. Spark timer
5. Thermal paper strip
6. Metal strip
```

The following description is tedious to write, but it ensures that your unknown reader will be able to repeat your experiment.

```
This apparatus consists of

1. A ramp 12″ long by 2″ wide with a 0.5″ groove
   running down the center of its length on
   one side. Two hooks at one end of the ramp
   will fit over the rungs of the ladder so
   the ramp is adjustable to different
   heights. A plastic gate at the top of the
   ramp will hold the ball in place.

2. A steel ball bearing of 0.5″ diameter.

3. A ladder 10″ tall that will support the
   ramp.

4. A spark timer made by Sparko, Inc., of
   Electra, Washington, Model #ST100, consist-
   ing of

   a timer with a digital dial for setting
   different time intervals between sparks,
```

a plug for a 110 volt ac outlet, and

two wires <u>that will attach to the metal strip.</u>

5. A copper strip 12″ long and 0.5″ wide with two leads (eyes) at one end.

6. A strip of thermal paper 0.5″ wide by 12″ long with a printed grid. Mfd. by Papco Inc. of Sawmill, Kentucky. Serial #42-TP for <u>recording the sparks between the ball and the copper strip.</u>

Note that the underlined words are not descriptions of the parts per se but rather of how they fit or relate to other parts. These are not necessary, but they are very helpful to your imaginary reader who may have never seen this equipment before.

For commercially manufactured parts or equipment or nonstandard laboratory supplies, designate the company of origin and the serial or model number. While this may seem like a lot of extra work, it becomes scientifically significant in chemical and biological experiments, where the quality of supplies and live subjects (experimental mice, etc.) may vary significantly from supplier to supplier. And it might help you at some later date if you have to restock supplies or replace parts.

Of course, there is no need to include extraneous information, such as the color of the ramp or the temperature of the room, although it is better to err on the side of excessive description. The importance of this practice is highlighted when results of an experiment can't be replicated, and researchers must conclude that some mysterious differences in the materials, methods, conditions, or apparatus are to blame.

DESCRIBE THE ASSEMBLY OF YOUR APPARATUS

Before describing the assembly of your apparatus, first assemble it yourself, perhaps taking notes on a scrap paper. Then write the procedure for assembly in the lab notebook. Give clear and complete directions. Most of us have had bad experiences trying to decipher poorly written directions for assembling toys or operating simple machinery. Try to keep those experiences in mind to avoid afflicting someone else with the following sort of instructions:

```
Turn on the spark timer after setting it to 10 and
hooking it to the metal strip. But first set up
the ramp and the ladder. Be careful of shocks from
the metal strip, so don't put the ball on top af-
ter you turn it on, but before. Also remember to
put the thermal paper on top of the metal strip
before putting the ball where it is supposed to
go.
```

As technical writing guru Dr. David Carson puts it, *"Pretend your reader is assembling a bicycle from one thousand parts for his child, and it's midnight, and he's had a couple of drinks."*

If chemicals or animals or certain parts of the apparatus pose danger (for example, electrical shock, radioactive contamination, poisons, or other biohazards) make sure to note those dangers and cautions clearly in your lab notebook. Similarly, if animals or chemicals require special handling or conditions, also note these clearly *before* the instructions describing those procedures.

```
CAUTION! Never touch the metal ball while it is on
the ramp and the spark timer is on. The contact
strip carries a high voltage current, and the
spark is strong enough to singe your skin. Make
sure you place the ball on top of the ramp before
turning on the spark timer.
```

Some other examples:

```
NOTE: Always pick up a mouse around the abdomen,
using your thumb and forefinger to gently squeeze
its jaws closed. Never pick up the mouse by the
tail or head.
```

```
CAUTION! Be sure to wear rubber gloves when han-
dling HCL.
```

```
CAUTION! Make sure all biohazard procedures are
followed when handling the test tube.
```

Sample Setup Description

SETUP

1. Locate the leads on the metal strip. Put the metal strip into the groove on the ramp, making sure the leads stick out from the end of the ramp that <u>doesn't</u> have hooks.

2. Place a 12″ length of thermal paper on top of the metal strip. Attach one lead to one of the wires from the spark timer and then attach the other lead.

3. Hook the ramp hooks onto the ladder at the 4″ mark.

4. Place the metal ball on the top of the ramp, making sure the gate is set to hold it in place.

5. Set the spark timer for 10 sparks per second by turning the dial on the spark timer to "10."

6. Plug the spark timer into a regular ac outlet.

Notice that the author includes very specific—even obvious—information, like reminding his reader to plug in the spark timer.

Another thing to remember when giving instructions is that it's hard to translate into words the location of objects that would be immediately apparent in a picture or when you're looking at them directly. As a result, it is important to orient your reader with directions like *up* and *down, left* and *right,* and to distinguish between different ends or sides of an object.

When possible, *describe the apparatus in both pictures and words.* You need not be an artist to draw the apparatus; a simple line drawing will suffice in most instances. Label parts clearly with arrows and pointers in the diagram. If there are many parts and labels will crowd the drawing, number the parts clearly and list the parts by number below the illustration.

DESCRIBE THE METHOD OR PROCEDURE OF YOUR EXPERIMENT

The method or procedure of your experiment is the set of steps you take to manipulate the subject of your study using your apparatus under controlled circumstances. In chemistry, the experiment might involve the mixing of chemicals. In astronomy, it might mean applying a new procedure to analyzing spectroscopic data. In biology, it might mean exposing living organisms to new environmental or chemical conditions. In geology, zoology, botany it might mean collecting samples. But the experiment is the heart of science, and designing the experiment well and correctly recording the data it yields is the heart of the experiment.

In explaining the experiment, you are both giving instructions and describing how data is yielded or recorded. For instance, running our sample experiment is really quite simple and is a continuation of the instructions for setup.

PROCEDURE

Turn on the spark timer.

Release the catch holding the ball at the top of the ramp.

Explaining the way you've collected the data is also relatively simple in this experiment.

DATA COLLECTION

The thermal paper shows dots recording the position of the ball at 0.1-second intervals in its path down the ramp. The dots are burn marks made by sparks between the metal strip on the ramp and the metal ball, caused by a current running from the spark timer to the metal strip through the paper.

Of course other experiments may require an elaborate explanation of the methods. We will treat some of these when we review the materials and methods section of the science article in Chapter 11.

PREPARE DATA SHEETS

A data sheet is nothing more than an organized system of blanks where data will eventually be entered. Usually it consists of tables demarcated by lines, with headings for columns and labels for rows. For this reason, graph paper is particularly suitable. The importance of a data sheet is that it becomes a template for your tables of raw data and in some cases, for the first few steps in analyzing data relationships.

In order to prepare your lab notebook to receive data, you have to understand beforehand the nature of your experiment, its purpose, and the expected outcomes. You must also understand your apparatus and the kind of data it will yield. Will you be simply reading data points from an instrument? Will you be taking measurements yourself? What are the important variables? Usually, one of the variables is time, and others will be measures of the characteristics of the phenomenon or subject you are studying, or outputs from manipulating that subject. In addition, you may want to create room on a data sheet for the first simple calculations—or analyses—of the data.

In the mock experiment of the accelerating ball, having defined the experiment and assembled the apparatus, you are now ready to prepare data sheets in anticipation of conducting the experiment itself. The purpose of the experiment is to measure the position of the ball at regular time intervals as it moves down the ramp. You anticipate that the distance between measurements—the velocity—will increase progressively. At the very least, then, for each "run" or iteration of the experiment you will need a column for the times, t_n, which will be measured in tenths of a second by each spark, and the positions of the ball, p_n, or how far down the ramp it has moved as indicated by the spark marks on the thermal paper.

However, you know that eventually you will want to plot the average velocity of the ball between each spark mark by measuring the distance between spark marks and dividing it by the time elapsed between spark marks (which will always be 0.1 seconds). And you also know that what you are really after is the acceleration of the ball,

Time [t_n] in secs	Position [p_n] in cm	$p_n - p_{n-1}$ in cm	Avg. Velocity [V_n] in cm/sec = $\dfrac{p_n - p_{n-1}}{t_n - t_{n-1}}$	Avg. Accel [A_n] in cm/sec² = $\dfrac{V_n - V_{n-1}}{t_n - t_{n-1}}$
0.00	0.00	0.00	0.00	0.00
0.1	3.6	3.6	0.36	3.6
0.2	14.5	10.9	1.09	7.3
0.3	32.7	18.2	1.82	7.3
0.4	58.2	25.5	2.55	7.3
0.5	90.9	32.7	3.27	7.2
0.6	130.5	39.6	4.05	7.3
0.7	178.9	48.4	4.75	7.3
0.8	233.6	54.7	5.47	7.2
0.9	295.7	62.1	6.21	7.4
1.0	365.0	69.3	6.93	7.2

FIGURE 3.2
Lab Notebook Data Sheet for the Rolling Ball Experiment

since the theory you are testing predicts that bodies acted on by an unbalanced force will accelerate. Acceleration is equal to the change in velocities during a time interval, or $(v_n - v_{n-1}) \div (t_n - t_{n-1})$. So rather than keeping your data in two separate entries, you create one master data sheet on which you will record your raw data on site, and still leave room for the basic calculations.

Note that columns 1 and 2 are for recording the raw data. Columns 3, 4, and 5 provide places for further calculations which the author anticipated.

FOLLOW GUIDELINES FOR RECORDING DATA

Now you are ready to record your data, but you should remember the two principals of a lab notebook when doing so. You need to

CHECKLIST #3

GUIDELINES FOR RECORDING DATA

☐ Record data from your observations in the order in which you made those observations, that is, chronologically.

☐ Make sure each data point has a number and a dimension or unit of measurement (denoting weight, length, time, energy, volume, temperature, and so on, or a relationship between dimensions such as velocity, rates, and so on).

☐ Record everything in ink.

☐ Date and sign each page.

☐ Enter all raw data directly into the notebook. It is unacceptable to record raw data on scraps and then transfer them to the notebook because in doing so, you may make errors, you will certainly waste time.

☐ Indicate clearly the units or dimensions of measurements. The meaning of raw numbers can quickly be lost or forgotten.

☐ Make corrections and deletions by crossing out words or figures with a simple single line in ink. Do not blacken out or erase them. You may want to refer to corrections later.

☐ Leave as little blank space between entries as is possible.

☐ Cross-hatch or otherwise fill blank spaces.

1. Guarantee the integrity of the data, and

2. Ensure repeatability of an experiment.

The guidelines for recording data in a notebook are similar to those noted in the more general checklist for using a lab notebook (page 26), but they bear repeating (see Checklist #3).

SHOULD YOU SUBSTITUTE THE COMPUTER FOR A HANDWRITTEN LAB NOTEBOOK?

In an age of electronic word processing and calculation, the computer is an indispensable tool. Many of the automated procedures in the modern laboratory make the computer incomparable as the first and most accurate means of capturing data. Laboratory software is a big business. New integrated packages permit you to record data from instrumentation, analyze the data according to well-established methods, devise your own analyses, and generate tables, charts, and graphs of the data. You can import these into many word processors, inviting you to do all the work on the computer from note taking to writing reports. Indeed, it is probably inevitable that the computer will eventually replace the handwritten notebook. With the advent of portable, laptop, and notebook computers this evolution even extending to the field scientist.

Multimedia capabilities make it possible to do things that no handwritten lab notebook could ever hope to: take data records and integrate them with graphical representations that provide vivid animation of dynamic models, fluids, and data trends or changing relationships. Of course, all of these features can be integrated with word processing to produce finished reports without ever touching pen to paper.

However, the computer's greatest strength as an information processor is also its greatest weakness for scientific procedure: it records and presents data in its most plastic and abstract possible form, as electronic bits. As a result, it is too easy to manipulate, alter, and lose data and observations. Compare the solidity of ink marks on paper to the ephemeral nature of electronic blips inside a computer, and you get the idea. *Using a computer makes protecting the integrity of your data more difficult,* even though computers make it simpler and apparently more precise to record that data.

Furthermore, computers only record what you instruct them to record: they do not have our five senses. We can see and react to the unexpected, and in science, it is sometimes the unexpected that produces the most exciting and important results. Seemingly irrelevant observations may turn out to be necessary for proper interpretation of results. A truck passing by a laboratory can shake recording equipment and alter readings from sensitive instruments. The accidental mixture of two chemicals can produce surprising effects. Computerized recording systems usually offer attractive templates for the manner in which raw data are to be recorded and reported. As a result, a preliminary sort of analysis has already occurred, since choosing one template over another begins to organize the data. If the results are unusual or unexpected, however, a template might hide an important anomaly.

Daryl W. Preston and Eric R. Dietz in *The Art of Experimental Physics,* tell the story of how Burton Richter at Stanford Linear Accelerator and Samuel C. C. Ting of MIT discovered a new subatomic particle because they refused to ignore a single anomalous data point. As a result, Richter and Ting shared the Nobel Prize in physics in 1976 for their discovery of this new kind of heavy particle.[8] The moral of the story? *If too much analysis of data is performed automatically, the scientist can miss spurious or anomalous data points. And anomalous data points can be significant.* The other moral is: *Don't let your expectations of outcomes lead you to ignore results that do not match those expectations.*

In short, the lab notebook provides a medium for connecting what goes on "in here," in your mind, and what goes on "out there," in the world. My advice is that you continue to keep a written record in addition to relying on the computer's considerable and growing assistance. If you decide to use the computer to keep your lab notebook observe the protocols in Checklist #4 on page 38.

ANALYZE THE DATA BRIEFLY

The lab notebook should include a brief explanation of why you analyzed the data in the way you did. This is helpful because it will also clarify in your own mind why you are performing certain mathematical operations. Your mental operation may go something like this:

> I have to show that the ball accelerated, so in order to do that I have to get the different velocities of the ball at successive points. In order to get that, I have to measure the distance the ball traveled between each of the points and divide it by the time it took to cover that distance, at least to get average velocities.

But notice that this is the reverse of the order of the calculations and operations you need to perform. So it is helpful to run through them mentally and then commit them to paper in order:

Measure the distance traveled between each spark mark by counting the grid marks, each grid mark = 1 mm. $(p_n - p_{n-1})$ Determine the average velocity of the ball between each spark mark by dividing the distance covered by the time elapsed between spark marks = $t_n - t_{n-1}$ or 0.1 seconds.

CHECKLIST #4

USING THE COMPUTER AS A LAB NOTEBOOK

☐ Use the word processor as your main program, not your data recording package.

☐ Treat the word processor just as you would the handwritten notebook, following the same steps and protocols. DO NOT ERASE DATA, except perhaps to correct a typographical error.

☐ Make frequent backups of your data and store them safely.

☐ Import data and illustrations from other programs into your word processor. Keep track of what program they came from and all other identifications (date, time, and so on).

☐ Continue to record your own observations of the experiment instead of relying only on automated data recording.

☐ "Lock" your files when you're done with them, making them "read only" so that they cannot be written over, by you or anyone else.

☐ If you need to make changes, do so as additions rather than editing the files.

☐ Date and time each entry so that all entries will appear sequentially. If you insert a new entry into an older entry, distinguish it and mark it with date and time.

☐ Note the name, manufacturer, and address of all software you used, including the application you used to assemble your notes.

☐ Note the name and vendor of the data recording applications (software) and instruments (hardware) under Methods and Materials.

☐ Note the name and vendor of the data analysis applications under Presentation and Discussion of Data.

$$\frac{(p_n - p_{n-1})}{(t_n - t_{n-1})}$$

NOTE: For the sake of convenience, I recorded this as v_n, even though it actually measures the velocity of the ball at some time $t_n - x$, where x is

less than 0.1 seconds but greater than 0.05 seconds, since the ball is accelerating. If the numbers seem anomalous, I will recalculate using the
method to determine the absolute velocity by taking the derivative or slope of the curve at each
t_n.

Calculate acceleration, equal to the change in velocities during a time interval, or

$$\frac{v_n - v_{n-1}}{t_n - t_{n-1}}$$

NOTE: This calculates the <u>average</u> acceleration of
the ball between t_n and t_{n-1}. Again, if the numbers seem strange, recalculate by determining the
<u>absolute</u> acceleration = the derivative of v_n at any
t_n.

The author here wisely included a caution ("NOTE") about potential problems with his methods of calculation, since these were
only average values for velocity and acceleration. By keeping track of
his decision not to calculate absolute values, he guarded against criticisms and left a reminder to himself to try another method of calculation if this one becomes unsatisfactory.

DRAW BASIC TABLES AND GRAPHS

As the next obvious step in analyzing the data, it helps to use visual
representations and calculations in the form of graphs, tables, and
charts. Draw these right in your lab notebook if you haven't done so
already (see Figures 3.2 and 3.7).

In preparing visuals, you ought to decide beforehand how to best
represent the data. Plotting the data points in a table format will help
you keep your calculations in order and will help to reveal some basic
relations in the data. If you haven't left columns in your original sheet
for recording the raw data, then create room for a new table for further calculations.

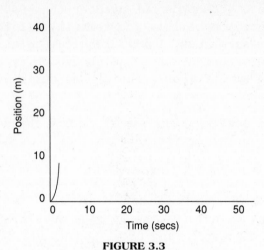

FIGURE 3.3

Graph Using Too Large a Scale for the Data

It is obvious from the table that the velocity is increasing, since more distance is traveled by the ball after each tenth of a second. But is there a more precise trend in the data? At what rate is the velocity increasing? Even before performing the calculations, graphing these data points will help determine and show relationships visually.

Moving from table to graph is simple. To show velocity increasing, let the horizontal axis represent *time* and the vertical axis *position.* You also must be sure to choose a scale of the drawing that will show your data. To take an absurd instance, in the graph above (Figure 3.3), if time were measured in minutes rather than tenths of seconds and distances in meters rather than centimeters, the data points would crowd into one indecipherable corner of a large graph, most of which would be left blank.

The opposite error is not planning the scale of your graph so that it shows all relevant data points (see Figure 3.4). The problem with this graph is that it doesn't show data points for the last 0.3 secs in the rolling ball experiment.

This graph of the position of the ball with respect to time (Figure 3.5) shows all the relevant data points in an appropriate scale. The exponential curve suggests that the velocity increases as the ball rolls down the ramp. The author has hand labeled the graph. Note the use

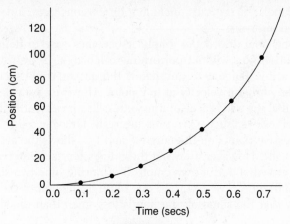

FIGURE 3.4

Graph Using Too Small a Scale for the Data

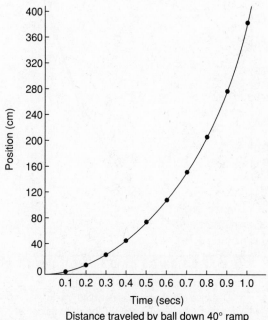

Distance traveled by ball down 40° ramp

FIGURE 3.5

Graph with Appropriate Scales

of clear labels for the axes, including dimensions (*secs* and *cm*), and numbered intervals.

Having now drawn the graph, it becomes easy to demonstrate other relationships without performing calculations. For instance, by drawing a line tangent to any point, the author could have represented the *absolute* velocity at any point. However, proving the hypothesis that the ball is accelerating only calls for calculating the *average* velocities over successive time intervals. Drawing a line between two successive points on the curve t_n and t_{n-1} shows the average velocity visually. However, drawing these lines for each interval would create a crowded and messy graph. By drawing only two such lines (Figure 3.6), one close to t_0 and one close to the end of the run, we can show that the slope of one line is less steep than the slope of a

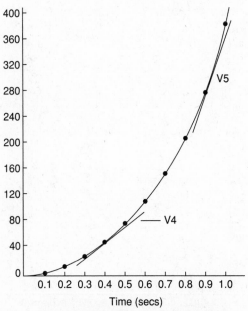

Distance traveled by ball down 40° ramp
with average velocities V4 and V5 shown as tangents

FIGURE 3.6
Graph of Lab Experiment Showing Velocities

Time Interval (secs)	Distance Traveled by Ball / 0.1 sec (cm)	v_n (m/sec)	a_n (m/sec^2)
0.0	0.0	0.00	0.0
0-0.1	3.6	0.36	3.6
0.1-0.2	10.9	1.09	7.3
0.2-0.3	18.2	1.82	7.3
0.3-0.4	25.5	2.55	7.3
0.4-0.5	32.7	3.27	7.2
0.5-0.6	39.6	3.96	7.3
0.6-0.7	48.4	4.84	7.3
0.7-0.8	54.7	5.47	7.2
0.8-0.9	62.1	6.21	7.4
0.9-1.0	69.3	6.93	7.2

FIGURE 3.7

Lab Notebook Data Sheet with Distance, Velocities, and Accelerations

subsequent line, thereby indicating an increase in velocity, or *acceleration.*

This graph visually answers the question about changes in velocity, but now it is a good idea to go back and perform the calculations not only for average velocity, but for acceleration just to be sure. These prove conclusively what the graph already suggests visually.

INTERPRET THE DATA BRIEFLY

Interpreting the data is a natural extension of analyzing it. Indeed, it is quite difficult to separate the two activities conceptually. One way to do so is to think of *analysis* as all those operations on the data that lead to absolutely certain answers. By contrast, *interpretation* involves all those operations on the data that leave some measure of uncertainty about answers. Both should be recorded in your lab notebook.

- **Find generalities about the data by applying mathematical or statistical methods and by matching data to different hypotheses or theories.** For instance, this lab experiment leaves room for further interpretation. The mission of the lab has been accomplished. The researcher has already determined from using the average acceleration that the acceleration is apparently constant and approximately equal to 7.3 m/sec^2 or so. But he expected the acceleration to equal gravity (g = 9.80 m/sec^2). So curiosity about this difference between what theory predicts and what he got as results of his experiment drives him to use calculus to determine the absolute acceleration of the ball down the ramp. Perhaps the difference was due to some aspect of using the average acceleration. Common sense suggests that the absolute acceleration will be very close to the average acceleration, but he wants to be sure. So he is not too surprised to discover that actually acceleration is equal to 7.27 m/sec^2. He notes this curiosity or anomaly in the lab notebook.

```
Theory predicts that a falling body will ac-
celerate at g (= 9.80 m/sec²). Yet my calcula-
tions show that the ball rolling down the
ramp actually accelerated at somewhat less
than that, 7.27 m/sec². I speculate that the
ramp impeded the downward motion of the ball,
slowing it. Further, I hypothesize that the
difference between the actual acceleration
and g is proportionate to the angle of the
ramp. I must look into this further, perhaps
by trying different angles of the ramp or
looking more closely at the literature.
```

- **Interpreting the data also means making _qualitative_ judgments.** From a calculation of the precise mathematical generalizations about the data, you should also move to a verbal characterization of the data.

```
The data show that the ball accelerates as it
moves down the ramp. However, the calcula-
tions above show that the acceleration is
```

CHECKLIST #5

STEPS IN INTERPRETING DATA

☐ Find generalities about the data by applying mathematical or statistical methods and by matching data to different hypotheses or theories.

☐ Interpreting the data also means making *qualitative* judgments. From a calculation of the precise mathematical generalizations about the data, you should also move to a verbal characterization of the data.

☐ Decide which one of competing explanations of the data makes more sense or explains (fits) more of the data.

☐ Note specific points of agreement or disagreement with the theory or hypothesis you were testing.

---

significantly less than gravity (by about 25.8%).

For example, proving mathematically that the velocity increases and giving the precise numbers of that increase (a quantitative interpretation) means that the ball accelerated (a qualitative interpretation).

- **Decide which one of competing explanations of the data makes more sense or explains (fits) more of the data.** In this case, the point of the experiment was to verify a well-known and proven theory about which there is no disagreement in the scientific community. Other experiments may require sorting through more ambiguous interpretations of the data.

- **Note specific points of agreement or disagreement with the theory or hypothesis you were testing.** Our sample experiment calls for a relatively straightforward interpretation. After drawing the graph, it becomes quite clear that velocity increases. The sharp observer would notice that the increase is not linear but exponential.

```
The data show that the distance traveled by
the ball increases—the ball accelerates—
proportionate to the square of tₙ. Thus the
first derivative, the velocity, increases
linearly, and the second derivative, the
acceleration, remains constant, verifying the
original conjecture or hypothesis.
```

A curious thing about interpreting data is that virtually any data set permits an almost unending string of interpretations and discussions about it. For instance, although the overly simple running ball demonstration in this chapter does not call for extending an analysis of the data, the researcher, out of curiosity, went on to note that although gravity is the "unbalanced force" acting on the ball, the value of acceleration is *not* equal to g, (the value of acceleration of a free-falling body under the influence of gravity = 9.80 m/sec^2), but rather to some fraction of that value.

DEFINE AND CALCULATE THE PRECISION, ERROR, OR STANDARD DEVIATION IN YOUR OBSERVATIONS

This is one of the most important parts of the scientific process. Every measurement and observation involves some degree of error. Instruments can only read quantities to a certain finite limit, beyond which their measuring abilities cannot go. Statistical methods all involve, by definition, only probabilities, not certainties. Human observations are prone to all sorts of errors. Environmental influences can alter or disrupt experiments. Sometimes the model or theory introduces error by discounting certain effects that would introduce a consistent measure of error. For instance, nonlinear effects like friction are often eliminated or approximated in the models of simple mechanical systems.

Each discipline has its own methods for error calculations apart from universal methods, like calculating standard deviation. Every means of analyzing and recording data, every instrument, has its own measure of error.

DRAW CONCLUSIONS BRIEFLY

In general, the lab notebook is not a good place to engage in an extended discussion of conclusions. If the experiment was a success, simply state that you proved what you set out to prove. You need not sound formal, but you should be clear.

```
The ball accelerated down the ramp while it was
being acted on by gravity. This is more evidence
of the general law that an unbalanced force acting
on a body will accelerate that body. But while
gravity was the unbalanced force acting on the
ball, the acceleration of the ball was equal to
7.27 m/sec², much different from what we expected
for g (=9.80 m/sec²).
```

If the experiment uncovered surprising or anomalous results, you will undoubtedly have to perform other experiments, do more research into the theory, or define the problem better, sending you out of the context of the experiment. On the other hand, you shouldn't be reluctant to use the lab notebook to jot down speculations and conjectures or notes to yourself regarding ways to pursue more research.

```
Could there have been another force? Why is accel-
eration slower than theory predicts? Does friction
account for the difference? Was there some error
in our experimental setup? Perhaps it has some-
thing to do with the angle of the ramp.
```

SOME FINAL WORDS
ABOUT THE LAB NOTEBOOK

Keeping a lab notebook is really a humble and humbling activity, but it is the foundation of science. Keeping a good lab notebook will plant your feet on the ground and remind you of the fundamentals of doing science: *integrity, thoroughness, observation, accuracy, and keeping clear records for future communication.*

4

From Lab Notebook to Lab Report

Your college laboratory course has probably required you to hand in a lab report based on your lab notes. This is good practice for the way you will write as a professional scientist. In the real world lab reports are a sort of in-between creature. They can be as informal as a written supplement for a weekly presentation to a research group, or as formal as a paper submitted to an external agency or contractor having legal and fiscal ramifications. Many lab reports are directed at an "in-house" audience—a supervisor or colleague in the same institution, or even in the same research program. External lab reports go to a sponsoring agency or corporation as part of a contractual obligation, or as part of a review by private or government granting agencies. As a result, some lab reports are eventually intended for a somewhat less expert reader—corporate executives or managers, for instance. In these cases, the lab report may have the feel of an interim report on work in progress, or it may resemble the formality and generality of a research article. In all cases, it is important to have a clear sense of your mission and your audience.

Your lab or institution may have very particular guidelines for the format of a lab report, so consult with a colleague or supervisor about these requirements and be sure you understand the audience for whom your report is ultimately intended. As always, *local rules take precedence.* The lab *report* builds solidly on the work and writing you have already done in the lab *notebook.* It also anticipates the parts of the scientific report or article that you may eventually write based on it. In fact, while there may be significant differences between some lab reports and some research articles, many lab reports become publishable articles with only a few modifications. For that reason, this chapter will compare and contrast the lab notebook and the lab report, and the lab report and the article intended for publication in a journal. We discuss the skills that come into play when you write a full-fledged scientific article intended for a journal in Chapters 7 through 11.

LAB NOTEBOOK VERSUS LAB REPORT

How do you develop lab notebook entries into a lab report? In evolving the lab notebook notes into the lab report, you must write more extensive and polished versions of the sections outlined in the checklist below.

CHECKLIST #6

PARTS OF THE LAB REPORT DEVELOPED FROM THE LAB NOTEBOOK

☐ Introduction   *cover page* ☐

☐ Statement of Problem   *table of Content* ☐

☐ Methods and Materials

☐ Presentation and Interpretation of Data

☐ Conclusions

These will be discussed further in the chapters devoted to writing journal articles and reports.

Since the lab notebook is handwritten "on the fly," there is little chance for editing. As a result, the primary differences between the lab notebook and a lab report concern presentation (style, layout) and the detail and length of the introductory, analytical, interpretive, and concluding sections. It's not likely that you would ever be asked to include *all* the following parts of a lab report in your lab notebook, but any combination of these may be required. Below, they are listed in the order in which they would appear in the report itself. In the following sections, we will review how to handle each of these in turn.

CHECKLIST #7

PARTS OF THE LAB REPORT
NOT FOUND IN THE LAB NOTEBOOK

☐ Letter of transmittal

☑ Cover page

☐ Abstract or summary

☑ Table of contents

☐ List of illustrations

☐ Glossary of terms

☐ More polished illustrations and graphs

☐ Extensive literature review

☐ Bibliography

Letter of Transmittal

Unfortunately, very few courses will ask you to write one, so many scientists write their first letter of transmittal on the job. For the sake of practice, you might ask your instructor for permission to include a letter of transmittal when you submit your lab report.

If you are reporting out of house (that is, to another institution or to a granting agency) or in house *to a person more than one step away in your institution's organizational chart,* then a letter of transmittal should accompany your lab report. A letter of transmittal is both a courtesy and an important bureaucratic (record-keeping) procedure. It follows the standard format for a business letter. At the very least, the letter of transmittal should repeat the information on the title page. It should also identify your relationship to the receiver. You may want to use the letter to communicate some important general information, including a brief summary of the findings or even *recommendations or implications not contained in the report.* You might want to include the dates on which the research was actually conducted.

So a letter of transmittal, even to your instructor in a lab class, should include some basic information (see Figure 4.1).

Dear Prof. Boering,

   Here is my lab report for <u>Experiment 7: The Rolling Ball.</u> I completed the work on 22 November 1994. I had difficulty with the original set-up of the apparatus because the spark timers are pretty beat up from all the use they get. I suggest you buy some new ones. I modified the leads to the spark timer to increase the voltage, making the burn marks on the thermal strip easier to read.

   My results show that the experimental data agree with those predicted by theory and that the ball accelerates in accordance with the formula
$a = g \sin q$.

Sincerely,

J. C. Maxwell

FIGURE 4.1
Student Cover Letter to Lab Instructor

The more elaborate letter in Figure 4.2 (on page 52) pretends that the ball and ramp lab demonstration in the previous chapter was conducted not by students in a lab class, but by a team of researchers working in an independent scientific laboratory, under contract to a high-tech corporation. As a result, the letter of transmittal includes more business information than normal because it addresses the problems of a contract that is about to expire. It is a good example of the range of information that can be included in a letter of transmittal for a lab report.

Two things about this letter should stand out in your mind. The first is that the letter makes the report itself virtually redundant. That is, the letter is self-contained. The assumption behind this tactic is that the person reading the letter is interested in results and conclusions and may not have the time or inclination to wade through the report itself. Furthermore, the reader (in this case, Mr. Galileo) may very well need to use the letter in corporate meetings where not everyone in the audience is familiar with the scientific details. The second interesting part of this letter is its businesslike approach to soliciting further support for scientific research. In other words, the letter of transmittal is part scientific summary and part business letter.

Title/Cover Page

The purpose of a title/cover page for a lab report is to identify completely and unambiguously the experiment(s) reported inside, as well as to acknowledge all parties responsible for the work. To this end, it might include any combination of the following pieces of information.

Niskayuna Gravitech Laboratory

PO Box 9299 • Niskayuna, New York 12309

TEL: (518) 381-1134 FAX: (518) 381-1135

Date   15 December 1993

Addressee   Mr. K. C. Galileo, Vice-president for R&D

Gravitron Inc.

32 Feetpersec Drive

Heaviside, MA 02139

Subject line   RE: Enclosed report, "Effect of an unbalanced force on a ball

(optional)   bearing traveling down a 40° ramp"

Salutation   Dear Mr. Galileo:

Enclosed please find a report on our investigations under-
taken by our lab on November 20 through December 10, 1993
as contracted by your letter of November 3, 1993.

Body   As the report shows, it is clear that gravity does indeed
produce acceleration in a friction-reduced ball bearing traveling
down a 40° ramp. However, our figures show that, surprisingly,
the acceleration does not match the predicted value for
$g = 9.80$ m/sec^2. Rather, our experiments show that the actual
acceleration is approximately 25% less or 7.27 m/sec^2 on
average.

You asked us to give our analysis of our data. No theory
to date accounts for this discrepancy. At the moment, we are
working on an hypothesis that suggests the decrease in the
actual acceleration is proportionate to the angle of the ramp by
the following formula:

$$a = g \sin \theta$$

where a is the actual acceleration and g is gravity and θ is the
angle of the ramp. If we are correct, the immediate implications
for gravitron development are clear.

Further   Further research along these lines are not covered under

contact info   the terms of our present contract. Perhaps we can meet

& thanks   soon to discuss continuation of this promising line of research.
In the meantime, we would be pleased to answer any ques-
tions you have about the report. Thank you for your support of
our work. We look forward to hearing from you soon.

Sincerely,

Signatures   Valerie Whitfield, Ph.D.

Dana Eli, Ph.D.

Benjamin Abrams, Ph.D.

FIGURE 4.2

Sample Letter of Transmittal

WHAT: The title of a lab report should be specific enough so that the experiment will not be confused for any other work done by the authors or, even more restrictively, any other work done in the same laboratory. Otherwise, the guidelines for creating titles follow those for giving titles to articles or reports for journals (see Chapter 6).

WHO: Names of researchers: The names of the researchers as the researchers themselves wish them to appear, and their titles, listed in order of their principal roles in the design and conduct of the investigation.

WHERE: The site of the laboratory or research, which should coincide with the authors' affiliation.

WHEN: Date of transmittal of the report, not the date of the conduct of the experiment.

SPONSORS: Complete identification of the sponsors, including grant or contract numbers. Sponsors usually have require-

Niskayuna Gravitech Laboratory
Niskayuna, New York 12309

The Action Gravity's Effect on a
Ball Bearing Traveling on a
40°-Inclined Plane

by
Valerie Whitfield, Ph.D.
Dana Eli, Ph.D.
Benjamin Abrams, Ph.D.

15 December 1993

Sponsored by
The National Serious Foundation
Grant #S24ND-99

and

Gravitron Inc.
32 Feetpersec Drive, Heaviside, MA 02139

FIGURE 4.3
Sample Title/Cover Page

ments for how they are to be named in any lab report or article and you should consult with them.

For the cover especially, neatness counts.

Abstract or Summary

Even in a lab report it is helpful to summarize your research in terms of an abstract. You will find a longer treatment of this important skill in Chapter 7, but some preliminary words are appropriate here.

Depending on the agency or audience for the report and their requirements, the abstract could be a very brief restatement of the conclusions reached, or a more extensive recounting of the problem, the method, the results, and conclusions.

When reporting to readers who have more general knowledge or needs, you may want to substitute an *Executive Summary* for the abstract. An executive summary usually recounts only the conclusions, or the problems and the conclusions, in more accessible, less technical terms. Even in these summaries, you are encouraged, to use the active voice ("The authors conjecture that. . . ," "This report analyzes. . . ," "Our results show. . . "), although the norm in abstract writing remains the passive voice ("The experiment was performed. . . "). (See the section on *passive voice,* pages 214–219.)

Theory predicts that an unbalanced force acting on a body will accelerate that body. This experiment tested this theory by measuring the effect of gravity on a ball bearing rolling down an inclined plane. Our results show that the ball accelerated, though significantly less than g (= 9.75 m/sec^2). The authors speculate that the actual acceleration of the ball is equal to some proportion between g and the slope of the plane and then we suggest lines of future research.

Table of Contents

The table of contents should follow the outline of the lab report, listed with the page numbers on which each part begins. Include all appendices as in Figure 4.4.

TABLE OF CONTENTS

Introduction: Statement of Problem and Hypothesis 1

Literature Review 2

Methods 4

Description of Apparatus 5

Data and Results 6

Interpretation of Results 7

Conclusion 9

Literature Cited 10

Glossary 11

Appendix I: Copies of Lab Notes 12

Appendix II: Copies of Data Sheets 18

Appendix III: Equipment and Supplies 20

Appendix IV: Description of the Statistical Analysis Program 21

FIGURE 4.4

Table of Contents for the Rolling Ball Report

Not all lab reports must follow this precise outline. For instance, the literature review can be included in the discussion of the problem.

Introduction

The twofold purpose of the introduction is to state the problem or the purpose of the run of experiments and explain why it is important. In most experiments or laboratory exercises conducted in college courses, one, two, or a few sentences will suffice, since the important contexts are almost certainly known by the audience. The same holds true for in-house reports, for instance from you to a lab director or research professor sponsoring your work.

(A) The purpose of this experiment is to measure precisely the extent to which acceleration of a friction-reduced ball bearing is impeded as it rolls down an inclined plane.

(B) The purpose of this experiment is to measure the effects of niacin deprivation on the

development of bone marrow in laboratory
mice.

(C) This reports the measurements of blue wavelengths in radiation spectra from globular
clusters NGC 288 and NGC 362.

However, it doesn't hurt to expand slightly to indicate that you
have a grasp of how this bit of knowledge is situated with respect to
the larger field and to practice for the sort of introductions you are
likely to write in a longer journal article or research report. The three
sentences below are good companions to the ones above (A–C).

(A) While an unimpeded object should accelerate
at gravity ($g = 9.80$ m/sec^2), an inclined
plane should impede the downward movement.

(B) While no clear causal connection between
niacin and bone-marrow formation has been
established, epidemiological evidence suggests that humans with niacin-deficient diets
have lower growth rates and bone density.

(C) Determining the relative color luminosity
of stars from these clusters will help us
determine the ages of these clusters, which
in turn will help us refine our model of how
galaxies form.

It is also a good practice to mention or cite here other research
articles or texts that are most pertinent to the experiment you conducted, and which helped define the problem most narrowly.

Hypothesis or Expected Outcome

In this section, you should state what hypothesis, theory, or theorem
the experiment is designed to prove. You may need to cite literature
or texts that describe those theories or hypotheses. This section may
simply state what outcome you expected from the procedure. It may
also include the more general theory from which you formed the hypothesis. (See Chapter 9, "How to write about hypotheses, models,
and theories.")

Literature Review

If you are not reviewing or citing the literature on which your experiment is based in each of the individual sections, then add a full literature review section at this point in your lab report. Rather than giving full citations in the body of the text as you might in a lab notebook, use the citation method that generally applies to your discipline. (See Chapter 10, "How to cite and list the references.")

Methods Section

Explain the method you used to gather the data in greater detail than you did in the lab notebook. If your method is one that others have devised, cite the literature that describes the method. (See Chapter 11: "How to write the method and materials section.")

Interpretations of Data/Conclusions

Since most laboratory exercises that you perform as a student are just that—exercises—the outcomes are known. Consequently, there is very little "news" in your lab report. Furthermore, because outcomes are known beforehand, you generally you will not need to defend, argue for, or persuade your audience about your data, your interpretations, of your data, or your conclusions.

But here, as in other writing assignments you will do for science courses in college, in order to reap any benefit from these assignments, the challenge is for you to imagine what a professional audience for a lab report would require. You have to break through your actual course situation, which is highly artificial, to pretend that you are describing your professional work for a professional audience. When writing, try to imagine that:

- The experimental apparatus is new and of your own devising;

- The outcome of the experiment is *not* already known;

- The format of your presentation of data was *not* prescribed beforehand but selected by you as the best possible format for presenting this particular data set;

- Your actual audience is not your instructor, but rather one of the general audiences for a lab report in the professional world: a supervisor in a corporation or university who has hired you to gather data, analyze a specimen, make observations, or run an experiment which you may or may not have devised.

(See Chapter 12; "How to present results" and Chapter 14, "How to write about your interpretation of results.")

Sketches of Apparatus and Other Illustrations

These can still be simple *line drawings*, labeled clearly with names in neat, printed letters or with numbers referring to either the names of the objects or the steps in the procedure, followed immediately by a list with corresponding numbers. However, in transforming the notes from your data book to a lab report, you can now take those crude drawings, graphs, and charts and make them neater, using a word processor or a graphical presentation program on the computer, or rulers and india ink on good paper with typewritten or neatly lettered labels and headings.

Some investigations will call for *photographs* of phenomena. It is easy to imagine instances in astronomy, biology, zoology, medicine, fluid dynamics, chemistry, geology, and many fields of engineering where that might be the case. If photographs constitute primary data or evidence, they should be included in the lab report and listed along with illustrations.

Conclusion

Depending on your audience for the lab report, you will probably want to add specific recommendations for further research in your concluding sections, or explain the conclusions you reached in greater detail. This permits you to use a somewhat more intimate tone than you might for a formal research report. For example, to pursue our rolling ball experiment, you might recall that the researcher found an anomalous result. The conclusion might be phrased this way:

```
Our experiment proved that the ball accelerated
down the ramp while it was being acted on by grav-
ity. This is more evidence of the general law that
an unbalanced force acting on a body will acceler-
ate that body. However, since gravity was the un-
balanced force acting upon the ball, the accelera-
tion of the ball should equal g (9.80 m/sec²).
```

Yet, the actual absolute acceleration of the ball was equal to 7.27 m/sec^2, a figure approximately 25% lower than g.

We speculate that the difference can be explained by the fact that the ramp, set at 40° for the purpose of this experiment, impeded the downward motion of the ball and thus the action of gravity on it. We further hypothesize that the actual absolute acceleration is proportionate to the angle of the ramp according to some constant or relationship we have not yet determined. Consequently, in order to clarify these results, we suggest that future research investigate variations on this experimental design using different angles of the inclined plane as well as possible theoretical explanations.

If you are reporting to an outside agency or corporation, you may need to include information for a supervisor or external party that will give them a sense of the "big picture": the consequences of the specific results for their larger programs, goals, or applications. So the author could have added yet another paragraph.

It is crucial for future designs of the gravitron that we understand the precise mathematical nature of this relationship and its theoretical underpinnings, since prototypes of the gravitron require a ball-and-ramp configuration in its operation.

More formal strategies for writing conclusions in the lab report are virtually identical to those for the research article, so please refer to Chapters 14 and 15, "How to write about your interpretation of results" and "How to write conclusions."

Bibliography or Literature Cited

Include a full listing of the sources used in your literature review in the introductory section. These should directly follow the last page of your conclusion. List the works you consulted under one of the following headings:

```
Bibliography

Literature Cited

References and Sources
```

Follow the standards for reference that apply in your discipline. See Chapter 10, "How to cite and list references," for more detail.

Nomenclature/Glossary

One of the items unique to a lab report is the glossary, a list of terms that are special to the procedures or theories discussed in the lab report and their definitions, arranged alphabetically. This is a good exercise for you and proof to your instructor that you understand the words you use. In a professional setting, it is an important courtesy to your readers, particularly if they include people with varying levels of expertise. Begin the glossary on a separate sheet, either directly before or after the bibliography. Give the sheet its own header, using one of these terms or phrases:

```
Nomenclature

Glossary

Definitions of Technical Terms
```

What words do you include in a glossary? You should apply the same rules of thumb as you would when determining whether to define a term in the body of your report. The most general rule of thumb is this: *If you aren't sure all the members of your audience are familiar with the term or understand your usage of it, then define it and list it with its definition in the glossary.*

Absolute velocity: The speed of a moving point at any instant of time. It is calculated by the equation

$$v = \lim_{t \to 0} \frac{\Delta s}{\Delta t} = \frac{ds}{dt}.$$

Average velocity: The average speed of an object during a time interval, calculated by the equation

$$\frac{(p_n - p_{n-1})}{(t_n - t_{n-1})}.$$

Motion: A change in position during an interval of time.

Spark timer: An apparatus that surges a current of electricity across a gap between two metal terminals for a very brief duration, causing sparks at regular intervals.

Unbalanced force: A phenomenon that adds energy to an object through one vector or in one direction (For example, gravity).

Appendices

Appendices contain material that is relevant to the report but peripheral to the main body. Use a separate appendix for each category of supplementary material. For instance, you might include separate appendices for

- Photostat copies of raw data sheets from your lab notebook;

- Photostat copies of handwritten notes taken in your diary/chronology;

- Samples of your calculations and error-checking routines, especially if you relied heavily on computer software to perform your data analysis;

- Descriptions of computer programs, including flowsheets or the programs themselves on disk or printout if they are non-commercial products (for commercial programs, identify name, company, and address directly in the body);

- Lists of technical reports supporting your method or describing operation of the apparatus.

The purpose of including such "background" information is to reinforce the basic rules of experimental reporting: you want to be sure that other researchers can replicate your work or, if other researchers want to examine your findings more closely, they can reconstruct your procedures for arriving at conclusions. Blaming calculation mistakes or incomplete data on transcription problems, equipment malfunction, or computer error is unacceptable. You need to know how the computer derived its analysis, since the computer is your tool, not an impersonal third party or responsible agent in itself.

FINAL WORDS ABOUT THE LAB REPORT

The lab report is the first step outside the laboratory. It is the first time you move your relatively private work and thinking into a wider sphere and try to express them for an audience. And although there is a natural evolution from the lab notebook to the report, take a moment to recognize the significance of this step by putting on your best clothes, metaphorically speaking. This would not be a bad time to consult Chapter 17, "Revising and Editing." Double check your facts and reasoning. Edit your work carefully. Make the presentation as neat as possible. Choose your words with care, but be clear and simple. And remember the importance of communication in the entire process of science.

5

Preparing to Write the Research Paper

The general outline of the scientific paper has not changed much in about a hundred years. For instance, *Preparation of Scientific and Technical Papers,* written in 1930, outlines in simple and clear terms the parts of the basic scientific report,[9] many of which remain unchanged today:

    I. Title: The title should consist preferably of a few words indicative of the contents that are most emphasized. Great care must be exercised to employ words that contain the elements both of brevity and comprehensiveness and permit of easy and accurate indexing.

  II. Introduction:

    A. Nature of the problem; scope; bearing; importance

    B. Review of important literature on the subject

    C. Object [goal] of work

    D. Time and place of work

 III. Materials and methods

    A. Description of the equipment and materials employed

    B. Explanation of the way in which the work was done. Emphasize the features that are new.

 IV. Experiments and results

    A. Detailed description of the experiments

    B. Description of the results

V. Discussion of results

    A. Main principles, causal relations, or generalizations that are shown by the results. Choose one or several main points which you wish to prove.

    B. Evidence (as shown by the data) for each of these main points

    C. Exceptions and opposing theories, and explanations of these

    D. Comparison of your results and interpretations with those of other workers

VI. Summary: A condensed account of the important contents, in a form suited to the requirements of abstract journals.

In an intriguing pair of footnotes, the authors suggest that the Experiments and Results section "may be compared to 'news' in a daily paper" and that Discussion of Results [Conclusions] "may be compared to an editorial in a daily paper."

Much has changed in the intervening years, and much of the book you are reading is based on new views of science that have emerged in that time. Yet what we have learned since then suggests that comparing the formal science report to their journalistic counterparts is still a good idea.

The science article requires more than one kind of writing or one set of skills. The science report is made up of different parts, and each requires different communication skills to succeed. The Experiments and Results section requires the skills of a reporter filing the news for a newspaper. The Discussion of Results section requires the skills of an editorial writer or a trial lawyer advocating a logical case or interpretation. The Materials and Methods section requires technical writing skills, such as those used in writing an instruction manual. The Introductory section often involves the skills of a good feature writer as well as a lecturer or teacher: there, you provide broader contexts, define new terms and relationships, and compare hypotheses and theories.

Chapter 18 will examine the problems that can arise when you bring strictly scientific attitudes to the style you use in writing about original research. The basic caution, objectivity, and impersonal nature of good science practices can lead to stuffy, overly-conditional and obscure writing. It helps to think of yourself as a very rigorous journalist getting all the angles on an interesting new experiment or set of data or exploring one of nature's arcane niches. Both you and the journalist have the same main job: to get the facts straight and communicate them to your audience.

PREPARING TO WRITE

Before sitting down to write an article, it helps to perform an exercise called "pre-writing." Try to step back from the primary nature of your material. Get the sort of perspective that will help you the most when you actually do compose your article. Basically, your goal is to see the forest where before you've been roaming among the trees. As an aid to prewriting, I suggest you write down the answers to the questions in Checklist #8 on page 66.

FROM LAB REPORT TO RESEARCH ARTICLE

The lab report and the research paper are very similar. Many professional journals even include sections for shorter reports that are essentially lab reports. And if you look closely at the organization of most research papers, you will find that they include many of the same parts as a lab report (see Checklist #9 on page 67).

However, there are some important differences between a lab report and a formal scientific paper. Almost all of them stem from the fact that your audience is now wider and more varied than it was for your lab report.

Style

A lab report can be pretty spare in its tone, whereas an article can afford to be—indeed, almost has to be—more expansive, especially in setting the context, gauging the merits of different points of view, and explaining interpretations. We will examine specific matters of style for each section of a research article in subsequent chapters.

Scope

A lab report might discuss only one experiment or a very small number of iterations of the same experiment. It may also represent an

CHECKLIST #8

QUESTIONS TO ASK YOURSELF BEFORE WRITING THE ARTICLE

☐ Do I (we) have a story to tell, news to break, or some important information to add? Describe:

☐ What is the single most important aspect of this research or article I propose to write? Describe:

☐ Am I describing (circle all that apply)

the results of research?

a new methodology?

a new theory?

a new interpretation of old data?

☐ Who contributed to/is responsible for the research? (List in order of contribution.)

☐ What contribution can they make to the writing of this report?

☐ On which works by other researchers/theoreticians/scientists does this research or discussion build ? [Attach bibliographical list.]

☐ With whose research or theories does it differ?

☐ Of what larger story is my story a part?

☐ What did I think I was going to find before I began?

☐ Have I checked my results?

☐ Will this data be best presented in a table, chart, graph or other visual medium?

☐ What are the consequences of this work or report?

☐ Is it sufficiently new and distinctive from other reports? What reports are most like it? (Add to bibliographical list)

☐ What does it add to the body of knowledge?

☐ On whom would it have the most impact? Who most needs to know about this research? (Describe your audience for the article, and/or list journals where you would like to see it appear. Aim high.)

☐ Who would best understand and appreciate the consequences?

☐ What is the most interesting way to present these results without, of course, sacrificing complete accuracy?

CHECKLIST #9

PARTS OF THE RESEARCH PAPER

☐ Descriptive title

☐ Abstract or Summary

☐ Introduction

☐ Statement of problem

☐ Methods and Materials section

☐ Presentation of data

☐ Interpretation of data

☐ Polished illustrations and graphs

☐ Extensive Literature Review

☐ Bibliography

☐ Conclusions

---

interim report of work in progress on a larger project. In contrast, an article can report a sequence of experiments or an entire research program. In fact, one of the common reasons why an article might be rejected by a journal is that the work does not offer a sufficiently distinctive contribution, that is, because it looks like a fancy lab report, with not enough *new* material to warrant publication.

A lab report may also include proprietary information—sensitive results or information—that may not be ready for publication to a wider audience for scientific, legal, economic, or security reasons.

Subject

A lab report is restricted to reporting experiments and their results. An article is the proper vehicle to discuss scientific matters that do not deal directly with experimentation: theories, new models, new procedures and methods, or the reinterpretation of others' data.

Definitions

A lab report generally does not have to define technical terms, whereas a journal article may have to define certain terms in order to ensure a commonality among its readership.

Introductory Remarks

A lab report contains fewer introductory remarks, whereas a journal article should include some material of a more general nature, such as explaining the significance of a problem or its relationship to theory, or the motivation in adopting a certain approach to a problem. Journal articles also take greater care to define the importance of the work in the context of other work in the field.

Literature Search

A lab report generally includes a minimal account of the literature unless you need to establish background or authority for an experimental procedure or a new interpretation of data. A research article needs an extensive and thorough citation of all the literature that pertains directly to the problem at hand in order to ensure that proper credit is given to other researchers in the field and to ensure that the question is properly defined in light of previous work.

Interpretive Remarks

Most lab reports will have interpretive remarks that are necessary only for very specific aspects of the data or the theoretical underpinnings of the experiment, since the audience for the lab report is usually familiar with the problem. A research article should include extensive interpretation of the results.

Conclusion

Lab reports may not reach any general conclusion apart from merely reporting the data and, perhaps, recommending further research. Most lab reports when they do reach conclusions reach very specific ones. Research articles, because they should cover a wider territory, need an extensive conclusion section, which might include definite conclusions, possible conclusions, statements about the conditions under which the conclusions are true or untrue, possible alternative interpretations, speculations, and recommendations for further research.

Finally, there is the most salient difference, the one from which all the other differences mentioned above flow. That is the matter of audience. Who is your audience for a research paper or article?

Audience

In the normal setting of a science course, your only audience is the person who will be grading your paper, the professor or instructor. As with other forms of scientific writing you do as a student, it is again helpful to imagine the audience you will face when writing a research article for a journal.

Your real audience will first be the editor of a journal where you would like to see the paper published. The editor's function in most journals is to see that the paper meets requirements for length, style, format of presentation, and subject or scope. In almost all journals, the editor will then send the paper out for "peer review"—a process by which colleagues in your field will read the paper, evaluate its contribution and its style, and vote on its acceptability for publication in the journal. Of course, as you become more specialized and more well-known in the field, it becomes more likely that you will personally know the reviewers and vice versa. For that reason, and in order to protect objectivity, most journals practice "double-blind" reviewing, in which reviewers don't know your name and you never find out theirs. Many journals practice simple blind reviewing, in which your name is included on the submission, but the reviewers remain anonymous.

In many instances, reviewers will recommend your paper for publication but suggest (or even demand) modifications and revisions. In other cases, reviewers will reject a paper for some technical reason but suggest that you try resubmitting the paper after meeting their objections. Finally, if all goes well, your paper will reach its wider, intended audience: the community of specialists in your discipline, or even the more general scientific community at large.

As a consequence of this elaborate process, the most significant problem in writing the paper becomes finding the proper *tone* or *pitch.* That is, you will need to balance your desire to demonstrate your very specialized expertise and knowledge with the equally important desire to communicate to everyone in your audience. This is not easy. But as in other kinds of writing about science, it is generally better to be overly clear than dense and difficult to understand. Be as clear as possible and define any terms that might be misunderstood by your wider audience.

6

How to Write Titles

As in other parts of writing about science, imagining your audience's needs is a good place to begin titling your paper. Even if your paper is for a course, it is good practice to imagine that your paper is going to be published. You may be surprised at how important titles really are.

If you go back to the flowchart of scientific communication (page 23), you will note that a project often begins with a literature search: scientists read other scientists' published work in order to find what's out there. So most readers will first encounter your title when they are searching for information. They might be logged on to a library computer that will search through the titles of articles in two ways:

1. By keywords you instruct it to search for, or

2. By a Table of Contents search in which you select a journal and the computer returns a list of titles in that journal.

Try, then, to imagine what you would want to see in the title if you were searching for your paper by subject. Including both a major title and a subtitle can help make your report specific, which is why some journals permit scientific papers to include subtitles, *but these journals are in the minority.* Most journals prefer (and the best titles are, I believe) single clauses or even sentences, rarely more than fifteen words long at the outside, containing a verb.

Along these lines, it is also helpful to scan the table of contents of the journals you have targeted for possible publication of your work. Note characteristics the journal seems to favor, such as titles with subtitles separated by a colon, very technical titles, or titles with verbs.

Well-formed titles usually include one or two (but not all) of the following elements:

- **The name of the problem, hypothesis, or theory that you tested or discuss.**

71

Is There Evidence for Sexual Dimorphism in
the Corpus Collosum?
A Physical Interpretation of the Haicheng
Earthquake Prediction
Origin of the Concept of the Black Hole in
Astrophysics and Its Role in Cosmology

- **The name of the phenomenon or subject you investigated.**

Variations in Strontium Isotopes in Seawater
from 3 Million Years Ago to the Present
Efficient Multistep Photoinitiated Electron
Transfer in a Molecular Pentad
Identification of a Banded Terrain in the
Venusian Mountains of Ishtar Terra

- **The name of the method you used to investigate a phenomenon or a method you have developed for application.**

The Use of β-Thymine for the Study of Okazaki
Genetic Fragments
The Possible Application of Remote
Geochemistry in Planetary Exploration
The Use of Nonlinear Programming to Correct
the Numerical Integration of the N-Body
Problem

- **A brief description of the results you obtained.**

Adenoviruses Enable Viral and Cellular Genes
to Transform Primary Cells in Culture
The Code of Ant-Plant Mutualism Broken by
Parasite

- **The most vivid titles contain a verb.**

Interleukin-1 <u>Regulates</u> Alloreactiviy in Vivo
The Nucleus of Halley's Comet <u>Contains</u> an
Active Polar Region

```
Tyrosine Increases Blood Pressure in Hyper-
    tensive Rats
```

Unfortunately, titles that use verbs are rare in scientific journals. Much more common are dense strings of nouns and adjectives. Sometimes what might be a verb gets buried, causing confusion over the title's actual meaning.

X: Deformation potential acoustic photon scattering limited mobility in narrow quantum wells[10]

Here, I believe, "limited" could act as a verb. But since it can also be an adjective, it gets lost amid the other adjectives and nouns. "Scattering" could act as either a noun or a verb. Compare the following titles (which have been artificially converted into noun strings) with their better, unpacked versions above:

X: A Three-Million-Year-Old-to-Recent Seawater Strontium Isotope Variations Study

X: Venus's Ishtar Terra Mountain Banded Terrain Identification

X: Okazaki Genetic Fragment Study β-Thymine Employment

While these are grammatically correct, they are difficult to decipher. The author has taken relationships between objects and disguised those relationships in nouns and adjectives. For a more elaborate discussion of noun strings nominalization and why scientific prose tends to abuse it, consult the section, "Use verbs; avoid nominalization and noun strings" in Chapter 18: "A Scientific Approach to Style."

When writing a title, omit obvious words and phrases, especially self-referential ones like:

X: A Study on . . .

X: A Report on the Results of an Experiment on . . .

X: An Investigation of . . .

These are general tactics to avoid, but for every suggestion there are hearty exceptions. For instance, it is generally a good idea to avoid using abbreviations or acronyms, but in many computer science journals, acronyms are quite common and necessary. Similarly, it is generally good counsel to avoid using symbols, but in many mathematics and particle physics journals Greek symbols are necessary. Finally, for most purposes extremely specialized jargon in the title itself is a bad idea, but in highly-specialized journals it is a common practice and may, indeed, be necessary.

7

How to Write Abstracts

WHAT IS AN ABSTRACT?

An abstract is an accurate representation of the contents of a document in abbreviated form. It should be prepared by its author(s) for publication with the research report. Writing abstracts is also useful in helping you consolidate your ideas for publications and machine-readable databases.[11]

At very least, the abstract should reveal the scope of the paper and the topics discussed. As one expert on abstracts has said, the task of the abstractor is "to convey what the author himself has done, why he has done it, and by what steps he has arrived at his conclusions, together with those conclusions. Any other points are irrelevant."[12] It should be self-contained; in other words, it should not refer to the paper itself for further clarification. And it must balance brevity with informativeness.

When it is time for you to submit a paper for publication to a scientific or technical journal, you must include an abstract. Therefore, it is a good idea to practice writing abstracts for papers you write in science courses. Writing abstracts is also a good discipline in its own right: it helps you get a perspective on your work and define for yourself its most salient (important) features.

WHEN DO YOU WRITE AN ABSTRACT?

In a word, last. The abstract should be the last thing you write before submitting work. But the other "when" question is: When do you *need* to write an abstract? There are several circumstances in which you will need to write an abstract or an abstract-like document:

- when you submit an article for publication, or in some instances, after an article is accepted for publication;

- when your dissertation for a higher degree (M.S. or Ph.D.) is accepted; or

- when your lab report will be disseminated to an audience that needs a summary of its contents.

WHERE DOES AN ABSTRACT APPEAR?

When writing a paper for a course or an institution, an abstract may not be required, but it is a courtesy to your reader and an important means of conceptualizing your work. Place the abstract between the cover page and the Table of Contents, or, as a second choice, at the beginning of your paper.

If your paper is published, the abstract might appear in three places: at the top of an article, often just beneath the title and author(s) line; in an abstracts index, which you can find in the reference section of your library; and/or in databases of abstracts that are maintained by listing services for computerized (on-line) searches. Virtually every major scientific discipline has its own abstracts index. Some have additional indexes. Chances are your university library subscribes to most or all of the important abstracts indexes and databases. These are listed in Appendix B.

WHY DO READERS NEED ABSTRACTS?

In writing the abstract, it is helpful to know why someone would want to read an abstract in the first place. In other words, what is the reader looking for in an abstract? The answer lies in the fact that the abstract is a research tool. Every practicing scientist needs to sift through an enormous volume of information in order to narrow a search for more specific information relating to his or her research. After locating the titles of likely prospects, a scientist will read abstracts in order to narrow the search.

In many cases, the abstract is the only part of your article that someone will read. To that end, abstract services collect only the abstracts, together with the bibliographical information (that is, where the article to which the abstract refers was published), from scientific papers and, in some instances, a list of *key words.* These services then order and index the abstracts in systematic ways to aid others who are searching the literature.

There are even computer programs that will automatically sort abstracts according to key words and subject, with varying degrees of efficiency. At the very least, researchers can use computers to call up key words. The goal of a reader will be to glance through many abstracts as quickly as possible. Since the reader will be interested in sorting through your abstract and thousands like it quickly, you ought to address him or her with *clarity* and *directness*. Along with the abstract, include a full bibliographical citation so that the person who reads the abstract will know where to find your article. The abstract also serves a secondary function: by reiterating the contents in a more general way, a well-written abstract helps readers understand those contents when they read the article in full.

Answer the questions in Checklist #10 before writing the abstract.

CHECKLIST #10

PREPARING TO WRITE THE ABSTRACT

☐ Who will read this abstract, and under what circumstances?

☐ Why would another researcher be interested in this work?

☐ What is the scope of topics covered in this report?

☐ What are the most significant aspects of this report?

☐ What is the minimum necessary information the researcher will need in order to understand these most significant aspects?

☐ Have I included bibliographical information if I am sending this abstract out by itself?

RULES OF THUMB FOR WRITING THE ABSTRACT

When you write the abstract you will probably be tempted to be as brief as you can at all costs. As a result, you may find yourself lapsing into a kind of telegraphic language—dropping articles (*a, an, the*) and relative pronouns (*this, that, which, who*), and relying on noun strings and nominals rather than verbs. However, your primary purpose in writing an abstract is to communicate the most salient features of your article within the space allotted. Deleting these little words makes deciphering meanings more difficult. Other common stylistic habits found in abstracts—using passive voice and sentence fragments—also tend to make reading more difficult.

CHECKLIST #11

RULES OF THUMB FOR WRITING ABSTRACTS

☐ Write complete sentences.

☐ Use correct grammar.

☐ Don't refer to the text of the paper in the abstract.

> **X:** As the data this paper presents will show. . .
>
> **X:** For more specific details, see the "Methods Section" of this paper.

☐ Communicate a *crucial* piece of information in every sentence.

☐ Maintain the same level of generality or specificity throughout.

☐ Use active voice as much as possible.

☐ Avoid compacting information into noun strings and nominalizations.

☐ Don't delete prepositions, adjectives, articles, and relative pronouns.

☐ Never include information that doesn't appear in the article.

☐ Don't editorialize, evaluate, or hype, in an effort to generalize, summarize, or encapsulate.

> **X:** . . . this <u>brilliant</u> deduction. . .
>
> **X:** . . . a <u>disappointingly</u> low number of correlations. . .
>
> **X:** . . . one of the more <u>incredible</u> phenomena. . .
>
> **X:** . . . these <u>striking</u> results. . .

WHAT YOU CAN LEAVE OUT

It is hard to specify what you can leave out of any abstract because scientific papers focus on different areas: for instance, you can generally omit descriptions of methodological apparatus, but valid scientific papers can be and have been written about the application of a new telescope, new procedures for separating chemicals, or a new means of tracing subatomic particles. In these instances you would naturally include descriptions of them in the abstract. The following are usually not discussed in an abstract unless they are the primary focus of the article:

- the data and representations of the data themselves,

- the method you used to analyze the data,

- elaborate description of the subject or phenomenon,

- detailed discussions of competing hypotheses or methods, or

- discussions of other work in the area—literature citations and so on.

TYPES OF ABSTRACTS

Librarians and abstract service specialists loosely categorize abstracts into three types: *informative, indicative,* and *descriptive.*

Informative Abstracts

Far and away the most common and most useful abstract is the *informative* abstract. An informative abstract gives the reader a sense of a major part of the picture without filling in the details. It's like a sketch or outline of figures in a drawing without the colors or shadings added.

A good way to construct the abstract is to devote a sentence or two to the major parts of the larger paper so that the abstract is a study in miniature of the paper:

Problem

Hypothesis

Method

Results

Conclusions

If space permits, it is often a good idea to include a sentence at the beginning describing the significance of the problem (contextualizing) and a sentence at the end describing the wider significance of the work or subsidiary but important conclusions. In other words, if space permits, you can even give contextual information in an abstract, as long as it is discussed in the paper itself.

For instance, the following abstract, adapted from Apostolos P. Georgopoulos, et al., "Mental Rotation of the Neuronal Population Vector," was published in *Science,* the journal of the American Association for the Advancement of Science. It involves some rather complex ideas, yet it boils down the essence of a paper that is the equivalent of six typewritten pages, including diagrams, to just 209 words.[13]

INTRODUCTION: Identifying how cognitive or mental operations match neural activity in the brain is a fundamental problem in cognitive neuroscience.

PROBLEM: A rhesus monkey learned the complex physical and cognitive task of moving its arm orthogonal and counterclockwise (CCW) to the direction of a target light. As the light changed its position from trial to trial, the monkey continued to move at 90° and CCW from that direction.

HYPOTHESIS: We hypothesized that the monkey first imagined a mental image of a vector between the light and the direction of its arm motion, and then mentally rotated this vector.

METHOD:	We tested this hypothesis directly by recording the activity of neurons in the motor cortex that are sensitive to direction while the monkey performed its task. We computed the pattern of action in these neurons in successive time intervals during the task. The results created a neuronal population vector (npv).
RESULTS:	This npv rotated gradually from the direction of the light to the direction of the arm movement.
CONCLUSIONS:	These results provide direct evidence for the hypothesis that the monkey imagined and then rotated a line between the light and its mental image of the vector of motion. [165 words]
SUBSIDIARY CONCLUSION:	It also proved that measuring neuronal population vectors is a useful tool for identifying how neuronal activity matches cognitive (imaginative) tasks in the brain of primates. [209 words]

Bringing the abstract in at about 200 words and still briefing the reader on each part of the paper is a good goal.

Indicative Abstracts

The *indicative* abstract is a guide to the contents of an article that does not reveal what those contents are in any detail. Indicative abstracts tend to indicate the subject and scope of an article, and sometimes the method by which a problem was solved or a phenomenon tested, without telling what the solutions were or what conclusions the article reaches except in the most general of terms. In other words, an indicative abstract would include information about

- the problem,
- its significance,
- possible solutions or hypotheses explaining it, and
- the methodology used to test a hypothesis or a solution.

In broad ranging or complex articles, you might want to write an indicative abstract rather than attempt to communicate the specific import of your research, as in discussions of pure theory. On the other hand, only in rare instances will this satisfy the criteria your readers, and most journals, have for an abstract. For instance, look at how anemic the abstract about the rhesus monkey looks when it is rewritten in indicative form.

PROBLEM: A rhesus monkey was trained to move and rotate its arm opposite to the rotation and movement of a target light that changed its position from trial to trial, a complex physical and cognitive task.

HYPOTHESIS: We hypothesized that the monkey first imagined a mental image of a vector between the light and the direction in which it was trained to move its arm, and then mentally rotated this vector.

METHOD: We tested this hypothesis directly by recording the activity of neurons in the motor cortex that are sensitive to direction while the monkey performed its task. We computed the way these neurons fired or "voted" in successive time intervals during the task, creating a neuronal population vector (npv).

Indicative abstracts do have the advantage of tending, consciously or not, to make readers curious about your work by posing questions but withholding specific answers. So, by their very inadequacies as sources of conclusive information, they may draw readers to the article. However, they have the serious disadvantage of being less serviceable for readers who use abstracts as their primary source of information.

Descriptive Abstracts (Executive Summary)

A *descriptive* abstract presents only the most general view of your subject, scope, and/or conclusions and recommendations. It is rarely serviceable for formal articles, reports, and journals. A descriptive abstract is often suitable for essays or technical reports intended for a more general readership (for example, in a popular science magazine or for a class made up of students with a variety of majors).

If all elementary particles are treated as strings, a consistent quantum theory emerges that accounts for all four fundamental forces. If this theory is correct, it will transform our ideas about space and time.

In this regard, the descriptive abstract closely resembles to the executive summary, which is useful for in-house reports, grant applications, and cover letters to editors. For example:

This study provides evidence for the hypothesis that a rhesus monkey imagines or mentally rehearses the direction in which it will move its arm before moving it. It also suggests that measuring the reactions of neuronal populations gives clues to cognitive events.

or:

In this study we show that gravity acting on a body produces acceleration in that body.

An executive summary would normally include a brief description of the subject, a complete report of the findings or conclusion, and, where appropriate, some recommendations.

This project studied the waves of energy produced by controlled detonations of explosives. We discovered that a detonation sweeps through an explosive as a supersonic shock wave, driven by the energy-releasing chemical reactions that the wave induces. Controlling this shock wave may in turn contain the direction of the explosion, directing the force of the explosion in a more concentrated fashion against its objective. Based on these findings, our recommendation is to concentrate future efforts on discovering such controls of the shock wave.[14]

SOME FINAL WORDS ABOUT ABSTRACTS

Whole books have been devoted to writing abstracts in science. Abstract are one of the most important parts of professional science writing, yet very few students during their college careers get much practice in writing them. It takes practice to get the knack. You will also find that writing abstracts is an important cognitive exercise that provides you with a concrete overview of your own work. Writing the abstract forces you to pare away the inessential and define the essential.

8

How to Write the Introductory Section

The *introduction* to a research paper should accomplish three things:

1. It should provide a larger context for the problem.

2. It should state and explain the problem in specific terms, restricting the scope of the problem to the one actually described in the paper. In some instances, the introduction should also suggest an answer to the research question in the form of an hypothesis.

3. It should give some sense of the paper's organization.

The major challenge in writing the introduction is knowing what to include or how broadly to begin in creating a context for the topic.

TAKING TOO BROAD AN APPROACH

I wish I had a dollar for every student paper I've read that began with some wonderfully sweeping vista.

X: "Ever since the dawn of mankind, when the earliest cave dwellers first discovered fire. . . "

X: "From the very moment the universe was born. . . "

The impulse behind these opening statements is a good one: The writers sense that it is important to establish a broad context and relevance for their work. It might even be possible to construct a scientific paper in which these sentences might pass muster. However, these sorts of introductions almost certainly begin with too wide a field of vision.

The introduction should orient the reader not with respect to the whole universe or all of human history or to fundamentals, but to unmistakably important and relevant contexts for the problem at hand.

TAKING TOO NARROW AN APPROACH

On the other hand, it is much more common—and in some ways more unsettling—to read scientific reports that plunge right in with extremely specific, technical statements. These introductions give the reader no orientation and set no context for understanding the importance of the research.

X: Guanine nucleotide binding proteins participate in eukaryotic signal transduction.

X: The probability for dissociation of CH_4 on $Ni(111)$ to produce an adsorbed CH_3 species and an adsorbed H atom has been measured as the function of the translational energy of the incident CH_4 molecule.

X: The source of turbulent mixing in the stably stratified, nondouble-diffusive parts of the ocean interior is thought to be instability of internal wave fluctuations.[15]

These may be suitable for short technical notes or correspondences, and you may even find that these sorts of introductions predominate in very specialized journals. But you should not assume that since they are so common, they represent best practices.

Such introductory statements may define the problem and "locate" the reader, but only in the very narrowest sense. They presume a reader who is already very close to the subject. In fact, they presume an audience that knows almost exactly what the author knows. There is the danger: You may think that the purpose of the work is obvious to other experts like yourself, but can you be sure? And can you be sure that only specialists—in this narrow sense—are reading your work? Common sense dictates that you try to broaden the context and make your introduction more explicit, even if only with a brief sentence or two.

FINDING THE MIDDLE GROUND

Many scientists have a natural fear of stating the obvious. When writing the introduction, many authors in the sciences think something like this:

> If I state the obvious, then my readers may think that I am trying to state something new when in fact I'm presenting stuff that's old hat to them. Therefore, they will think I am less knowledgeable about my subject than I should be, and I will appear foolish or inexpert.

There are two problems with this thinking. First, it is very difficult to decide what is "obvious": what one person understands clearly may be rather obscure to another. And certainly, in some senses, since you are writing the paper and you know the subject, it is *all* obvious to you. So there's a sliding scale of obviousness, with you at one end and some unknown reader at the other end for whom all of this is news.

It is much worse to err on the side of obscurity than on the side of giving too much information. Remember, the primary goal of your writing is to communicate. If you lose 25 percent of your audience because you did not locate the subject generally enough or explain the subject clearly, then you have failed in your primary mission.

Finding the Proper "Pitch"

A better way to approach the introduction is to think about finding the proper "pitch." In order to do so, you must know your audience and orient them.

Use the Introduction to Explain

State as clearly as possible the problem that your paper addresses and what special factors you considered in defining it.

Use the Introduction to Contextualize

Place the problem in context by citing the work of others who have also attacked the problem. Explain what is *new, important,* and *rele-*

vant, in your approach even if you think this is going to be obvious to many of your readers. Explain how it will extend or contrast to the work of others. This will help your reader locate your work in relation to others. If you can't describe the intrinsic interest of your work, at least for somebody somewhere, then you probably don't have much to report and should go back to the drawing board.

Use the Introduction to Define

Define new terms and concepts and explain special uses of familiar terms.

Here is an introduction to a research paper by Fujita, Lazarovici, and Guroff, published in *Environmental Health Perspective,* that does all the above while retaining its specificity:

CONTEXT:
Between 1948, when the first experiment on nerve growth factor (NGF) was published, and 1976, when the first report on PC12 cells appeared, there was relatively little progress toward understanding how nerve growth factor acts on its target cells.

EXPLANATION:
The reason for this difficulty is that the classical targets of nerve growth factor, sympathetic and sensory neurons, are difficult to harvest, difficult to culture, and above all, absolutely dependent on nerve growth factor for survival. Thus, any experiments directed toward the biochemical or molecular consequences of nerve growth factor action on these cells suffered from the criticism that the controls, those not given nerve growth factor, were dying. In short, it was difficult if not impossible to say whether a given biochemical response was a specific action of

nerve growth factor or simply a result of the fact that the cells
were not dying. Clearly, a tool was
needed with which to study the actions of the factor apart from living cells. Such a tool was provided
by the development of PC12 cells.

DEFINITION: These cells are currently the pre-
miere tool for the study of nerve
growth factor, but, more than that,
they have become a very important
model for the study of neuronal
differentiation. Indeed, the findings with PC12 cells, in some
cases, have implications for differentiation of cells in general.[16]

It is very likely that most of the readers of this article are more or
less familiar with this history of the problems involved in studying
nerve growth factor in living cells. Yet going over the history places all
the readers on a common ground and helps refresh the memories of
those readers who may not be sure of the precise problems involved.
And of course, it helps to inform novices in the field.

The next example, by Kapuleas, from the *Annals of Mathematics*,
illustrates how you can be extremely technical and specific, but still
provide the important context—in this case the historical context—of
a problem in topology, a branch of mathematics. Here, the language is
very technical, but despite the specificity of the subject, the author
has taken the time to give an historical background.

A soap film in equilibrium between two regions
of different gas pressure—in zero gravity—is char-
acterized mathematically by the fact that the
surface it defines has nonzero constant mean
curvature. It is an old problem in classical differen-
tial geometry to decide which finite topological
types of surfaces can be realized as complete,
properly immersed, or embedded surfaces of nonzero
constant mean curvature in $\underline{E}^3$. Very little is

known in this regard. For a long time, the only
known examples of such surfaces were, besides the
round sphere and the cylinder, a family of rota-
tionally invariant surfaces discovered in 1841 by
Delaunay [D]. In 1853 J. H. Jellet [J] studies the
star-shape surfaces of constant mean curvature. In
1900 Liebmann proved that a convex sphere of constant mean curvature in E^3 is round. S.-S. Chern
extended Liebmann's result to a certain class of
convex W-surfaces.

Hopf established that constant mean curvature
characterizes the round spheres among all topological spheres and asked whether it does so among
all closed surfaces. Alexandrov answered in the
affirmative for embedded surfaces. . . . Eventually
H.C. Wente in 1984 disproved the so-called Hopf
conjecture by constructing infinitely many immersed tori in E^3 of constant mean curvature.[17]

Even in mathematics, where problems sometimes seem to simply
materialize from some pure and abstract realm, there are historical
contexts which help situate the reader in relationship to your work.

A DIGRESSION ON THE QUESTION
OF WHERE PROBLEMS COME FROM

As a student you seldom get a chance to set your own problems and
pursue them experimentally. In the context of a course, most problems are assigned to you. But it is important to imagine the conditions
under which you would be defining and choosing your problems as a
professional scientist. Very few scientific projects are *sui generis*—
self-created out of thin air on the basis of a striking observation by a
solitary scientist.

Imagine that you are scientist about to embark on a new scientific
project. You were probably drawn to it by what others have written—
or not written—about the subject. Perhaps you have chosen to focus
on a particular scientific problem because you were inspired by a direct observation of nature. Perhaps you observed some anomaly:

something behaved strangely, in a way different from what theory predicts. Or perhaps you have always been fascinated by some aspect of nature: the blueness of the sky; the power of lightning; why children look like their parents; the way light works. Perhaps you had a humanitarian or utilitarian goal: you wanted to cure diabetes, make energy available to more people more cheaply, enable space travel, devise efficient ways to grow food. As you have become more expert you have defined more specific ways to approach these goals.

Part of becoming expert means learning what others have learned about research problems. As you get closer to defining your particular experiment or project, you read more narrowly, encountering more technical papers about a subject. You will be building on the work of others, directly and indirectly, and you want to make sure your work will contribute to and not repeat the work of others. In other words, you want to do something *new*.

New scientific problems, new research programs, tend to arise from the pool of information reported in journals and conferences by the network or community of scientists in the field. Scientists choose research problems because in reading the work of others or hearing a conference paper, they have learned something or something has struck their imaginations. While there are often other, institutional pressures on scientists to find a research problem, questions tend to arise from a larger pool of information.

DEFINE THE PROBLEM USING "PREWRITING" EXERCISES

A good way to define the problem is first to ask yourself what sort of general problem it is you're working on, and then ask more specific questions. If you can't write your problem in terms of a question, or if you can't explain it in simple or brief terms, chances are you aren't ready to write the report or even to undertake the research. You haven't defined the problem carefully enough, or the project isn't clear enough in your own imagination.

Writing can play a natural role in this part of the scientific method as well as in writing the paper. Writing specialists call this combination of mental exercise and writing "prewriting": preparation for writing the first draft of a paper or even embarking on a new project. In this exercise, you would write in order to define the problem by answering questions you pose to yourself.

What Am I Trying to Discover or Prove?

To show the usefulness of prewriting, consider the following excerpt from the introductory section of an article on the evolution of life on earth. It sounds as if it were taken directly from a prewriting exercise.

We will focus on certain lipid-like molecules called <u>aphipiles.</u> Amphipiles play a crucial role in understanding the origins of life because they have the ability to assemble themselves into membrane-like structures which form self-contained microenvironments. The following questions about amphipiles will help us understand the prebiotic conditions under which life may have formed:

1. What physical and chemical properties permit the self-assembly of certain molecules into membranous boundary structures?

2. What components of the prebiotic environment were probably used for assembling the earliest membranes?

3. How could macromolecular systems involved in early life processes become encapsulated in amphipiles?[18]

Which Kind of Problem Am I Working On?

There are four general kinds of problems in science based on what a researcher wants to accomplish:

1. *Define or measure a specific fact or gather facts about a specific phenomenon.* That is, explain: how a phenomenon behaves (under given circumstances); what it is composed of; how it works; and/or how it happened.

2. *Match facts and theory.* Discuss why no part of current theory explains these facts; explain why these observed facts, behaviors, or phenomena contradict what current theory predicts; and/or develop another theory that will explain certain facts better.

3. *Evaluate and compare two theories, models, or hypotheses.* Discuss how current theory leads to these two contradictory conclusions, or explain that the behavior of this phenomenon

under certain circumstances has not yet been tested to see if it agrees with current theory.

4. *Prove* that a certain method yields better data than other methods.

Now pose what it is you are trying to discover or prove as specifically, simply, and briefly as possible in terms of *why, when, how, where, what,* or, if you're a social scientist, *who.*

- Does <u>ras</u> p21 mediate insulin action?
- Can white dwarves have planets?
- Where do yellow-bellied sapsuckers migrate in April?
- When do retinal ganglia form in the human fetus?
- Does lowering heart rates affect coronary artherosclerosis?
- What is the chemical composition on Io, Jupiter's moon?
- What causes the uneven thickness and disruption in the late Quaternary sediment cover on the continental slope off New Jersey?
- Why does La_2CuO_4 possess antiferromagnetism?
- Who is most likely to be found attractive to members of the opposite sex, all other factors being equal: those with large pupils or those with small pupils?

RELATE THE PROBLEM TO THEORY

Undoubtedly, the answer to the question you've posed will either confirm or deny current theory. It makes sense, then, that you must

- explain the theory or model;
- describe what facts are already known that support or don't fit the theory;
- elucidate where or why the match or mismatch occurs; and
- state the problem in specific terms.

The following introductory paragraphs are taken from an article that tries to explain the origins of light elements in stars. It accomplishes the four tasks noted above in order.

EXPLAIN THEORY	Most of the elements that make up the solar system were forged during the course of stellar evolution. The process began billions of years ago when clouds of primeval matter condensed to form young stars. Within these stellar furnaces hydrogen and other light elements were fused together to form heavier nuclei. The heavy elements were then spewed out into space during either the cataclysm of a supernova (the explosion of a massive star) or the death of a red giant, the kind of star the sun will become in about five billion years. The cycle then began anew with the birth of the second generation star that was richer in its composition of elements.
DESCRIBE FACTS THAT DON'T FIT	As successful as this theory is, however, it cannot explain the existence of three light elements: lithium, beryllium, and boron.
STATE PROBLEM	How, then, were the three elements formed?[19]
	The nuclei of these three elements, which contain three, four, and five protons respectively, are extremely fragile and would rapidly disintegrate in the hot, dense and violent interior of most stars. In fact, any lithium, beryllium and boron initially present in the core of a newly formed star would actually be destroyed as the star contracts and heats up.

WHY IS THIS PROBLEM NEW OR DISTINCTIVE?

At this point in your paper, you are ready to place the research problem in proper perspective. If you are writing for a specialized audience, you probably don't need to define why your work is important in larger terms. But even so, you should not hesitate to explain the significance of your work within the narrow domain of your specialty. The most direct way to describe the significance of the problem is to explain what the consequences of solving it would be.

Answer the Question in Both Specific and General Terms.

The following examples answer the questions posed on page 93.

- Because if <u>ras</u> p21 mediates insulin action, then we have another clue in the puzzle of diabetes, which in turn might lead to a cure.

- Because if white dwarves have planets, that explains the erratic quality of their orbit, might portray the future of our own planet, and might suggest why there are so many planets in the galaxy.

- Because knowing their migratory patterns would explain other data about populations of this bird, leading to a better picture of the health of the species.

- Knowing when retinal ganglia form in the human fetus may lead us to understand, and eventually prevent, certain congenital eye deformities.

- If a slower-beating heart prevents artherosclerosis, then perhaps we should intervene with drug therapy in high-risk artherosclerosis cases.

- If La_2CuO_4 possesses antiferromagnetism, it might lead to a new source of superconductivity.

• If we know what causes the disruption on the
  late Quaternary sediment cover on the continental slope off New Jersey, then we will
  have both a different picture of how geological forces work on this area and a better explanation of how sedimentation of pollutants
  affect the ocean floor.

In some cases, the import of a question is extremely specific and discipline-bound. Are you simply testing or seeking confirmation of someone else's hypothesis? For instance, in the paper about Quaternary sedimentation off the Jersey shore, the authors directly confront a statement made by other geologists:

Our data, however, do not support the proposal
that the area has functioned largely as a derelict
landscape, receiving a mantle of . . . sediments
but lacking other, more active processes for at
least 20,000 years.[20]

Include Nonscientific Contexts if They Have Influenced the Interpretation of Scientific Results or Motivated the Research Project.

For instance, in the article about lithium, beryllium and boron on page 94, the authors merely generalize about the importance of their subject:

The question has long baffled researchers.

Although curiosity is a sufficient motivator in its own right for science, this is not really as satisfactory as it could have been. One is still left wondering, so what? To find the importance of the question, you have to read through the paper to paragraphs near the conclusion. The authors could have included these sentences in the introduction instead.

What do the abundances of the light elements imply
about the universe as a whole?. . . . [They] can be
used to infer the initial baryon density of the
universe [which in turn can be used to calculate]
Omega, the ration of the calculated density to the
critical density of the universe: the minimum density for which the gravitational force would be
sufficient to halt the present expansion of the

universe. If Omega is less than 1, the universe is said to be open and will expand forever. If Omega is greater than 1, the universe is closed and it will eventually begin to contract. If Omega is equal to 1, the universe will continue to expand, but the rate of expansion will slow asymptotically.

When You Revise, Move the Context-Setting Information up Front.

One of the important parts of revising a paper is deciding which information comes in which order. The most common problem, one obviously apparent in the excerpt above, is that on the first pass through a paper, you often *write to discover what it is you want to say.* On the second pass through, you should move those insights up to the front to set the context for the information you are going to reveal in the rest of the paper.

CHECKLIST #12

WRITING THE INTRODUCTION

- ☐ Answer the question: *What is it I'm trying to discover or prove?*
- ☐ Answer the question: *Which kind of problem am I (are we) working on?*
- ☐ Pose the central question in terms of *why, when, how, where, what,* or *who?*
- ☐ Explain the theory or model.
- ☐ Describe what facts are already known that support or don't fit the theory.
- ☐ Elucidate where or why the match or mismatch occurs.
- ☐ State the problem in specific terms.
- ☐ Answer the question in both specific and general terms.
- ☐ Include nonscientific contexts if they have influenced the interpretation of scientific results or motivated the research project in the first place.
- ☐ When you revise your work, move the context-setting information up front.

9

How to Write about
Hypotheses, Models,
and Theories (HMT)

The scientist is like the man in the joke who is looking for his wallet on a city street late at night. A policeman watches him as the man looks over and over a little patch of sidewalk under a pool of light cast by a single streetlight. Finally, the officer can't contain himself any longer.

"And what do you think you're doing?" he asks.

"Officer, I'm looking for my wallet," the man says.

"But you've been looking under that light for half an hour. There's obviously nothing there, why don't you look somewhere else?"

"But officer," he replies, "it's too dark everywhere else!"

Although you may not realize it, when you choose a problem you are already looking under the streetlight. You have come armed with a whole set of lights—theories, models, and hypotheses. These conjectures, predictions, and speculations filter and even dictate what you will observe and what questions you ask. These direct your attention and shed light; it is more difficult to look in places you haven't even defined yet.

Discussions of hypotheses, models, and theories (abbreviated and lumped together here as "HMT") normally flow directly from or are included in the introductory sections of research reports. In many instances you will want to return to them in your concluding remarks, after the results of your observations are in. However, writing about these three abstractions requires its own set of skills, so we will spend some time pondering them.

Because of their size and coherence, some theories and models may seem more permanent than they are. The history of science is the history of revising theories and models, discarding one temporary structure in favor of another. For that reason, maybe it is better to think of them not as provisional scaffoldings which will be torn down once you erect a cathedral, but as nomad's tents—temporary dwellings where science lives until it's time to move on to new territory. Where the Truth may be forever elusive, and theories come and go, the Search is eternal.

Another way to look at it is to pose yourself this question: Is science more like reading from a book of facts or more like participating in an on going conversation?

You may have difficulty knowing whether you are working with a hypothesis, a model, or a theory, and distinguishing all three from hard-and-fast law or the real thing in nature itself. So let's spend some time distinguishing them before lumping them together as HMT.

THEORIES

What a particular researcher discovers from a research project is confirmation or denial of an hypothesis. These confirmations or refutations accumulate to help paint a larger picture: a theory. Theories are elaborate, coherent narratives about how nature works, and they are often presented as such in textbooks and in the introductory sections of research papers. Theories gain acceptance because they are convincing: they do a good job of explaining most of the available evidence. Some theories are very speculative, like The Big Bang Theory, which in the absence of overwhelming evidence one way or another cannot be easily refuted. Other theories are well established but still retain grand elements of supposition and mystery, like the Theory of Gravitation, the Theory of Evolution, or Quantum Theory. Others are good, coherent pictures where some of the corners haven't been painted in yet, like Plate Tectonic Theory. All share this feature: In the absence of absolute confirmation, they cannot achieve the status of law.

At any given time, a niche of the universe can be explained by several different and competing theories. The same sets of data can imply all sorts of competing interpretations. One of the most common, naive errors about science is the belief that it deals with hard-and-fast laws—the Truth with a capital "T"—or that there is always a single ruling theory to explain any problem.

MODELS

Theories give rise to models, often presented in mathematical or visual terms. A model is a precise, mechanical construction of how phenomena will behave. It is often, but not always, based on the theory. For instance, Nils Bohr's theory of the quantum nature of the atom suggested a concrete model, with electrons grouped in discrete quanta orbiting around nuclei made of protons and neutrons. Yet, Bohr deduced it in the absence of direct observations of actual atoms, from mathematical and indirect physical evidence. Similarly, Watson and Crich's idea that the DNA was arranged in pairs of nucleotides along a twisted ladder or double helix, suggests a model which fits much of the evidence. However, the neat image of the double helix that this model presents and that they popularized bears only a faint resemblance to the actual appearance of supercoiled DNA in their natural state in the living cell.

By contrast, there are certain models that evolve in the absence of a good theory to explain them. Sometimes you can collect data from observations and find regularities among them without understanding why those regularities exist, especially with help from the computer, which can visualize complex mathematical relations for us. When you plot the data on a graph or evolve a physical picture of something you cannot observe directly, you have created a model without necessarily understanding why the model has that shape or those characteristics. One of the surprising success stories of our age is chaos theory, which presented many computer-generated pictures of complex, organized systems based on pure mathematics. Only afterwards did scientists in different disciplines recognize similarities to phenomena like alluvial plains and then apply chaos theory to explain them.

When you blueprint a picture of a geographical formation deep beneath the mantle of the earth, you are creating a model. When you suggest an order of biochemical events that led to the origination of life, you are proposing a model. When you design software that will depict the changes in metallic structures under stress, you are also creating a model. Like theories, models help guide future research and set the program for study, but *models are not the real phenomena themselves and ought not to be confused for them.* The assumptions you make in your models will influence the data you receive, because they will focus your attention on some aspects of a phenomenon to the exclusion of others, so in some senses, all models are partly self-fulfilling prophesies. In an age of computer simulation, when good models can render animation of events that are very lifelike, in real time, it is easy to forget that models are partly fictional constructions, products not only of rigorous logic but also of the imagination.

HYPOTHESES

An hypothesis is a rigorous exercise in prophesy: a prediction about what you will find after you conduct your experiment based on existing theory, evidence, and logic. Sir Isaac Newton said, *"hypotheses non fingo"*: "I do not feign hypotheses." He knew that it was tempting to perform an experiment and then concoct an hypothesis to match it after the fact, making himself look smarter. So he shunned this practice. Newton might also have been cautioning us to approach problems without preconceptions so that our conclusions would be based solely on deduction from observations without prejudice. Certainly, Newton's greatness was partly a result of his rigorous practice of deriving facts and laws from his empirical investigations—from experiments and direct observations—and not from hypotheses.

Despite these real dangers, hypothesizing is a vital and creative part of the scientific method. Right on the heels of defining a problem comes the irresistible urge to suggest an answer or a set of possible answers. It's unavoidable, inevitable, a formal way of wondering and speculating.

Formulate the Hypothesis with the Help of Prewriting

Prewriting can play an important role in formulating the hypothesis. By posing questions you can define your hypothesis. The first and most obvious question to ask is: What do I expect this experiment to reveal? Why? You can write down the answer in a personal way:

```
I expect this experiment to show . . . because . . .
```

Next ask: How does my hypothesis directly answer the question posed by the problem? In many instances, the hypothesis can be as simple as the problem. Let's take examples of problem statements from the previous section and see what sort of hypothesis statements they produce:

PROBLEM: Does <u>ras</u> p21 mediate insulin action?

HYPOTHESIS: Yes.

PROBLEM: Can white dwarves have planets?

HYPOTHESIS: No. White dwarves are too gravita-
               tionally dense to have planets.

PROBLEM: Where do yellow-bellied sapsuckers
               migrate in April?

HYPOTHESIS: To the eastern shore of Maryland.

PROBLEM: When do retinal ganglia form in the
               human fetus?

HYPOTHESIS: Earlier than previously expected.

PROBLEM: Does lowering heart rates affect
               coronary artherosclerosis?

HYPOTHESIS: Yes, under certain circum-
               stances:. . . (Specify).

PROBLEM: What is the chemical composition on
               Io, Jupiter's moon?

HYPOTHESIS: [List of chemicals].

PROBLEM: What causes the uneven thickness
               and disruption in the late
               Quaternary sediment cover on the
               continental slope off New Jersey?

HYPOTHESIS: Seismic disruption.

PROBLEM: Does La_2CuO_4 possess antiferromagnetism?

HYPOTHESIS: Yes, because. . . .

PROBLEM: Who is most likely to be found attractive to members of the opposite sex, all other factors being equal: those with large pupils or those with small pupils?

HYPOTHESIS: People with large pupils (the Cleopatra Effect).

PROBLEM: How were light elements originally formed if not through the explosion of a supernova or in the collapse of a red giant?

HYPOTHESIS: Light cosmic rays (protons and alpha particles) interacted with heavy nuclei (carbon, nitrogen, and oxygen) in the interstellar medium, or heavy cosmic rays integrated with light nuclei in the interstellar medium.

Now I am going to tell you something you may find shocking: many professional scientists admit that they write their hypothesis section *after* they've already conducted the experiment. They *fingo!* to bring the hypothesis closer to the actual data they discover. At first glance this may seem like patent dishonesty and quite contrary to the strict allegiance to integrity that is the bedrock of science. But in fact, from a communication point of view, it makes quite a bit of sense: the account of the hypothesis is another opportunity for you to provide a context for the information that is to follow. If there is a wild mismatch between the hypothesis and the actual data, then any elaborate account of the hypothesis is in some senses (and in some cases) wasted from the reader's point of view. On the other hand, if the hypothesis is constructed *ex post facto* to represent the data that is to come, then the reader is prepared to understand those data in the context of an organizing idea that makes sense of them. So, while this may seem like a strategy for the scientist to save labor and face—and in many cases it undoubtedly is—it is also an attempt to portray a more coherent picture.

HOW TO EVALUATE AND COMPARE DIFFERENT HYPOTHESES, MODELS, OR THEORIES

How does the HMT fit in with other HMT or more general paradigms in your discipline? How will your work challenge or support the work of others? In most cases, you should locate your hypothesis in terms of where and whether it fits existing knowledge and current theory. Explain the current theory to which it relates. Where necessary, cite the literature that gives alternative views or on which you based your explanation, unless it is generally accepted and clear in your specialization. You may not be neutral in framing your hypothesis. It may challenge alternative hypotheses or even existing theory. It may actually imply a whole new theory. As a result, the hypothesis section of your paper might well contain quite a bit of drama. Here, your task is to:

- define and explain the competing HMT, including their deficiencies and strengths, and

- compare and contrast the specific points where they agree or disagree.

The following example taken from the astronomy journal Icarus follows a successful two-step procedure for accomplishing these tasks. The authors, Giese and Kührt, first define and explain competing theories or models, pointing out their deficiencies; and then define their own theory or model, explaining why it ought to be superior.

DEFINE OTHER THEORIES:	Astronomers often use the standard thermal model (STM) theory to infer the diameters of asteroids which have low thermal conductivity. The underlying assumption of the STM is that the asteroid has a smooth, spherical surface and that each surface element reaches instantaneous equilibrium when exposed to the sun.

EXPLAIN
PROBLEMS:

But the application of STM is problematical. It neglects the time it takes for heat to be conducted away from the surface. Further, the STM assumes that the light "beams" in order to explain observed data. In particular, STM is unreliable at wavelengths which are well into the blue slope of the thermal emission spectrum. Attempts to apply the STM to observations of the Martian satellite Deimos confirmed these problems.

OUR THEORY:

In this paper we show that a better agreement between the Deimos observations and theory is possible if we apply a rough surface model and eliminate the beaming parameter. We further refine the model by assuming that Deimos's surface is covered by small craters. Moreover we take into account that Deimos is elliptical rather than round and that its surface conducts heat. The results will show a better agreement between predictions derived from this model and actual observed data from Deimos.[21]

Note that the authors are adapting a crude model to the data by adding elements that refine it and make it more sensitive to reality.

DISCUSSIONS OF HMT REQUIRE ESPECIALLY CAREFUL WORDING

If you want to discuss hypotheses, models and theories at length or if you are forwarding a highly original hypothesis there are special challenges in writing. On the one hand you are advocating your ideas, but on the other hand you are engaging in speculation. The result is a special need for care in your prose.

Look at the way Harry F. Noller and Carl R. Woese, writing in *Science,* discuss the inadequacy of any model or hypothesis currently available before presenting their data:

```
Although in one sense we have learned a lot about
ribosomal structure during the past two decades,
we nevertheless can still give no more than a su-
perficial description of how their transcription
mechanisms work. Our failure to understand the
essence of this mechanism might, of course, re-
flect the inherent complexity of the ribosome; but
it could equally mean that we have yet to focus on
its essence. For technical reasons, if not con-
ceptual prejudice, almost all effort up to now has
gone into characterizing ribosomal proteins and
various protein factors associated with transla-
tion rather than translation itself. However, the
rapid methods for sequencing nucleic acids now
make it feasible to characterize the large rRna's
in detail and so to begin inquiry into the role,
if any, these molecules play in RNA
transcription.[22]
```

At first glance, this passage seems overly-cautious, abstract, and even overly-emotional. But there is nothing at all wrong with its style. It *is* complex, using phrases like

```
Although in one sense we have . . .

we nevertheless can still give no more
    than . . .

but it could equally mean that we have yet
    to . . .

For technical reasons, if not conceptual
    prejudice,. . .
```

Yet these complex phrases are required by the difficulty of grappling with things that the authors—and science—have not yet fully understood. We might even say that the tone of the passage is *editorial:* the authors are arguing for—trying to persuade their audience to accept—a point of view. In particular, they are urging their readers, fellow research scientists, to "focus on the essence" of the ribosome by turning their attention away from an exclusive focus on ribosomal proteins and toward nucleic acids, especially in terms of the role they may play in transcription. They imply that what prevents this proper focus is not only technical obstacles but "conceptual prejudice." In other words, molecular biologists have shied away from an aspect that may have seemed too complex or irrelevant! And all this within the introduction of a report on experimental research.

Here is a discussion of a theory about subatomic nature by Claudio Rebbi from a *Scientific American* article, "A Lattice Theory of Quark Confinement."

As the experimental evidence has accumulated, it has begun to seem that if quarks are real particles at all, they must be permanently bound within nuclear particles. Any theory of quark interactions ought to account for this phenomenon, which is called quark confinement. It is easy to construct pictorial models of particles such as the proton in which the constituent quarks are confined. For example, the quarks can be thought of as being fastened to the ends of an unbreakable string, they are then free to move about with the volume defined by the length of the string but cannot wander away from each other. It is a formidable task, however, to formulate a theory that can account for the permanent binding of quarks and the structure of nuclear particles without violating the constraints imposed by the theory of relativity, quantum mechanics, and the principles of ordinary causality.[23]

Let's look at some of the phrases and words Rebbi uses to mark his discussion of theory and speculations in this short excerpt:

it has begun to seem

If quarks are real particles at all, they must be

any theory . . . ought to account for

For example, quarks can be thought of as . . .

It is easy to . . .

It is a formidable task, however, to account
    for . . . without violating the constraints
    imposed by [other parts of the theory]

As a result . . .

should be able to

have taken to calling

it should be possible to make them in experi-
    ments

a series of increasingly accurate [mathemati-
    cal] approximations [the results of which] do
    not carry the same force as a logical deduc-
    tion from accepted first principles.

Nevertheless,

the numerical results have provided strong evi-
    dence for the confinement of quarks.

The effect of these phrases and words is complicated and we should examine it closely. On the one hand, it shows the author is being careful to warn the reader that this model is nothing more than an attempt to explain a very difficult phenomenon. By using all these conditionals, Rebbi is admitting his model is highly conjectural; all these conditionals put it up in the air, like castles in the clouds.

On the other hand, by using phrases like "must be," "ought to," "should be," and "nevertheless," Rebbi constructs a sense of the *necessity* of this model. Furthermore, by introducing the model as mental ("it can be thought of"), he asks his reader to imagine along with him the lattice theory of quark confinement. Accompanied by some persuasive illustrations and good numerical data, the result is a balanced discussion of the theory as both a speculative and promising explanation of existing data.

What advice can you glean from our analysis of these passages?

- When comparing HMT, use especially careful wording. The advice given in Chapter 2 about squirrel writing may not apply here. At times, the overly cautious phrases are needed to accurately portray the contingent, conjectural, or speculative nature of an hypothesis or model.

- When discussing HMT that you will refute or modify, be especially careful to give it its due by:

defining it carefully,

explaining under what circumstances it *does* work,

explaining under what circumstances it *does not* work and why, and

explaining the relationship of your alternative to the original.

WHERE TO PUT YOUR DISCUSSION OF HYPOTHESES, THEORIES, AND MODELS

Many papers save their discussion of opposing points of view or theories for later sections when they interpret data or draw conclusions. However, putting the theory discussion first, or at least reviewing the theories at hand first if only to return to them later, has certain advantages: it helps frame the experiment and the data it produces. The author "clears the air" and prepares the reader to understand the significance of the work reported in the body of a paper. This strategy does not prevent you from returning to a more forceful discussion of competing viewpoints, armed now with data, in the interpretive or concluding sections of your paper. Introducing your experiment or more narrow discussion with a larger consideration of theory early creates a narrative structure like this:

A. *Putting discussion of HMT up front*

1. Current theory suggests this: [define and explain].

2. There are competing hypotheses to explain the data, Hypotheses A, B [define and explain].
3. However, we have an alternative hypothesis to forward, Hypothesis C [define and explain].
4. We have designed this experiment to test the aspects of a phenomenon that Hypothesis C describes but that A and B don't. If the experiment yields positive data, then not only is Hypothesis C proven but the other hypotheses will then seem less adequate.

or like this:

5. Here is current theory [define and explain]. We propose an alternative theory because of objections of the following nature [define and explain].

Saving the discussion of opposing opinions for the Discussion of Results or the Interpretive section creates this sort of argument:

B. Saving the HMT discussion for later in the argument:

1. We formulated an Hypothesis D based on Theory T.
2. We conducted the experiment to test it and received these results.
3. We can make the following generalizations from the data.
4. There are various hypotheses normally used to explain the subject: Hypotheses A, B, and C.
5. However, while each of these hypotheses explain some of the data, none explains as much of it as well as our Hypothesis, D. The consequences for Theory T are as follows: . . .

Both of these "narratives" make good reading and are completely legitimate. But cases are rarely so cut and dried as option B implies. Sometimes more evidence is needed to clarify a position. And sometimes more evidence muddies the waters, forcing you to write something like this in the interpretive or concluding section:

The data reported herein support aspects 1, 2, and 3 but contradict aspects 4, 5, and 6 of Hypothesis D. While Hypothesis D is not completely satisfactory, no one has yet offered a better hypothesis.

So you basically have two choices about where to place your HMT discussion: (A) in the front end and back end, or (B) in the back end alone. Though (B) may sound more efficient, (A) is likely to render a clearer picture of your work and save you some backpedaling at the last moment. At least introduce the HMT discussion in the introductory section before returning to it in your conclusion.

CHECKLIST #13

WHAT TO INCLUDE IN THE HMT DISCUSSION AND WHERE TO PUT IT

☐ What do I expect this experiment to reveal? Why?

☐ How does my hypothesis directly answer the question posed by the problem?

☐ How does the hypothesis fit in with other hypotheses or more general theory? How will my work challenge or support the work of others?

☐ Define and explain the competing theories, models or hypotheses, including their deficiencies and strengths.

☐ Compare and contrast the specific points where they agree or disagree.

☐ When comparing HMT, use especially careful wording. The advice given in Chapter 2 about squirrel writing may not apply. At times, the overly cautious phrases are needed to accurately portray the contingent, conjectural, or speculative nature of an hypothesis or model.

☐ When discussing HMTs that you will refute or modify, be especially careful to give it its due.

☐ It is generally a good idea to least introduce the HMT discussion in the introductory section before returning to it in your conclusion.

10

How to Cite and List References

WHY CITE THE LITERATURE?

Science is a collaborative activity. Even when you are working in solitude on an experiment that you designed yourself, you are working within a larger architecture of science that has been designed and built by many hands. Where and how did you first become curious about your problem or topic? Was it from your direct observation of nature? Were you first inspired by a discussion, perhaps in a class, a textbook, an article, or a symposium?

The theory you use to make sense of your problem, the experiments you devise, the methods you use to interpret your data, your conclusions and speculations—chances are, these were the work of others. They provide the context in which your work will be recognized as important, judged, and understood. So you cite the literature.

Since science is essentially a report of the new, it is crucial that you let your readers know what is old. Also, because matters of priority in discovery and thinking have absolutely real practical value—they translate into fame and promotions and pragmatic support for professional work—it is your ethical responsibility to note what work you performed versus what you have built on the foundations laid by others. Citing literature is the means for doing so.

As you probably know, academia takes breaches of these ethical responsibilities very seriously. Penalties for plagiarism are increasingly severe, including expulsion from college and even legal action for infringement of copyright. If you present someone else's words or ideas without acknowledging your source, you have stolen ideas, work, time, and credit, and lied about what you have done and thought and said. If someone else's ideas have inspired yours, that person deserves credit. If you have loosely based your own conclusions on someone else's guesses, that person deserves a footnote or citation. Changing words around so that you are not using direct quotations does not absolve you of this responsibility. If someone else's words are so enticing and apt, use them verbatim, put quotes around them, and cite their source in a bibliographical listing. If you've lost a crucial reference and can't retrieve it in time to hand in a paper, you can't use it.

WHERE TO CITE THE LITERATURE

It has become more rare in modern professional articles to find a separate section devoted exclusively to a review of literature. More often, references to the work of others is found throughout a research article, with good reason. There is almost no place in the research report, except perhaps for the account of direct observations, where your work does not stand on or relate to the work of previous scientists and authors.

HOW TO CITE A REFERENCE
FROM THE TEXT

- Every citation should occur immediately following the piece of information to which it relates.

- Every citation refers to a listing in the bibliography.

In other words, do not save your citation for the end of a sentence, but insert the citation directly into the sentence as a parenthetical remark or as part of its declaration. In the following example, the numbers 11–14 represent the listing in the bibliography that follows the article. Avoid bunching the citations at the end of the sentence like this:

```
X: We used the same method explained by Hartke
   et al. to refine the data from the Lector
   Experiments in order to develop a model which
   differs significantly from those offered by
   the Formalists [11][12][13][14].
```

or this:

> **X:** We used the same method explained by Hartke
> et al. to refine the data from the Lector ex-
> periments in order to develop a model which
> differs significantly from those offered by
> the Formalists.[11,12,13,14]

For papers requiring reference to the number of the bibliographic entry on the line, write this:

We used the same method explained by Hartke et al.
(11) to refine the data from the Lector experiments (12) in order to develop a model which differs significantly from those offered by the
Formalists (13,14).

For papers requiring reference to the number of the bibliographic entry in superscript (above the line), write this:

We used the same method explained by Hartke et
al.[11] to refine the data from the Lector experiments[12] in order to develop a model which differs
significantly from those offered by the
Formalists.[13,14]

Note the style subtleties:

- If two citations follow each other as numbers in parentheses or in superscript, separate them with a comma.

- Always list the numbers in ascending order.

For papers requiring reference to the name and date of the bibliographic entry, when there is one author, write *(author, year)*; two authors *(first author, & second Author, year)*; or if there are many authors, *(first author, et al., year)*:

We used the same method as (Hartke et al., 1989)
to refine the data from previous experiments on
these treatment samples (Recto & Verso, 1991) in
order to develop a model which differs significantly from those offered by the Formalists
(Bringsjord, 1992; Meteer, 1993).

Note style subtleties:

- The period goes outside the parentheses of the final citation in a sentence.

- If two citations by name and date follow each other in parenthetical references, separate them by a semicolon.

- If there are two authors, list them both (Recto & Verso, 1989).

- If there are more than two authors, name the first and then et al., which is short for *etalia*, or "and others" in Latin: (Hartke, et al.). Note the period after al.

HOW TO LIST REFERENCES:
THE BIBLIOGRAPHY

Every literature citation should include at least these pieces of information:

- name(s) of author(s),

- title of vehicle or venue (book, magazine, conference, or journal),

- date, and

- page numbers.

Depending on what sort of publication you are referring to, you will also want to include the title of the article, place of publication (in the case of a book, report, or conference paper), volumes and numbers (in the case of journal articles), and editors (in the case of an edited volume).

Apart from these constants, however, there is an extremely wide variety of citation methods and protocols among disciplines or even among journals within a discipline, and a range of information you need to include in each citation, depending on its source. What follows is a review some basic bibliographic methods. However, for more complete information on citation methods specific to your discipline or the journal you have targeted for your writing, consult the style guides of the journals you read most often or of your discipline. Every professional journal has something like a "Note to

Contributors" or "Guide to Authors," usually one page long at the front or back, which explains the protocols for submitting manuscripts, formatting illustrations, and using citations. Furthermore, some disciplines have sponsored publication or style manuals which are extremely valuable:

Biology:

Council of Biology Editors, *CBE Style Manual*, Fifth Edition. Betheseda, MD: CBE, 1983. Available from American Institute of Biological Sciences, 1401 Wilson Blvd., Arlington, VA 22209.

Chemistry:

American Chemical Society, *The ACS Style Guide: A Manual For Authors and Editors*. Washington, DC: ACS, 1986. Available from ACS, 1155 Sixteenth St., N.W., Washington, D.C. 20036

Mathematics:

American Mathematical Society, *A Manual for Authors of Mathematical Reports*. Providence, RI: AMS, 1973. Available from AMS, P.O. Box 1571, Annex Station, Providence, RI 02901.

Physics:

American Institute of Physics, *Style Manual,* Fourth Edition. New York: AIP, 1990. Available from AIP, 335 East 45th Street, New York, NY 10017.

Social Sciences:

American Psychological Association, *Publication Manual*, Third Edition. Washington, DC: APA, 1983.

NOTE!

The order of information listed within each of the following examples may be different from the ones required by your discipline, journal, or course instructor.

- **Order of citation:** If cited by number in the text, either in superscript or parentheses, list the references in the order of their citation using the number of the citation and a period on the line.

16. M. N. Reguiero, P. Monceau, and J.-L. Hodeau, "Crushing C_{60} to Diamond at Room Temperature," <u>Nature</u> 355, (16 Jan 1992): 238.

17. C. Kottmeier, "Winter Observations of the Atmosphere Over Antarctic Sea Ice," <u>Journal of Geophysical Research</u> 95, no. D10 (Sept 20, 1990): 16, 551-60

- **Author names:** If the citation in the text is by number, list the first names or initials first and then the last names for all authors, as shown above. If cited by name in the text, list the references alphabetically by the last name of the first author. List all other authors. Many science publications prefer initials for all except the last names of the authors.

Kottmeier, C. "Winter Observations of the Atmosphere Over Antarctic Sea Ice." <u>Journal of Geophysical Research,</u> 95, no. D10 (Sept 20, 1990): 16,551-60

Reguiero, M. N., Monceau, P., and Hodeau, Jean-Louis. "Crushing C_{60} to Diamond at Room Temperature." <u>Nature</u> 355, (16 Jan 1992): 238.

- **Paper titles:** Give the full title of the article, report, or paper, including subtitles. Some journals ask that you do not capitalize any but the first word in a title, but it is generally best practice to capitalize all words except articles and prepositions. Separate the author names from the paper titles with a period. If the last listing is an initial, then it already has a period and another one is not needed (see examples above). Many journals do not require you to list the title of the article, they rely on the page numbers for a researcher to locate the paper. But for virtually all writing you do for college courses, you should include the title.

Young, P. R., and Huang, H. C. "Iodide Reduction of Sulfilimines: Evidence of a Minor
Role for Catalysis by Hydrogen Bonding in the
Decomposition of Sulfurane Intermediates."
<u>Journal of the American Chemical Society</u> 109
(1987): 1810-13.

- **Journal titles:** It is acceptable to abbreviate journal titles, but all have standard abbreviation formats. If you are unsure, expand the title to its full form.

Young, P. R., and Huang, H. C. "Iodide Re-
duction of Sulfilimines: Evidence of a Minor
Role for Catalysis by Hydrogen Bonding in the
Decomposition of Sulfurane Intermediates."
<u>J. Am. Chem. Soc.</u> 109 (1987): 1810-13.

- **Book titles:** Book titles take italics. If your typewriter or word processor cannot generate italics easily, underline the title. Give the entire title of a book.

Peers, John. <u>1001 Logical Laws.</u> New York:
Fawcett Columbine, 1979.

Gleick, James. <u>Chaos: Making a New Science,</u>
195. New York: Viking Press, 1985.

- **Books with editors:** Give the names of the editor(s) first, then the title.

Paras, I., ed. <u>Anticipations of Scientific
Revolutions: Deterministic Chaos in Nineteenth Century Physics.</u> London: Butterfly,
1985.

- **Chapters in edited volumes:** Don't forget the page numbers.

Sween, G., and Argyros, A. "Dissipative
Structures in Darwinian Far-from-Equilibrium
Structures." In <u>Anticipations of Scientific</u>

<u>Revolutions: Deterministic Chaos in Nine-
teenth Century Physics,</u> edited by I. Paras
and K. Mednick, 222–40. London: Butterfly,
1985.

- **Theses and dissertations:** Give the author's name, title of thesis, level for which the thesis was written, university, and date.

  Cramer, S. "Morphological Resonance in
  Dipthero-hydroxy Menisci." Ph.D. diss., Yale
  University, 1984.

- **Reports and government publications:** Give the author of the report where available, the title of the report (underlined or italicized), agency or institution, publication number, location or address of agency, and date.

  <u>American National Standard for the Preparation of Scientific Papers for Written or Oral
  Presentation.</u> ANSI z39.16-1979. American National Standards Institute: New York, 1989.

  U.S. Task Force on PCB, <u>PCBs and Bacterio-
  phage Solutions.</u> EPA-600/78/987; U.S. Government Printing Office: Washington, D.C., 1978.

- **Unpublished material:** This would include notes taken from lectures, reports handed out in conferences, material accepted for publication but as yet unpublished, and personal communications. Give as complete an identification as possible of the date, place, and nature of the communication, as well as the author's (or source's) affiliation.

  Benzon, W. "Visualization and Cognitive
  Function Models for AI Implementation," <u>Jour-
  nal of Artificial Intelligence and Vision</u> (in
  press).

  Gold, L., Albany Medical Center, Albany, New
  York. Personal communication. 12 May 1991.

Lemis, P. "Effects of 5-hidroxy triptamine
on secondary atrial arrhythmias." Paper presented at the Conference on Secondary Cardiac
Arrhythmias, Vail, Co., 8 February 1992.

Steiner, D. Lecture notes on nuclear fusion.
Rensselaer Polytechnic Institute, Troy, New
York, 23 October 1990.

- **Abbreviations:** The following words are quite common in literature listings. If the table below does not show an abbreviation, spell out the word.

TABLE 10.1

Word	Abbreviation
chapter	chap.
edition	ed.
editor, editors	Ed., Eds.
number	no.
page, pages,	p., pp.
revised edition	rev. ed.
second edition	2nd ed.
Technical Report	Tech. Rep.
translator(s)	trans.
volume	vol.
volumes	vols.

FINAL WORDS ABOUT CITATIONS

The essence of citations are four C's: **courtesy, collegiality, context, and cooperation.** It is a courtesy (as well as a legal obligation) to acknowledge colleagues and other researchers who have influenced your work. It is also a service to your readers, who will naturally want to know other references to the subject that interested them in your article, and it helps provide a context for your work.

11

How to Write the Materials and Methods Section

The materials and methods section (M&M) is like technical documentation or an instruction manual. It is a straightforward factual summary of the apparatus and procedure by which you performed the experiment, a sort of script. The premise of the M&M section is that your colleagues reading it should be able to repeat the exact experiment or conditions of observation in their own laboratories or work. If the procedure you used was mostly standard, your report should *emphasize the features that are new.* But like a good technical manual, it should take nothing for granted, being sure to describe all aspects of the materials and methods for gathering data that another scientist would need.

Of course you still have important choices to make. You can't explain every action you took, or explore every blind alley. We all like our audience to appreciate the work that went into our results, but again, the audience's need to know comes first.

PARTS OF THE M&M

All methods and materials descriptions should include:

- The design of the experiment.
- Subjects and or material on which the experiment was performed.
- Preparation of subjects and/or material.

- Apparatus: machinery and equipment used to perform actions on the subject and/or materials. Include illustrations.

- Procedure: the sequence of events, step by step, in handling subjects/materials or recording data.

- Means by which data was recorded—

  by computer,

  by hand after direct observation,

  by hand after reading out an instrument (a thermometer, for example), or

  by some recording instrument (camera, tape recorder, spectroscope, etc.).

WHAT IS METHOD?

After you choose the problem, you must decide how to attack it. What will you do to your subject in order to get it to yield its answers? What sort of evidence do you need to get an answer? Do you need a set of comparison data—a parallel control study—in order to understand the data you get from your experiment?

Sir Francis Bacon compared the scientist to a lawyer. He said that the scientist should put Nature on the witness stand and "trick" it into yielding its secrets. This idea of the scientist as Nature's cross-examiner captures some of the flavor of modern scientific methods. Most research projects today require a combination of complex assemblies of measuring instruments and equipment, elaborate and precise procedures, and computer modeling and analyses in order to observe, collect, and decipher data. Science does tend to put nature into some very uncomfortable and artificial circumstances, and the apparatus of laboratory science can appear to be a rigorous and glorious set of technological or instrumental "tricks."

Think of the cloud chamber in which particle physicists study the tracks of subatomic particles after they collide. We cannot observe these particles directly because they are so minute, and their interactions occur in such vanishingly brief instants of time. So physicists have devised this highly artificial means for capturing a trace, a trail on a photographic plate, of an extremely ephemeral event. Analyzing the characteristic markings on the trail yields clues as to the nature of the subatomic beasts the physicist is tracking.

Only in rare cases do scientists observe nature with their naked senses, without some artificial medium to extend their vision. Astronomers certainly capture images of raw nature, but they must use the intervention of telescopes and spectroscopes to do so. Many naturalists—botanists, ecologists, zoologists, ethologists, entomologists, anthropologists, psychologists, and so on—try to be as unintrusive as possible in gathering their data from the field. Similarly, ethnomethodologists, who represent a growing subset of social scientists in anthropology, psychology, and communications, have attempted to emulate naturalists in their observations of human behavior. Their goal is to try to catch humans in their most naturalistic state. Yet even—or perhaps especially—social scientists come armed with theories and models that direct their attention and with methodologies for gathering data that restrict which kinds of data they are prepared to record and observe.

Whatever method you choose in whatever discipline, you've got to leave a record of it that is clear enough so that you or another researcher can reproduce it. This is one of the most important functions of the scientific report. And if proving the efficacy of a new method is the point of your work, the methods and materials section should be the most interesting part of your paper. In any case, it is your obligation to indicate how you performed your experiment. You must do this clearly, identifying unusual or non-standard equipment, and describing in thorough detail your experimental design and procedure.

POINTS TO CONSIDER IN THE M&M

- **Describe the experimental method and apparatus in a way that ensures others can reproduce them.**

    The level of specificity in the following example gives a good sense of how careful the M&M description should be:

```
We performed all runs on I_3- at 353 nm on a
Hitachi 100-60 UV-vis spectrophotometer,
equipped with an automatic cell changer and a
thermostated cell compartment which main-
```

tained temperature at 18° C. We kept the ionic
strength at 1.0 with KCl. We determined the
pH of each cell at the end of reach run with
a Corning pH meter equipped with a combined
glass electrode. We calculated catalytic constants for buffer catalysis from the slopes
of these plots.[24]

• Define clearly the subjects, including human subjects, or materials on which you performed the experiment.

Our subject group was four hundred undergraduate males between the ages of 20 and 22
years old who had no previous history of
learning disorders and who were experimentally naive—that is, none had participated in
any other experiment. They were all students
at the University of Rhode Island or Brown
University.

• When chemicals are involved, describe the amounts and purities.

In the following example taken from the chemical journal *Tetrahedron,* note how the authors include instructions for preparing two slightly different chemicals, **2** and **7** acrylate, in the same description by noting only the one step that is differ-ent, thereby saving a lot of verbiage.

PREPARATION OF ETHYL-α-AZIDO-B (3-CARBAZOLYL) ACRYLATES (2 AND 7)

Ethyl azidoacetate (5.16 g, 40 mmol) and a
solution of the appropriate 3-formylcarbazole
1 or **6** (10 mmol) in dry ethanol (10 ml) were
added dropwise under nitrogen at −30 °C for 6
hours, poured into cold water (100 ml), and
then extracted with diethyl ether (for **2**) or
dichloromethane (for **7**) (3 × 30 ml). The com-

bined organic layers were washed with water
(3 × 10 ml), dried over anhydrous sodium sul-
fate, and filtered. Concentration to dryness
yielded a crude material which was recrystal-
lized from the solvent.[25]

- **When live animals are involved, identify precisely their
species, genus, and strain, and breeding origins:**

Mice. BALB/c and C.B-17 mice were used
throughout these studies. BALB/c mice were
obtained from Simonsen Laboratories, Inc.
(Gilroy, CA). C.B-17 (BALB/c strain congenic
for C57BL6 IgH) were bred at the University
of Texas Southwestern Medical Center (Dallas,
Tx). Both male and female mice (8–12 wk) were
used, and the sex was noted at necropsy. Mice
were housed in sterilized cages within a
pathogen-free environment tent.[26]

- **If you have devised special apparatus or any part of the
experimental procedure is innovative, be as elaborate
and careful as possible in your description of these.** Remember: someone who has never seen the equipment or performed the experiment will have to rebuild it or reenact it in order to replicate your experiment.

- *Illustrations* **will almost certainly be helpful if an apparatus is rare or of your own devising.**

- **Use the active voice to distinguish between a human
agent performing an action and a machine or part of an
apparatus performing an action.**

     In this first example, using the passive voice allows the
briefer important information to come first and, because it is
clear what or who is performing the action (the spectrometer)
passive voice does not create ambiguity.

UV-vis spectra were recorded on a PEλ5 spectrometer, equipped with an Oxford C28009A
cryo-tip cell for low temperature studies.

However, in the next two sentences, it is ambiguous as to whether the experimenter or the apparatus is performing the action:

```
Spectra at 78 K were corrected for solvent
(3MP) volume contraction (25%). CD Spectra
were obtained on a Jasco J-600 spectropo-
larimeter by taking the difference between
those of the pigment and the bleached sample.
```

How were the spectra corrected? Automatically? Or did a human hand make the calibration? Similarly, who calculated the difference between the spectra of the pigment and the bleached sample? Here is a rewrite for clarity, using the active voice:

```
We calibrated the PEλ5 spectrometer for sol-
vent (3MP) volume contraction (25%). To ob-
tain the CD spectra, we took separate spectra
readings on a Jasco J-600 spectropolarimeter
for the pigment and the bleached sample and
calculated their difference.
```

This is especially important when you describe actions performed by a computer, since many computer actions take human terms (anthropomorphically): *recall, run, analyze, plot, generate, model,* and so forth.

X: Data were recorded directly from the seismograph onto a Macintosh using MacQuake software. A 3-D view was modeled by computing the
mean activity in 0.01-sec intervals and then
plotted onto a graph, which was compared to
previous graphs of the same geographic locale
during quietus. The graphs were superimposed
(Fig. 2). The difference was analyzed. It was
concluded that the primary mantle shifted to
the east 0.17 m ± 0.02 m, and that therefore
the Oahuaca quake had significant effects
more than 200 km from the epicenter.

Again, questions remain in the reader's mind: Who or what modeled the mean activity and plotted the graph? Who or what superimposed the two graphs? Who or what analyzed the difference and drew conclusions about the results? Here is a rewrite that eliminates these ambiguities by using the active voice:

```
Data for 20 Feb 1993 were captured directly
by a Macintosh SE-30 using MacQuake software
(Cupertino, CA). We used the same software to
generate a 3-D model and then to plot the re-
sults of this computation onto a graph (Fig.
2) based on MacQuake's automatic computation
of the mean activity in 0.01-sec intervals.
Using MacQuake facilities, we recalled previ-
ous graphs of the same area during quietus
(16 Feb 1993 and 9 Feb 1993), superimposed
the three graphs, and analyzed the results.
On the basis of these, we concluded that the
primary mantle shifted to the east 0.17 m ±
0.02 m, and that therefore the Oahuaca quake
had significant effects more than 200 km from
the epicenter.
```

- **When particular measuring instruments or other non-standard apparatus are involved, describe them in sufficient detail so that other experimenters can reproduce them.**

- **Note and emphasize clearly any dangers, hazards, or potential ill results that might occur during an experimental procedure.** Call attention to these hazards by including them in a separate paragraph in the Methods and Materials section of your paper labeled CAUTION or CARE MUST BE TAKEN or NOTE ON HAZARDS.

- **Some study designs are so common that you need not identify them in detail.** In these cases, you can refer to the procedure by name (if it has one) or by a brief description, and a citation of the source where the study originated or where the study is described in detail.

- **Describe the procedure.** Apart from the design of the materials, equipment, and subject, you now need to describe how you manipulated them—the procedure—in order to get your results. In many instances, you can combine these into one description, explaining what the apparatus is and what it does, how accurate it is, and what errors it may introduce, as in the following description of meteorological data collection near the North Pole, adapted from an article by Kottmeier, "Winter Observations of the Atmosphere Over Antarctic Sea Ice," published in the *Journal of Geophysical Research:*

During both Polarstern winter cruises, buoy networks were installed on the sea ice. In this paper, we use the data gathered by seven buoys deployed during the October–December cruise along the southeastern Weddell Sea Coast. . . .

The buoys are manufactured by Polar Research Laboratories Incorporated, United States. They have an ice-strengthened hull of nonmagnetic alloy, and they are floatable in case the sea ice melts. They measure air temperature with a thermistor within a radiation-shielded and self-aspirated housing 1 m above the ice surface. The hull temperature is measured with the same kind of sensor approximately 2 m below the surface. A propeller anemometer and a wind vane are mounted on a tripod mast at a height of 3 m. Air pressure is measured with a pressure-sensitive quartz transducer.

A data logging system within the buoy collects and averages the sensor data and trans-

mits them to two polar-orbiting satellites
every minute. The buoys' locations are determined from the Doppler shifts of the transmitter signal observed at different satellite
positions. The accuracy of the buoys' positions depends on the oscillator stability of
the buoy transmitter, on the movement of the
buoy, and on the inaccuracies in the satellite orbit. Argos Collect Localisation Satellites Company [1988], which is responsible
for the satellite data transmission, reports
that the buoys are accurate to within 150 m
in 95% of cases.[27]

Note that the authors are careful to explain the limitations of
the device as well as its attributes.

For some experiments, it is advisable to separate the description of materials from the explanation of the method. In
many disciplines, papers regularly include a separate section
entitled Experimental Design or Procedure after describing the
equipment, materials, chemicals, and subjects. The same descriptive skills apply.

CHECKLIST #14

THE METHODS AND MATERIALS DESCRIPTION

☐ Describe the design of the experiment.

☐ Describe subjects and or material on which the experiment was performed.

☐ Describe preparation of subjects and/or material.

☐ Describe apparatus: machinery and equipment used to perform actions on the subject and/or materials. Include illustrations.

☐ Describe procedure: the sequence of events, step by step, in handling subjects/materials or recording data.

CHECKLIST #14 (continued)

☐ Describe means by which data was recorded:

by computer,

by hand after direct observation,

by hand after reading out an instrument (a thermometer, for example), or

by some recording instrument (camera, tape recorder, spectroscope, etc.).

☐ Describe the experimental method and apparatus in a way that ensures others can reproduce them.

☐ Define clearly the subjects or materials on which you performed the experiment.

☐ When chemicals are involved, describe the amounts and purities.

☐ When live animals are involved, identify precisely their species, genus, strain, and breeding origins.

☐ If you have devised special apparatus or any part of the experimental procedure is innovative, be as elaborate and careful as possible in your description of these.

☐ *Illustrations* will almost certainly be helpful if an apparatus is rare or of your own devising.

☐ Use the *active voice* to distinguish between a human agent performing an action and a machine or part of an apparatus performing an action.

☐ When particular measuring instruments or other nonstandard apparatus are involved, describe them in sufficient detail so that other experimenters can reproduce them.

☐ Note and emphasize clearly any dangers, hazards, or potential ill results that might occur during an experimental procedure.

☐ Call attention to these hazards by including them in a separate paragraph in the Methods and Materials section of your paper labeled CAUTION or CARE MUST BE TAKEN or NOTE ON HAZARDS.

☐ Some study designs are so common that you need not identify them in detail. In these cases, you can refer to the procedure by name (if it has one) or by a brief description, and a citation of the source where the study originated or that describes the study in detail.

12

How to Present Results

Presenting your results is the meat of your report. This is where you finally get to tell your audience what it is you've discovered, invented, or confirmed. This is the news report. It should also be the simplest section to write since, like Sgt. Friday in *Dragnet,* your audience is interested in "the facts, just the facts."

To make your report effective, however, you need to organize things. A raw, unedited presentation will seem both amateurish and ineffective. So you gather the data and organize them into a coherent format. Your goal in choosing a format is to reveal the *significant* data, those that relate most closely to your problem and most clearly reveal an answer (or lack of an answer).

- **Report qualitative observations using the five unmediated senses when possible and relevant.**

    The following sentences are based on a report in the British journal of science, *Nature,* about an experiment on Carbon-60 (*buckminsterfullerenes*), the newly discovered form of carbon shaped remarkably like a soccer ball. The researchers were attempting to convert fullerene into diamond. After placing the fullerene inside an "anvil" which subjected it to extremely high pressures, they collected what was left. Note that the authors use their unmediated hearing, vision, and touch.

```
Each time we subjected sample A to this pres-
sure, we heard a loud explosion inside the
anvil. Despite this, we were able to recover
the entire samples, which were still sur-
rounded by their pyrophilite rings. They were
```

```
disk-shaped, with a diameter 1 mm and height
0.1 mm. They were brittle, and cracked and
broke with handling, giving rise to faces
with sharp dendrites. The samples became
transparent, with an amber or reddish-brown
hue. A small amount of black powder remained
on the surface and on the boundary of the py-
rophilite sample.
```
[28]

- **Describe only the *relevant* data, but *all* of the relevant data.**

    One of the common complaints of many teachers and even of journal editors who must read student papers is that the authors do not discriminate between important and unimportant data. Many science papers I read have the feeling that the author is telling me, "Well, here it all is. I did my job. Now you decide: was this great research, or what?"

    It is simply a mistake to include everything, as if the reader may discover something in the data that the author has missed, or the authors are overly proud of their hard work and want none of it lost. It is *your* responsibility to determine what is significant data and to leave the rest in your lab notebooks or, if you are uncertain of your analysis, for an appendix which you can submit along with your paper. A well-formed table or graph will represent a compilation of all your data and highlight the important features. Thoroughness does not mean being exhaustive (and exhausting to your reader), it means deciding completely what you need to say and saying it.

- **When possible, present the data in terms of a graph or a chart.**

    Visual presentations (other than photographs) organize the data. However, using one will require that you refer the reader to it from the text. Do so simply, placing your reference to the visual in its natural place in the sentence, making sure the visual is nearby.

```
As Photograph A shows . . .
The results from this run (Table 3-2) . . .
```

```
Many different patches of grey appeared (Fig.
11), with striking similarities to those from
our previous sample (Fig. 10).
As shown in the data from Experiment #6,
Table 7 . . .
Comparing satellite photographs A to B re-
veals remarkable shifting in the ozone hole
over the Northeast region of the United
States.
While the percentage of T-cells was as low as
4.7% (Table 6, column 2) . . .
As shown in Figure 4 (middle row) . . .
When we integrated all the velocities from run
1 they equaled those of run 2 (Table 9-1).
```

If a visual is small enough, try to present it right in the text to which it refers. If it is large, include it on its own page inserted between pages of text, or place all illustrations and tables in an appendix in the order in which you refer to them in the text. For guidelines on how to assemble visual elements, see Chapter 13: "How to Compose and Use Visual Material."

- **Briefly describe the method you used to analyze data.**

    Most methods for evaluating or analyzing data are standard: computing means, averages, ratios, or percentages; finding common arithmetic factors; using calculus to differentiate or integrate; calculating standard deviations and probabilities. You do not need to elaborate on these. Furthermore, many disciplines have common methods for analyzing data, and these need not be explained, either. Here is how astronomers writing in *Science* explained a common method for computing the orbit of a newly-discovered comet:

```
Following the usual practice for a newly-dis-
covered comet, Marsden (2) computed parabolic
orbital elements under the assumption that
this object was traveling in a nearly para-
bolic trajectory around the sun in a period
greater than 200 years.[29]
```

- **You will need to explain more extensively when your data analysis requires special manipulations, when you have made certain assumptions, or when you have excluded certain data for special reasons.**

Later in the same astronomy article, we encounter this careful explanation of a calculation:

The total visual magnitude of a comet represents the total integrated brightness of the visible coma (tail) and is a good indication of the comet's activity. A representative power-law formula for calculating the visual magnitude is:

$$\underline{m}_1 = 13.0 + 5 \log \Delta + 12 \log \underline{r} \qquad (1)$$

where Δ and $\underline{r}$ are the comet's geocentric and heliocentric distances, respectively. This equation provides a fairly good fit for posthelion observations in the range of 0.66 AU $< \underline{r} < 2.48$ AU. (Use caution when applying this equation to perihelion observations in 1991, since comets typically have asymmetric light curves with respect to perihelion).[30]

CHECKLIST # 15

PRESENTING RESULTS

☐ Report qualitative observations using the five unmediated senses when possible and relevant.

☐ Describe *only* the relevant data, but *all* of the relevant data.

☐ When it will help clarify or organize, present the data in terms of a graph or a chart.

☐ You will need to explain more extensively when your data analysis required special manipulations, when you made certain assumptions, or when you excluded certain data for special reasons.

FINAL WORDS

Your presentation should be clear and direct. Like a good journalist filing a report from the scene of a crime, you should use the active voice, short sentences, and unambiguous terminology. Avoid coloring the incident in order to prejudice or lead your audience to certain conclusions. Be concrete. Include visual material such as illustrations, photographs, tables, graphs, and charts. These tell stories in their own right, like pictures and photos in magazines and newspapers or video-taped segments in a television report.

13

How to Compose and Use Visual Material

Scientific reports rely heavily on presenting information visually. Tables, charts, graphs, sketches, photographs, and illustrations or line drawings are the staples of scientific communication. Scientists expect visual representations of information. Of the hundreds of articles I read to find examples for this book, 95 percent contained some sort of visual presentation.

Photographs or illustrations obviously are meant to represent faithfully what is visible. They bear witness to what the researchers themselves have observed. But this also holds true for the other sorts of visual elements that accompany a good report: charts, graphs, figures, tables, and line drawings all have the purpose of bearing witness to an empirical observation, sometimes enhanced to clarify the important relations.

By far the most common purpose of an illustration is to represent numerical data from measurements taken in an experiment. Those numerical data often have to be subjected to various kinds of statistical manipulations before they make sense: anything from simple averaging, to being crunched through complex mathematical formulas by a computer.

There are two primary reasons for choosing to present information visually:

1. To make deciphering information or analysis of information easier and to describe relationships among data that are not apparent through other means.

2. To communicate visual aspects of a phenomenon or apparatus.

When using visual testimony, keep in mind that though communicating information this way may simplify the message, arranging data into charts or graphs and producing line drawings can be time-consuming and expensive. If you are considering publishing your work, you should know that editors frown on unnecessary figures and illustrations because of the expense they add to publication. Furthermore, a poor illustration will only confuse and frustrate the reader. However, if you keep sight of the fact that the purpose of your illustration is to bear witness, then you can choose wisely among formats for presenting data.

CHECKLIST #16

PROTOCOLS FOR ALL VISUALS

☐ Use visuals when they simplify information; that is, on occasions when words alone convey the information less efficiently and concisely.

☐ Information presented in a visual form should supplement, not duplicate, information presented in the text.

☐ All visuals should be self-contained: they should reveal or explain important information without reference to the body of the text.

☐ All visuals should be followed by a caption which directs the reader's attention to important aspects of the data or picture and explains them.

☐ All visuals should include a number (For example, Figure 17, Table 6), a concise title ("Temperatures 27–28 Nov, 1997"), and clear and proportionate labels.

☐ Every illustration should be cited in the text.

☐ The medium is the message: photos, line drawings, pie charts versus graphs each have their most appropriate uses. Simply by choosing one you are already cueing the reader to expect the information that follows to have a certain form and message.

For instance, given a pie chart (see Figure 13.1), readers instantly know that they will be looking at the apportioning or divisions of a whole (100%). By contrast, a bar chart emphasizes comparisons of absolute values (see Figure 13.2).

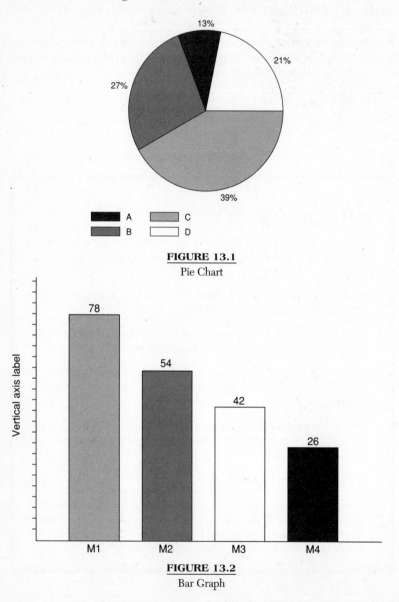

FIGURE 13.1
Pie Chart

FIGURE 13.2
Bar Graph

VISUAL PRESENTATIONS SHOULD SIMPLIFY INFORMATION

Visual arrangement of information should make information easier to understand. This can be illustrated with something as simple as a basic table. Imagine that a meteorologist measures temperature in a controlled environment simulator at varying time intervals beginning at time $t_0 = 0:00$. There are many ways the author could present pertinent information, but here are four examples:

A. At 0.00 hours the temperature was equal to 14°C;
at 10:05 hours the temperature was equal to 10°C;
at 16:10 hours the temperature was equal to 4°C;
at 22:51 hours the temperature was equal to 0°C;
at 32:19 hours the temperature was equal to −6°C.

B. t_0 (time) = 0.00, T (temperature °C) = 14°;
$t_1 = 10:05$, $T_1 = 10°$; $t_2 = 16:10$, $T_2 = 4°$;
$t_3 = 22:51$, $T_3 = 0°$; $t_4 = 32:19$, $T_4 = −6°$.

C.

Time	Temperature (°C)
0:00	14
10:05	10
16:10	4
22:51	0
32:19	−6

D.

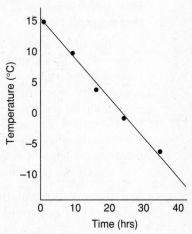

Which of these, A–D, is easiest to decipher? Of the four, B makes the reader work hardest just to sort out the data and their relationships. It was easiest for the author to create, however, and would be cheapest for a journal to publish. A is a little easier to sort out, but is hypnotically repetitive and just plain inefficient.

C simplifies the data enormously, just by the simple trick of arranging the data in columns and rows. It was easy to produce on a word processing program and would not be expensive to reproduce in a journal. Yet, it requires of the reader at least one step of analysis: scanning the row of figures and abstracting from them the downward trend. It would take at least another step to visualize mentally that the progression is more or less linear. On the other hand, the table gives the exact data points without ambiguity.

Clearly, D has immediate visual impact. It shows forcibly both the **trend** (downward) in the data and the **nature of the trend** (linear) without any further analysis by the reader: the temperature fell more or less steadily over 33 hours. It also lets the author demonstrate a further level of analysis of the data: the average rate line does not intersect all the data points but rather, abstracts a trend from that data.

On the other hand, our meteorologist author has to consider a few questions before going through the extra labor of transforming the simple presentation of data in a table C to the more elaborate presentation of the data in the graph chart D:

- **How much easier will you make it on the reader by plotting a graph?**

  After all, the simple conclusion the author wants readers to make —that temperature fell more or less steadily—can be derived quickly from table C. Furthermore, editors frown on the unnecessary inclusion of visuals: they're expensive, and time-consuming for the layout department of a journal. On the other hand, cognitive studies show that *scientists tend to be more visual* than the rest of the population, so you want to present your data visually when it helps reveal relationships quickly. D reveals the crucial trend in data at a single glance.

- **Are there other relationships you wish to plot on the same graph that would require other tables or charts?**

  If so, then it might be worth graphing the data points. If not, then a table will probably suffice.

- **Are exact values important?**

  If so, notice that table C is more suitable than a graph D, which requires that the reader track values on the two axes in order to decipher the values represented by any single point.

CHECKLIST #17

A QUESTIONNAIRE FOR VISUAL PRESENTATIONS

☐ What is the most important feature of these data ? (Summarize in a sentence and use this sentence in a caption.)

☐ What would be the best way to represent it?

☐ What conclusion do I want my audience to draw from a brief glance at the data? Does my chart or figure make that conclusion easy?

☐ How finely-grained should the scale of representation be? What level of detail should I show?

CHECKLIST #18

COMPARISONS OF TYPES OF VISUAL PRESENTATIONS

☐ **Tables** or **lists** are simple ways to organize the precise data points themselves in one-on-one relationships.

☐ A **graph** is best at showing the trend or relationship between two dimensions, or the distribution of data points in a certain dimension (i.e., time, space, across studies, statistically).

☐ A **pie chart** is best at showing the relative areas, volumes, or amounts into which a whole (100%) has been divided.

☐ **Flow charts** show the organization or relationships between discrete parts of a system. For that reason they are often used in computer programming.

☐ **Photographs** are not very good at calling attention to a particular part within a larger structure. They are best at presenting overall shapes, shades, and relative positionings, or when a "real-life" picture is necessary, as in the picture of a medical condition or an electron micrograph of a particular microscopic structure.

☐ **Illustrations** are best when they are simple, unshaded line drawings. Remove all but the essential details in order to keep your line drawings as uncluttered as possible. They suit most purposes for representing real objects or the relationship of parts in a larger object.

TABLES

Tables are rows and columns of data showing their relationships (see Figure 13.3). In some journals, the column headings are called the "box heading" and all the row headings are called "box heading for the stub."

CHECKLIST #19

COMPOSING TABLES

☐ Number and title each table as *Table 00: Title.*

☐ Be sure to cite every table in the text.

☐ Give each table a caption.

☐ Use clear and concise column headings.

☐ Type a thick or double horizontal line below the headings and at the end of the table.

☐ If there is more than one footnote to a table, use lowercase super-script letters: [a, b, c,] and so on, starting a new sequence of footnotes for each table.

☐ Place footnotes below a line at the end of the table.

☐ Indent row subheadings.

☐ Align data in the field according to decimal places. Do not center numbers if that will offset them from decimal alignment.

☐ If data in the field have been assessed statistically, give means, sci-entific deviations, or errors in footnotes.

☐ Double-check data with your presentation of them in the text.

Title

Column Headings

Table 5.2: Results of the Rolling Ball Experiment, Run #17

	Time in secs	Position in cm	Change in Position in cm	Avg. Velocity in cm/sec	Avg. Accel in cm/sec^2
1	0.0	0.0	0.0	0.00	0.0
2	0.1	3.6	3.6	0.36	3.6
3	0.2	14.5	10.9	1.09	7.3
4	0.3	32.0*	17.9*	1.79*	7.0*
5	0.4	58.2	25.5	2.55	7.3
6	0.5	90.9	32.7	3.27	7.2
7	0.6	130.5	39.6	4.05	7.3
8	0.7	178.9	48.4	4.75	7.3
9	0.8	233.6	54.7	5.47	7.2
10	0.9	295.7	62.1	6.21	7.4
11	1.0	365.0	69.3	6.93	7.2

Row Headings

Field

Column

Row

Footnote

*Low numbers probably caused by jarring of apparatus during run.

Caption

As ball rolls down the plane inclined at 40°, acceleration remains nearly constant after 0.2 seconds after overcoming inertia.

FIGURE 13.3
Parts of a Table

GENERAL GUIDELINES FOR USING FIGURES

Figures include any visual element other than a table: graphs, charts, illustrations, photographs, and so on.

CHECKLIST #20

COMPOSING FIGURES

☐ Number figures with Arabic numerals (Fig. 1, Fig. 2, . . .) in the order they appear in the text.

☐ Be sure that you have cited every figure in the text.

☐ Give every figure a caption, complete and intelligible in itself.

☐ Place figures in sequence after the body of the text.

☐ Figures should generally be no larger than 21 x 28 cm or 8.5 x 11 in.

☐ Make line drawings with black India ink on Bristol board, heavy smooth paper, or high-quality tracing paper. If you are laser printing a figure, do so on good quality white computer paper.

☐ Draw symbols and letters so that the smallest ones are not less than 1/16th inch tall and the largest are not disproportionately large.

☐ Avoid gross disparities between thicknesses of lines and in the sizes of symbols and letters.

☐ Use a mechanical device (template, ruler, plotter, compass) for regular shapes and lines.

Graphs

- A **bar graph** shows the relative proportions of data. Each bar represents one or more divisions of data (see Figure 13.2, page 138).

- **Scatter graphs** (see Figure 13.4) are plots of individual data points, represented by dots, each of which shows a relationship between two variables. This is effective in showing the distribution of data for which no simple mathematical relationship is immediately apparent by looking at the raw numbers.

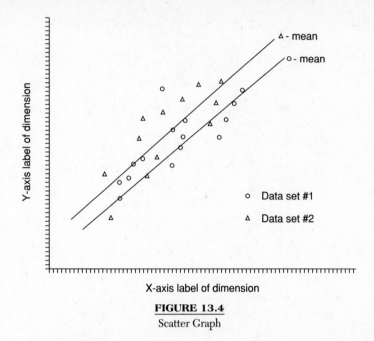

FIGURE 13.4
Scatter Graph

- **Line graphs** (see Figure 13.5, page 146) plot individual points, each of which represents a relationship between two variables, and then shows the lines between them in order to demonstrate a trend (as in the rolling ball graph). They can also plot multiple relationships, allowing the reader to simultaneously compare relationships at several levels. Line graphs can also plot a continuous relationship between two variables in continuous tracings of data on a graph, or "real time analog outputs," for example, in an electrocardiogram or seismograph (see Figure 13.6, page 146).

Unless you are preparing your graph on a computer or having it drawn by a professional, draw line graphs on graph paper.

Charts/Computer Flowcharts

Charts or schematic diagrams are usually boxes around text or symbols with lines between them, sometimes with arrows, showing relationships. Because they represent abstractions (like positions of officers or functions in a corporation, or the relationship among ideas),

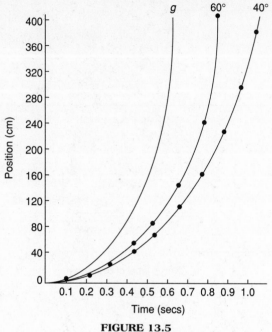

FIGURE 13.5
Line Graph

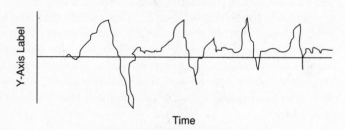

Time

FIGURE 13.6
Line Graph Showing Continuous Tracing of Data

charts provide a great service to the reader by making those relationships concrete.

In computer programming, the flow chart is elevated to an art form. It serves as a kind of blueprint of the sequence of operations needed to complete a program. Computer scientists have developed a

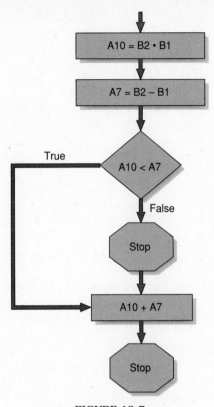

FIGURE 13.7
Flowchart of a Computer Program

system of protocols for different sorts of boxes: for instance, the dia-mond-shaped box in Figure 13.7 means a "decision" step. Notice that two lines come from the diamond leading to two different decision paths, one if the result of the operation in the diamond box is *true* and another if it is *false*.

Illustrations, Schematic Diagrams, and Line Drawings

Illustrations and line drawings depict the important aspects of a real phenomenon or system. You should think of them as something be-tween a blueprint and a cartoon: they are not meant to show *every*

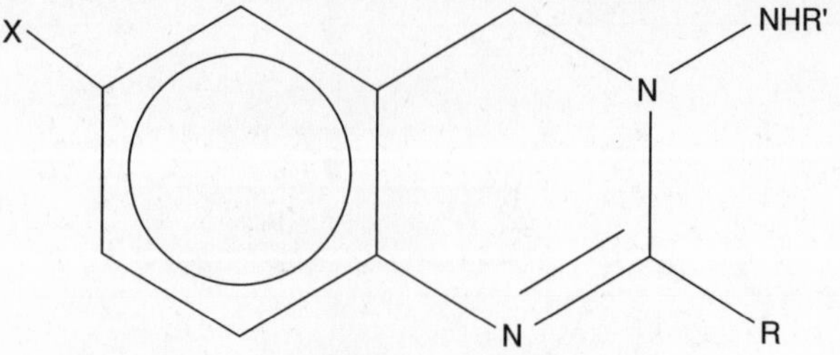

FIGURE 13.8
Chemical Compound Structural Diagram

part of an object, only its *salient* features. Unlike a cartoon, however, they generally do not exaggerate proportions.

Line drawings are very good at showing anatomical relations and models, particularly models of intangible or microscopic objects, like subatomic nature or cosmological phenomena or chemical compounds (see Figure 13.8).

Scientific texts use line drawings and schematic diagrams most frequently to show machinery, apparatus, or parts of a real object (For example, the anatomy of the cell, parts of a molecule, an apparatus or machine).

Note that Figure 13.9 (page 148), based on the original in *Scientific American,*[31] uses clear labels, and includes a figure title and an explicit caption, even if the caption is redundant of material stated in the body of the article.

FINAL WORDS ABOUT PICTURES

In his article "Faithful Witness," Alan Burdick, an editor of *The Sciences,* relates this anecdote about one of the origins of scientific illustration:

Andreas Vesalius' *"De humani corporis fabrica"* ("On the structure of the human body"—1512) was the first anatomy textbook ever accompanied by detailed illustrations. His work was controversial because it exploded many myths about how the human body was structured, especially those proposed by the classical Greek physician, Galen, "whose word was gospel in the medical community." Braced for critical onslaught, the Belgian anatomist sought to bolster the credibility of his *Fabrica* by introducing the testimony of faithful witnesses. These wit-

Fig. 9: Surface structure of a coral polyp tentacle

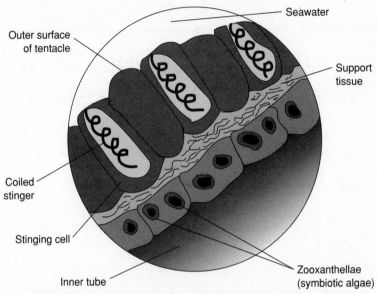

The tentacles of the coral polyp pull in food from the seawater, often stunning its prey with stingers, coiled to release at the slightest touch. Algae called "zooxanthellae" thrive in a symbiotic relation with the coral. The algae sustain the coral with oxygen and food, while the coral, in turn, provides a home for the algae in its tissue, supplying them with nitrogen and phosphorus.

FIGURE 13.9
Schematic Diagram

nesses were not, as one might think, living persons but, more boldly, elegant illustrations. . . .

Acting as faithful witnesses, the Vesalian illustrations made even the most distant reader a participant in the discovery. Through them, the claims of a solo anatomist extended to the public realm of science, to become, as Vesalius said, "common property."[32]

This is an excellent description of the primary purpose and function of any good visual representation in a scientific communication, whether it is a drawing, a photograph, or an illustration. *All illustrations present testimony about an empirical observation or a set of observations.*

14

How to Write about Your Interpretation of Results

"From a drop of water . . . a logician could infer the possibility of the Atlantic or a Niagara without having seen or heard of one or the other. So all life is a great chain, the nature of which is known whenever we are shown a single link of it."

—*Sherlock Homes' article in* A Study in Scarlet,
Sir Arthur Conan Doyle

After painstakingly gathering and describing the data, you must now *interpret it*. Interpretation transforms neutral data into evidence for a case. It changes raw information into a communication. Many science papers divide this part of the report into its own section, using a subhead "Discussion of Results," or "Interpretation of Data."

Interpretation means fitting information, which is generally neutral in and of itself, into a scheme or framework, a larger story. In science, that story or point of view is supplied by a theory, a model, or an hypothesis, which the evidence may either support or refute. In other cases, the evidence contributes important pieces to a larger puzzle. There may be no definite conclusion or interpretation, so you will have to clarify a gray area.

Interpreting your data calls for some of the rhetorical skills of a person who is defending a position or advocating a point of view. It's a little like a lawyer presenting his summary to the jury or an editorial writer trying to form opinions. However, you must not present an unbalanced view of your own data, suppress competing interpretations, or try to color or distort data in order to convince your audience. As a result of this complex mix of demands, reporting and interpreting data can be the most challenging section of a science paper. It can bring you face to face with the gray areas of scientific thought. Interpretation involves us in the discourse of uncertainty.

The bulk of your science education in high school and college and almost all of the textbooks you read, are devoted to *that which is known* (or at least, suspected with near certainty). Virtually all of your science courses teach you procedures and formulas which yield known outcomes. Yet science, when you practice it, will be primarily an exploration of *the uncertain and the new.* Think about how dull and irrelevant science would be if it only went over the same old territory, confirming old facts. It would be like listening to yesterday's evening news every night of your life. By contrast, the actual practice of science is devoted to exploring the unknown, the *terraincognita* where outcomes, interpretations, and even the laws of nature themselves may be in doubt.

MAKE A CONVINCING CASE

The two premises of most discussions or interpretations of results are:

1. The data are neutral, incomplete, or ambiguous until you interpret them.

2. There are competing interpretations of the data that appear to have equal merit.

If the data were revealing and complete and unambiguous on their own, you wouldn't need to explain them. Thus it is your job to give clear reasons what interpretations are possible and which ones are better or best. How do you convince your audience? You can't simply say, "Take my word for it." Certain forms of argument are most persuasive in a scientific context:

- **Arrange evidence:** Treat the data as evidence for a case. Arrange evidence in the order that illuminates what you are after.

- **Explain** your methods of analysis.

- **Use induction and deduction:** You are generally focusing on principles, relations, or generalizations which you induce from your data or deduce from known generalizations.

- **Invoke authority:** You may be relying not only on your own authority but on the authority of other scientists who have come to similar interpretations in similar circumstances to support your case. As a result, you might cite literature in this section.

- **Defeat opposing opinions:** You are entertaining opposing theories and explanations only to dismiss them as inferior to your conclusions, based on logic and evidence. So you might well be comparing hypotheses, models, and theories in this section as well as in the introductory and concluding sections.

- **Persuade:** You are trying to persuade your audience to agree with your interpretations of the data you have gathered, though you are doing so without distorting or suppressing any aspects of the data themselves.

For a scientific audience, the most fundamental tool of persuasion is logic. Ordering your presentation of data, interpretations, and claims in a logical order, using the language of logic, and distinguishing between what is certain and what is uncertain secures and preserves your authority.

Order Your Presentation of the Data Logically

There are two general patterns of logical presentation that are clear and easy to organize. The first is to assemble all the data and then draw conclusions from them. This is called *induction*. The second is to state general principles or models of how data fit together and then show that the individual data predicted by the model or generalization do indeed fit the data obtained. This is *deduction*.

Use Induction

Gather all the small facts that contribute to one larger conclusion into one paragraph and end it with the larger observation or conclusion. Here is how Robert Pirsig explains it in *Zen and the Art of Motorcycle Maintenance:*

> Inductive inferences start with observations of the machine and arrive at general conclusions. For example, if the cycle goes over a bump and the engine misfires, and then goes over another bump and the engine misfires, and then goes over another bump and the engine misfires, and then goes over a long smooth stretch of road and there is no misfiring and then goes over a fourth bump and the engine misfires again, one can

logically conclude that the misfiring is caused by the bumps. That is induction: reasoning from particular experiences to general truths.[33]

Use Deduction

Gather all the larger assumptions and their supporting data and end that chain of reasoning with the deduction. Pirsig writes

> Deductive inferences do the reverse. They start with general knowledge and predict a specific observation. For example, if from reading the hierarchy of facts about the machine, the mechanic knows the horn of the cycle is powered exclusively by electricity from the battery, then he can logically infer that if the battery is dead the horn will not work. That is deduction.[33]

In a fascinating article about the Anthropic Cosmological Principle, a controversial theory about the inevitability of intelligence arising in the universe, the author discusses how deduction normally works to apply a theory to developing a model or an hypothesis:

> A deductive theory begins by specifying the initial conditions of a physical system and the laws of nature that apply to it; the theory then predicts the subsequent state of the system. For example, one might deduce the present conditions on earth by specifying the initial size, mass, and chemical composition of the nebula from which the solar system condensed, then tracing the evolution of the sun and the planets under the influence of physical laws that describe gravitational forces, nuclear forces, and so on.[34]

In the example below, adopted from Norman H. Sleep et al., "Annihilation of Ecosystems by Large Asteroid Impacts on the Early Earth," in *Nature*, the authors discuss the possibility that a large meteorite hitting the Earth eons ago may have evaporated entire oceans and accounted for massive extinction of species—"global sterilization"—including whole ecosystems. They studied the impacts of meteorites on the moon to analyze the potential effects of a single impact at some time in Earth's geological history. They entitled this section of their report "Discussion and Uncertainties":

Given that 25% of the impact energy of a meteorite would be used to evaporate sea water, a total impact energy of 2×10^{28} J [Joules] would be needed to evaporate the entire ocean. That would take an object of mass 1.3×10^{20} kg hitting the Earth at a speed of 17 km s^{-1}. We can infer that the Imbrium projectile [a large asteroid that hit the Moon] is 1/11th of the total mass that collided with the Moon after 4.3 Gyr (4.3 billion years before the present). We therefore deduce that it is probable that between 3.8 and 4.3 Gyr, an object 31 times as massive as the Imbrium projectile, or 6×10^{19} kg, hit the Earth. Given the uncertainties inherent in such a model, which assumes that the scale and frequency of impacts will not vary, the last ocean-vaporizing impact may have occurred as early as 4.44 Gyr or as late as 3.8 Gyr. However, it is probable that the photic zone of the Earth vaporized as late as 3.8 Gyr, whatever the size distribution of impacts, since the larger fragmental asteroids would have sufficed. Thus, it is likely that there was a long time between the last impact to vaporize the ocean and the last to have evaporated the photic zone.[35]

Note that the authors use the language of logic to show the connections between their ideas: "we can infer," "we assume," "it is probable that," "we therefore deduce," and so on. Also note that the authors include doubts and uncertainties about their own model. (See the discussion of HMT in the previous chapter for systolic advice on how to handle such discussions.)

If you have decided to interpret your data in a separate section after presenting the data itself without significant comment, then you are undoubtedly presenting an inductive case. On the other hand, you may very well decide to mix the presentation and interpretation of data, in which case you will probably move from specific points to general conclusions and then back to specific points again, mixing chains of deductive and inductive inference.

Move from the Most Certain to the Least Certain Parts of Your Case.

When you report on an experiment, this principle almost always means moving in the following order:

- data,

- generalizations or analyses of data,

- conclusions with regards to your hypothesis, and

- inferences that you can make from these to larger issues.

In other instances, this means moving from known laws or well-established theorems to specific cases, as in the application of formulas.

- **Describe all important and nonobvious assumptions that went into the analysis of your data or construction of your statistical model.**

- **Along with the data, explain the certainty of all the data, or their standard deviations or error calculations.**

In order to preserve your authority, you should distinguish carefully between what is a fact and what is an assumption, particularly when you are analyzing your data. You should also note the certainty with which you present data. The following excerpt from the same article about collisions between Earth and asteroids does both:

The Earth should have been hit with many more projectiles than the moon because it has more surface area and larger gravity. Statistically, the Earth is also likely to get hit by larger objects. For the impact velocities we assume below, the moon is hit by 1/24ths of the objects and the Earth the remaining 23/24ths. At the same time, it is probable that none of the 16 largest objects hit the moon ($P \bullet 0.5$), because $(23/24)^{16}$ is $\bullet$ 0.5. Thus, if Imbrium is the largest lunar projectile after 4.3 Gyr, it is likely that 16 larger objects hit the Earth in the same period. The time and size of these objects are difficult to specify because of the small numbers involved. For example, the late impact of the Imbrium projectile on the moon could be a statistical fluke. . . . Conversely, it is

also possible to interpret that event to mean that
very few large objects hit the moon at all.[35]

LOGICAL LANGUAGE

A sheer presentation or list of facts is often insufficient to make a scientific case. Without their logical glue, most interpretations of data would not amount to much. Scientific prose needs the transitional words and phrases which signal the reader that data are logically connected and are part of an effort to persuade. They put data together to tell a story. Choosing appropriate transitional and modifying phrases is one of the most important ways to establish your objectivity.

- **Use phrases that indicate the logical relations between thoughts or facts:**

It follows that

Given fact A and fact B under circumstances C and with conditions D, it follows that E is true if and only if

Conversely,

We can [conclude, infer, deduce, induce, posit, derive, extrapolate, extend, assume] that

... from these data

It is [apparent, clear, unclear, obvious, inconclusive, illogical, inarguable] that

Evidently,

It is obvious then that

From this it follows that

To the contrary,

By contrast,

However,

Yet

Thus,

Consequently,

As a result,

Because

By induction,

Inductively,

By deduction,

Deductively,

If ... then

Tentatively we may conclude

It is important that you choose these markers carefully to establish your objective viewpoint.

BIASED LANGUAGE

There are three kinds of phrases you should avoid if you want to establish the correct balance in presenting your interpretations and conclusions and avoid appearing biased:

- **Avoid phrases that characterize the truth status of a statement.**

  X: Clearly
  X: As is well-known
  X: It is self-evident that
  X: It is perhaps true to say that
  X: It is generally agreed that
  X: It is inarguably the case that
  X: Doubtless
  X: Undoubtedly
  X: Incontrovertibly
  X: Obviously
  X: It is likely that
  X: There is no doubt that

- **Avoid phrases that characterize the assumed knowledge of the reader.**

  X: As you undoubtedly know
  X: It should not be necessary to stress/mention that
  X: All reasonable men think
  X: It is intuitively obvious that
  X: As you are by now well aware
  X: As should be apparent by now
  X: As you have seen from the above
  X: As a result, you can conclude that

- **Avoid words or phrases that color the qualities of an observation and that are not supported by further explanation or definition.** Any adjective or adverb that intensifies, diminishes, or characterizes a fact or interpretation, or causes or expresses emotion about it, is inappropriate unless supported by careful definition or explanation.

X: bizarre, magnificent, fascinating, incredible, awesome, terrible, thoughtless, unbe-
lievable, formidable, astounding, dismaying,
disappointing, unparalleled, absurd, exciting, fantastic, inconceivable.

Sometimes, you really mean, and need to say, that a conclusion is true only with certain conditions. Sometimes, you are speculating and must be careful to qualify your speculation as such, distinguishing it from a proper conclusion. In these cases, such biased language is indispensable.

HOW TO COORDINATE YOUR PRESENTATION OF DATA

In actual practice, it is often difficult to separate the presentation of data with discussion and interpretation of them. Quite frequently you may find that interweaving the two is the best route to follow.

The following excerpt is from an article on a series of experiments intended to study how worker honeybees prevent each other from producing males. (These researchers discovered that the workers remove male eggs that are the offspring of other worker males!) The report, written by Francis L. W. Ratnieks and P. Kirk Visscher is entitled "Worker policing in the honeybee." It is marvelously concise, an efficiency that comes from *interweaving the report of data and its interpretation.*

As you read the excerpt, note how the authors at each step explain the four experiments, report the results, interpret the results, and then explain how the subsequent experiment refined the previous one. They refer to an accompanying table that contains all the relevant data and their accuracy (probabilities = P's), but in their explanation they only refer to the important, conclusive data. In the last paragraphs included here they move into concrete conclusions and then, finally, into inferences and speculations.

EXPERIMENT #1:   In Experiment #1 we reintroduced
eggs to the part of the honey-
bees' source colony where the
queen resided. We compared the
number of eggs laid by mother-
queens and those laid by sister-
workers that were removed.

RESULTS: Workers accurately discriminated
                    between these classes of eggs
                    (Table 1): they removed all but
                    four of 204 worker-laid eggs
                    (2%), yet 150 of 237 queen-laid
                    eggs (61%) remained ($P < 0.0001$)
                    after 24 hours.

INTERPRETATION: This discrimination against
                    worker-laid eggs could result
                    from three possible factors: the
                    workers somehow "knew" the relat-
                    edness of eggs; they preferred
                    queen-laid over worker-laid eggs;
                    or they detected colony odors de-
                    spite the double screen we used
                    to separate them.

EXPERIMENT #2:   To differentiate between these
                    possibilities, Experiment #2 com-
                    pared the treatment of eggs laid
                    by the queen with those laid by
                    her worker daughters. We intro-
                    duced eggs into a new colony, so
                    none of the eggs were related to
                    the workers who removed them.

RESULTS: The results were still very close
                    to those of Experiment #1: 59% of
                    queen-laid and < 1% of worker-
                    laid eggs remained (Table 1.2) ...

INTERPRETATION: ... indicating that the caste of
                    the egg's mother alone determined
                    whether an egg was removed or
                    not. In trial 4 of Experiment #2,
                    we inspected activity more fre-
                    quently. The workers removed
                    worker-laid eggs rapidly, with

half gone within two hours and 90% within six hours (Fig. 1).

EXPERIMENT #3:   In Experiment #3, we tested an additional 11 colonies using similar methods, with the following changes: queenless colonies were not kept above queen-right colonies; queen- and worker-laid eggs used in a trial were not always from the same source colony; and we did not transfer the eggs to a cell which previously held a queen-laid male egg. Our goal was to isolate the possible causes.

RESULTS: All colonies showed significantly greater removal of worker-laid eggs, except one which removed both worker- and queen-laid eggs (Table 1.3).

INTERPRETATION: If worker eggs were not viable, this could explain the differences in removal. However, queenless honey bee colonies often rear many males, so at least a proportion of worker-laid eggs must be viable.

EXPERIMENT 4:   So we next compared the _in vitro_ viability of queen- and worker-laid by transferring eggs of each type that were no more than 24-hours old into a beeswax-lined Petri dish also containing a water-saturated piece of cotton. We incubated them at 35°C for four days, and compared the numbers hatching.

RESULTS: In five trials, 81 of 207 worker-laid eggs (39%) and 86 of 215 queen-laid eggs (40%) hatched ($\underline{P} = 0.90$) . . .

INTERPRETATION: . . . showing that the eggs were mostly viable. In fact, these viability results were probably lower than actual because of the dehydration or damage during transfer and incubation. Therefore viability was not a factor in removal.

EXPERIMENT 5:   Was there some marker in the organism itself? To test this we transferred one-day-old larvae from their natal combs.

RESULTS: In one trial, 47 of 57 queen-derived larvae (82%) and 24 of 33 worker-derived larvae (73%) remained after 24 hours ($\underline{P} = 0.70$).

INTERPRETATION: We concluded that, once hatched, there is little support for the hypothesis that workers discriminate between queen- and worker-derived larvae based on some marker in the organism itself. All attempts to isolate such a marker failed to alter significantly the accuracy by which workers removed worker-laid eggs.

SUMMARY: These results taken together provide strong support for the worker-policing hypothesis. Workers removed worker-laid eggs in all colonies. In Experiments

#1 to #3, only 0.7% worker-laid
versus 45.2% queen-laid male eggs
remained after 24 hours. Since
the egg stage lasts three days,
actual removal of worker-laid
eggs might have been still
greater.

SPECULATIONS: We can also make inferences from
these results about what sort of
cue the workers use to discriminate among eggs. Since workers remove the worker-laid eggs—but not
the larvae—we inferred that there
is some marker either on the egg
itself or on the inner surface of
the natal cell. However, when we
transferred eggs out of their natal cells in Experiment #2, workers still removed those eggs, providing evidence against the
possibility of a natal cell
marker. Since Experiments #2 and
#3 show that relatedness between
workers and the worker-laid eggs
are not a factor, we speculate
that there is an egg-marking
pheromone, specific to the queen,
by which workers can determine
which eggs should be preserved.
The workers discard eggs that
don't have this marker.[36]

Again, note the authors' explicit use of the language of logic:

We can make inferences from these results about

We inferred

Also note their explicit use of the language of comparative hypothesis testing:

CHECKLIST #21

DISCUSSION/INTERPRETATION OF RESULTS

☐ Order your presentation of the data logically.

☐ Use induction and deduction.

☐ Move from the most certain to the least certain parts of your case.

☐ Describe all important and nonobvious assumptions.

☐ Along with the data, explain the relative certainty of all the data, or their standard deviations or error calculations.

☐ Use phrases that indicate the logical relations between thoughts or facts.

☐ Avoid phrases that characterize the truth status of a statement.

☐ Avoid phrases that characterize the assumed knowledge of the reader.

☐ Avoid phrases that color the qualities of an observation.

☐ Do not hesitate to interweave your presentation and discussion/interpretation of the data.

☐ Explicitly state pivotal questions *as questions* in the body of your argument.

```
These results taken together provide strong
    support for the worker-policing hypothesis.

. . . providing evidence against the possibility
    of . . .

We concluded that . . . there is little evidence
    for the hypothesis that. . . .
```

Also note the very effective use of the question in the first sentence describing Experiment 5: "Was there some marker in the organism itself?" How simple and elegant! I encourage you to explicitly state pivotal questions *as questions* in the body of your argument. Using this tactic helps solidify the issues in the reader's mind.

15

How to Write Conclusions

The conclusion is where you take that last step and make sure you don't leave your audience wondering, "So what?" The purpose of the conclusion in a science article or report is to summarize your findings and generalize their importance. It is also the place where you can raise questions which remain unanswered, discuss ambiguous data, and recommend directions for further research. Finally, the conclusion is also the place where you can express a broader vision of the importance of your work.

There is a natural flow between your interpretations of data and the summary of your findings. In fact, it is sometimes difficult—and may be unnecessary—to distinguish between the two (as shown in the excerpt about honeybees in the previous chapter). However, it is helpful to ask yourself whether or not they are indeed distinct from each other. Try to separate which aspects of your interpretations are open to doubt, which rely on speculation, and which are certain. The conclusion is the appropriate place in your paper to make those distinctions.

STATE YOUR CONCLUSIONS

The first order of business in a conclusion is to state your rock-solid conclusions, if any, without fanfare.

```
We conclude that a ball rolling down a 40° ramp,
acted on by an unbalanced force will accelerate at
7.27 m/sec². This provides further evidence for
the general theory that falling objects accelerate
when acted on by an unbalanced force.
```

The next excerpt is taken from the concluding section of a recent *Scientific American* article about geology. In particular, it concerns the movement of a section of stable, extremely old continental crust on the border between South Africa and Swaziland called the Kaapvaal Craton.

Pulling together the above evidence yields an 800-million-year history of the drift of the Kaapvaal Craton, beginning 3.5 billion years ago. At that time, the craton was near the pole. By about 3.18 billion years ago it had wandered to the equator. The craton then moved more than 3,000 kilometers poleward so that 2.875 billion years ago it lay at least 30 degrees from the equator. By 2.69 billion years ago the craton had drifted back to the equator, but its orientation was significantly different than it had been 490 million years earlier.[37]

Note how the author moves to his conclusion from the evidence in very plain terms: "Pulling together the above evidence yields. . . ." Note also how he states as fact matters that are beyond the reach of his direct observation in statements such as: "The craton then moved more than 3,000 kilometers poleward"; "By about 3.18 billion years ago it had wandered to the equator"; and so forth.

RESTRICT OR EXPAND YOUR RESULTS

The next step in your conclusion would be to restrict or expand your results by stating probable conclusions or possible implications, adding conditions and being careful not to claim too much.

For instance, in the article quoted above about the probable age of the Earth's crust, the author goes on to consider less certain conclusions one might infer from his work:

Our work implies that the Kaapvaal Caton was drifting about as fast as modern continents since at least 3.5 billion years ago. Presumably, other continental fragments were behaving the same way. I should emphasize that despite the many advances

```
in methodology and instrumentation, studies in
magnetic traces leave considerable room for
error.³⁸[Emphases mine]
```

In taking this tack you are essentially warning the readers as to how and why they should not generalize your conclusions, or suggesting ways in which they can, indeed, generalize your conclusions. The useful words in accomplishing this task are those that communicate conditionals, restrictions, or contrasts:

implies that

Presumably,

However,

Nevertheless,

Yet

Furthermore,

only under the following circumstances

In most instances,

In these specific cases,

Specifically,

or those that permit the logical introduction of larger statements:

Therefore,

As a result,

Consequently,

probably

almost certainly

It is unlikely that

it is likely that

It is logical to conclude, then, that

We might therefore speculate that

It would not be unreasonable to suggest that

These results further suggest

In the following examples, note how the authors conditionalize their findings and conclusions by using restrictive terms (*only*) and logical terms, especially those denoting contrast or objection (*therefore, however, yet*):

```
Our results apply only to falling bodies when
their motion is impeded by an inclined ramp of
40°. We speculate that these results can probably
be generalized to other falling bodies by the cal-
culation of a proportion of g and the sine of the
angle of the ramp. However, we await further ex-
periment to verify this hypothesis.
```

The sort of caution exercised by Ursula Neissert in her article "How Many Genes to Start With? A Computer Simulation About the Origins of Life," exemplifies one of the great virtues of science: cautioning the reader to take no leaps of logic where none are warranted by the data.

```
A simulation of the origin of life by computer
should well be concerned with primordial transla-
tion. However, we did not touch upon this notori-
ously difficult problem in the simulation reported
here. Therefore the reader should not infer that
we have even developed or assumed a model of how
genetic material was translated in a primordial
environment.³⁹
```

COMPARE YOUR CONCLUSIONS
WITH THOSE OF OTHERS IN THE FIELD

The following is an excerpt from the conclusion to a paper analyzing the large earthquake that shook San Francisco, disturbing the World Series in 1989 (called "the 1989 Loma Prieta" by seismologists). In it, I have removed the technical information in order to highlight the words and phrases that the authors use to compare their final model of the earthquake with others presented in the same volume.

How does our slip model compare with the other
dislocation models presented in this volume?
Although there are significant differences between
our model and others, there is also remarkable
agreement concerning the overall nature of this
rupture. All researchers conclude that. . . . All
researchers find that. . . . All studies indicate
that. . . .

Although our model is similar in most respects to
the others, it differs substantially in two aspects:

First, . . .

By contrast, the models of Beroza (1991) and
Steidl et al. (1991) show . . . [different ver-
sions]. It should also be emphasized that. . . .

Second, [in addition to these previous differ-
ences] the other models require . . . whereas our
model suggests. . . . In particular, . . .

It is not clear why the slip distribution model of
Beroza has different characteristics than ours. . .
. Perhaps the . . . variability is partially due to
the difference in the applied [mathematical meth-
ods]. . . .

Finally, the authors try to find a reasonable middle ground among the competing theories and models:

Despite these many differences, however, it is important to note that even though the models vary,
the net sum of any of these models will be very
similar over long periods.[40]

The conclusion cited above goes on to explain why it restricts its ap-
plicability. In doing so, it also defines the questions about its topic that
have gone unanswered, another task of the conclusion.

DEFINE UNANSWERED QUESTIONS

This is an important part of your conclusion. It ties your work to the larger project of science and provides a strong sense of completeness or symmetry with the introductory section, especially if you introduced larger contexts there.

Here is another example from computer applications in space exploration and surveys of the earth's geography, written by W. L. Garrison in *Scientific Experiments for Manned Orbital Flight:*

```
Whatever the characteristics of a geographic in-
formation system, it must be able to respond to
queries put to it by scientists and non-scientists
alike. In certain respects this communication
problem may be similar to the kind of problems
posed by communicating with a computer. However,
in addition to the usual difficulties in program-
ming a computer, we can anticipate another class
of problems that may be even more difficult to
handle.
```

From here the author goes on to define those questions. His final words, however, are particularly poignant:

```
Nevertheless, it does appear that the design of a
geographic information system cannot avoid the
complexities that, up till now, have made life
difficult only for logicians and computer program-
mers.[41]
```

By now, it should be obvious to you that a good deal of science is an exploration of arenas of doubt. One of the first signs of a maturing scientist is that he or she abandons the idea that good science always demands authoritative answers to hard questions. In fact, as many of these concluding excerpts show, much of scientific writing is concerned with expressions of doubt: an attempt to navigate the tricky shoals of uncertainty.

Don't Be Afraid to Express Uncertainties

It is one small step from defining unanswered problems to suggesting that these problems become the focus of further research. However, you may not want to take that step, so I separate it here into its own item, illustrated by the following two examples:

Recommend Directions for Future Research

G. Hahn and M. E. Bailey do exactly that in their article for *Nature* about the evolution of the giant comet, Chiron.

The nature of Chiron's present orbit, one of transition between short-period and long-period comets, means that this and similarly chaotic orbits should provide important tests of cometary dynamics. Observations of its physical properties as it approaches perihelion in February 1996 may provide clues to its detailed evolution and composition, supporting or contradicting the past history we have proposed. Chiron plays a pivotal role in current theories of the formation and evolution of comets, and further observational and theoretical studies of this and related objects (such as Hidalgo 944) are eagerly awaited. Chiron should be considered a prime candidate to be explored by any cometary space mission planned for the next century.[42]

This excerpt is virtually lobbying other astronomers and perhaps even NASA itself to set the research agenda in the next century.

The author of the paragraph below expresses a fond hope that a missing fragment of the geological puzzle will turn up. He tacitly suggests that research should focus on finding it.

Perhaps further measurements of rocks from the same region . . . may yield a small fragment that escaped severe reheating during mountain-building events. The magnetic record in such a rock would be invaluable for decoding the Earth's evolution.[43]

In the excerpt below, Ursula Neissert moves from her positive answer about genetics, given her assumptions, to suggestions about
other simulations that would be needed to make her assumptions
more than speculative. In doing so, she frames questions for future
research rather nicely, noting how the answers would still leave
doubts.

```
To simulate primordial protein synthesis one would
have to make precise assumptions, however specula-
tive they may be, about how—and how efficiently—
primordial organisms translated genetic material.
Unfortunately, any simulation or model founded on
that much speculation could not in any way be con-
clusive.⁴⁴
```

Express a Broader Vision

You have a broader vision of why you are working in a particular niche
of science. The final paragraph of your research paper is an appropriate place to express this vision and draw these connections, especially
if they are not implicitly obvious to your readers.

```
Finally, as our knowledge of these physical and
biological processes grows and we reach a better
understanding of the nature of life and matter on
our planet, we may be able to design experiments
which, in conjunction with other space- and
ground-based facilities, will answer the more elu-
sive answers to our deeper questions about the na-
ture of other planets and the possible existence
of life forms on them.⁴⁵
```

No matter how specialized your work has or will become, there is
certainly a chain of reasoning or trail of significant connections which
has led you from larger, perhaps even philosophical questions, to
more specific ones. There is no reason to be shy about expressing
those connections. I personally believe your colleagues would appreciate these broader statements, if they are both brief and warranted,

---

CHECKLIST #22

WRITING THE CONCLUSION

☐ State your rock-solid conclusions, if any, without fanfare.

☐ Restrict or expand your results by stating probable conclusions or possible implications, adding conditions and being careful not to claim too much.

☐ Define unanswered questions.

☐ Don't be afraid to express uncertainties.

☐ Recommend directions for future research.

☐ Express a broader vision.

---

at the conclusion of your papers. And I believe that science itself would be healthier for it.

FINAL WORDS ABOUT THE RESEARCH REPORT AND ARTICLE

Besides reading a guide like this, the best training for writing the research article is to read others, especially in the journal closest to your discipline. But in order to profit from that exercise as a writer, you must read with a more critical eye, like one artist looking at another's painting. Examine not only the information you're getting but how you're getting it. Is the writing confusing? Do you find yourself reading sentences more than once just to untangle them, let alone understand the information they convey? Note what sorts of writing aids your comprehension.

When it comes to writing your own article, follow the bottom-up approach advocated in the previous chapters. Solid writing is founded on solid data and careful recording. Being prepared from the outset should make your final report easier.

Editing and revising require a special kind of attention. Your work is not really finished until you've rewritten it to satisfaction.

Chapters 17 and 18 deal in great detail with the skills and attitudes involved.

You will often find that science writing is a collaborative activity, and that the final article will bear more than just your name. Writing by committee tends to make the process much more difficult. My advice is that after you all meet to discuss the article, let one person have authorial responsibility and write the entire draft or as much as he or she can alone. Then let others contribute editorial changes and additions to the draft he or she produces. Of course, all authors have to approve the final product before their names go on it, but letting one person remain in control will generally smooth the way to collaborative writing.

Finally, the point which bears repeating: *remember your audience*. Writing is the extension of a conversation among colleagues.

16

How to Write about Science in Essays and Term Papers or Reports

"In whatever art or branch of science, the orator, if he has made himself master of it, as of his client's cause, will speak on it better and more elegantly than even the very originator and author of it can."

—*Cicero,* De Oratore

"I loved France. It was great. The only trouble was they have a different word for everything over there."

—*Woody Allen in monologue*

This chapter is intended to give you a short guide to ways of writing about science and expressing scientific material that fall outside the scope of a lab report or formal research paper. This part of the guide is intended specifically to help

- students who want to write essays, term papers, or reports about science;

- scientists who are interested in exploring their thoughts about science in essay form; and

- beginning journalism students who are interested in the science "beat."

When you write about scientific work that you haven't done yourself, you face special challenges. It's a little like translating from one language to another: you will rarely capture the nuances or all the information of the original research, because sometimes it will seem as if "they have a different word for everything over there." But this is actually not necessary or even desirable. Quite often, you are importing information from one domain into another and giving it a new context, giving a new meaning or "spin" to it.

This chapter does not tell you everything you need to know about writing essays, term papers, or term reports. There are many excellent handbooks and textbooks that will give you good advice about how to write a general research paper, including systems of citation and organization of material. For a listing of some of these, see Appendix B. My goal is to broaden your view of how you can communicate science beyond the strictures of a research or lab report and what you should know if you are a nonspecialist who wants to write about science for a college course or magazine.

FORMAL SCIENTIFIC REPORTS VERSUS TERM PAPERS AND ESSAYS ON SCIENCE

There are many fundamental similarities between writing a report on experimentation and writing a term paper or report. The term paper or report may even follow the same sort of format:

I. **Introduction:** begin with a contextualizing statement

II. **Statement of Problem:** define the problem, topic, or your thesis/perspective

III. **Hypotheses and Review of Literature:** describe different views of the problem

IV. **Present Data:** describe the subject in detail using facts synthesized from your research

V. **Interpret Data:** show how the subject, once we understand it in the way you've described it, provides evidence for one or another of the views

VI. **Conclusions**

VII. **Bibliography**

This is a most sensible and quite common outline for the term paper, if a little dull. Unless you are writing in a course where your instructor has explicitly asked you to follow this outline, you are not obliged by any professional convention to do so. For there is an important difference between writing a research paper that reports your own experiments—your own practice of science—for fellow professionals, and writing an essay or research report about someone else's work in the sciences.

In writing for an audience of professional peers, you should adhere to a relatively rigorous format, because pretty much the same sort of story is being told with each report and the rigorous guidelines are there for good reasons, as previous chapters have explained. But when you write a research essay or term paper, there is an enormous variety in the kinds of stories you can tell and the ways you can mold them to suit the subject you've chosen. Furthermore, you are writing for a general audience with relatively little or no knowledge about your subject, so it is best to make your story amusing and simple as well as informative.

Nothing makes my students unhappier than an assignment to do a "library research essay." Beyond the pain of grappling with the labyrinth of the library, tracking down references only to find they are missing, or trying to coordinate the flurry of paper such research produces, I think many of them feel that I have sentenced them to playing the role of a mere messenger, shuttling among encyclopedias, books, and journals. Many have told me that they view it as a cut-and-paste exercise, where they artfully rearrange the information they've "dug up," keeping track of quotations and sources on index cards, and trying to avoid plagiarism by carefully rewording ideas that originated with some other author.

In contrast to the lab or research report a scientist writes, in the term paper or research essay it is easy to believe—mistakenly—that your instructor only wants you to consolidate and synthesize facts that other experts have found. It is hard to find a way to insert originality into this process. Add to this the usual pressure of a deadline and it is easy to see why you might dread such assignments. This attitude might even contribute to plagiarism: If you don't feel you have much at stake in the process beyond the grade, and if you feel you don't "own" the information you are transmitting, it is easy to get confused about the difference between plagiarism and reporting.

Let me suggest an alternative view of these assignments. Writing these reports is not merely an exercise in hunting through a library or creating a synthesis, although those are necessary skills. It is an invitation to be original and make a contribution. By writing an essay you can bring a wealth of information or a point of view to an audience that it would not reach otherwise. You are educating in the broadest sense of the term. And you are beginning by educating yourself.

Furthermore, a term paper or essay can do things for science that a research article or lab report cannot. In it you can tell the parts of the story of science that never get told in a formal report. You can express the beauty and wonder and mystery and variety of nature. You can dramatize the excitement of discovery. You can explore the complex web of politics and economics and personalities that drive modern science. You can interpret the dry, technical material of journal articles and books for a more general audience, explaining the significance of obscure research. You can speculate about the future and draw connections among different disciplines. You can show the impact of science on society and culture. You can focus on the human side of science, the personalities and politics, the individual genius and complicated teamwork that goes into scientific discovery. You can even create opportunities for personal reflection. In short, the essay is your opportunity to represent realities of science in ways that formal scientific discourse itself cannot. In short, *by writing an essay or report you can make a significant contribution to knowledge.*

Not all new knowledge is arrived at through the scientific method. Sometimes new knowledge comes from seeing things in a new light or yoking disparate or hitherto alien things together for the first time, revealing unanticipated features or relationships. An essay can accomplish this in a way that the scientific report usually cannot.

Another of the great advantages an essay about science has over the formal scientific article is that while you still must be truthful and precise in your language, you are free to spread your wings stylistically. You may use metaphors, intense and descriptive language, elaborate analogies, and qualitative adjectives. You may become eloquent in describing a subject and go far afield in providing a context for understanding its importance. You can paint the big picture, argue for a position, and still make an important contribution to knowledge and to the institution of science as well as to the public good.

The following sections of this chapter discuss the steps in writing an essay, report, or term paper from a nonspecialist's point of view, the various approaches to telling the story, and the stylistic tools you can use.

STEPS IN WRITING THE ESSAY, REPORT, OR TERM PAPER

Choose a Topic

The first step is to choose a general topic, preferably one that already intrigues you. If possible, state it in the form of a question. Then imagine a preliminary answer or set of answers to that question. I advise my students to think of something they have always wondered about or been fascinated by, even if it seems simple or childish: Why is the sky blue? What is lightning? Why does it get cold in the winter? What causes diabetes? Why did the dinosaurs become extinct? How does an internal combustion engine work? Will computers ever think? Can we stop the aging process? What is the smallest known bit of matter? Who were the first people and where did they live? Even the most juvenile-seeming question can present a doorway into the most fascinating realms of science. Choosing a topic you're initially interested in gives you a head start in motivation and will help you sustain your interest when the going gets rough.

Begin Researching the Topic

Begin your research by finding books, magazines, and journals that address your topic, or by speaking directly to the experts. Note carefully where you got each piece of information. Write a complete bibliographical reference to the author(s), title of article, title of publication, date of publication, page numbers, and for books, the name of the publisher and place of publication. It's also a good idea to keep track of the library call number of each book or magazine in case you have to return to it.

One obvious trick to doing library research is to use the bibliographies of the books and articles you have already uncovered to find more information. I feel I have completed my research when I find the most recent expert article on a subject, read the bibliography, and discover that I've already found almost all of the references it lists.

If your information came from interviews, write down the names of your sources, their titles, the time, date, and place of the interview. Secure your subject's permission to use the information in a report.

Narrow Your Topic and Refine Your Thesis

Refine your topic by narrowing (or in rarer instances, expanding) its scope. One good way to refine a topic is to write down the main questions or problems in that topic:

```
What causes lightning?

What are the kinds of lightning?

How many streaks of lightning in each burst?

How and why does lightning cause damage?

Can the energy of lightning be harnessed?

What are the historical and mythological views
   of lightning?

Can lightning strikes be predicted? Prevented?

What is ball lightning? Streak lightning?

What is the effect of lightning on property?
   The atmosphere? On people who survive a
   lightning strike?
```

Similarly, one way to choose a thesis is to note the various competing hypotheses, theories, or opinions about a subject and who holds them.

Adopt an "Angle" or Point of View

Not all research papers have to follow the same format. Decide what is the most intriguing or interesting aspect of the topic. Think of different ways to tell the story. Should it profile a personality? Follow the evolution of an idea? Contrast different opinions? Try to persuade your audience to adopt a point of view? Try to move your audience to an aesthetic or intellectual appreciation for a subject? We will discuss various strategies and kinds of "stories" later in this chapter.

Write the Paper

Whole chapters of writing textbooks are devoted to each of the following steps in writing a paper, and again I refer you to a list of such textbooks in Appendix B. But all of them offer one common thread of advice: re-writing is the key to a successful essay.

- Summarize your subject, thesis, or approach in the form of an abstract or two- or three-sentence brief.

- Outline the paper.

- Write a rough draft.

- Rewrite and edit the paper, adding footnotes and a bibliography. Revise and rewrite it again.

KINDS OF SCIENCE ESSAYS

Some of the best models for the essay or term paper about science are found in popular science magazines and newspaper reports. Of all the kinds of stories you read in magazines and newspapers or watch on television, science journalism differs from conventional narratives in one vital aspect: where virtually all other journalistic stories concern the interplay among human characters, in science journalism, ideas, phenomena, or even raw information—an anomalous fact, an unexplained datum, a new theory or hypothesis or conjecture, a fascinating natural event, a wild speculation—can be the heroes and heroines of the story as well as the people, politics, and economics.

The scientist is almost always trying to tell this story:

> Here is what I discovered and how I did it. Here is its significance within a limited context. I assume if you are reading this then you comprehend the larger significance and context for understanding this work and so I don't need to spell it out, even though I think it's enormously important work. I may be excited about the subject, but I cannot let my excitement show.

When you write an essay, whether for a writing course or a science course, or even a newspaper, journal, or magazine, you are trying to tell any of a number of other kinds of stories, but almost certainly you are not trying to restrict yourself to the one a scientist is trying to tell through a research article or report in a professional

journal. Most magazine reports about science follow the general journalistic outline:

I. The "lead" or introductory sentences

II. The "billboard" or establishing paragraphs

III. The story

IV. The "exit" or concluding paragraphs

Leads or Introductory Sentences

Much of journalism depends on getting a good lead. Traditionally, this
has meant writing a first sentence that "hooks" the reader's attention
with a striking image, observation, or fact. The typical **expository
lead** simply tells the major idea or problem in a sentence or two, or
states a thesis. However, since magazines aren't usually as cramped
for space as newspaper reports, and since magazines usually accompany articles with flashy color, attractive illustrations or photos, and
eye-catching typographic elements, some of the pressure is taken off
that first sentence. Indeed, most magazine leads spread their drama
or "hook" over many more sentences and even paragraphs. In the following example, the first sentences offer simple facts. The real hook
comes out in the second paragraph, which is then called a "billboard"
in magazine parlance.

LEAD: When a beaker of water is put in a
freezer, it solidifies to form ice.
When a bar of hot iron is refriger-
ated, it may become magnetically
polarized. When samples of certain
metals, such as aluminum, are cooled
to extremely low temperatures, they
become superconducting, losing all
resistance to the flow of electric
current. When certain homogeneous
mixtures of liquids are cooled, they
become immiscible, dividing to form
two distinct liquids separated by a
boundary called a meniscus.

BILLBOARD: These phenomena are examples of phase
              transitions. A sample of matter is
              said to be in a certain phase (such as
              the solid phase or the superconducting
              phase) when it has a certain well-de-
              fined set of macroscopically-observed
              properties (such as hardness or lack
              of resistivity). The phase of a sample
              of matter is really an indication of
              the degree of order or disorder inher-
              ent in the molecules or atoms of which
              the sample is composed. . .

              Reappearing phases are actually a
              direct consequence of the interplay
              between energy and entropy, or disor-
              der, as that interplay is expressed in
              the motions and interactions of the
              molecules that make up the materials.
              Reappearing phases can be of great
              utility in studying physical systems
              because they make it possible to gain
              a more thorough and accurate descrip-
              tion of these microscopic interactions
              than would otherwise be possible.[46]

A **dramatic lead** begins with a very dramatic opening image,
thought, or fact, as in this article about tsunamis—giant tidal waves:

LEAD: After leveling 400,000 homes, the
              earthquake that struck southern Chile
              on May 22, 1960, appeared to have run
              its course. Along 600 miles of coast,
              whole streets lay submerged, buildings
              were demolished and boats were lost or
              sundered from their moorings. But
              oceanographers in Hawaii had been mon-

itoring the seismic and tidal data
from stations around the Pacific, and
they knew the earthquake would soon be
felt elsewhere. They traced the epi-
enter of the quake to the port of Ancud,
Chile, and predicted that the tumult
on the seafloor, where continental
plates had shifted, would trigger a
tsunami—one monstrous wave. Fifteen
hours after the Chilean quake, the
tsunami hit Hawaii, killing sixty-one
people. Seven hours later the Japanese
islands of Honshu and Hokkaido were
struck by a wall of water twenty-one
feet high, and 199 people were
drowned.[47]

Magazines and essays can afford to take oblique entries into their subject. In fact, it is one of the significant differences between an essay and a scientific article. An **oblique lead,** or a **nonsummary lead,** is one of the ways to establish tone and create drama or intrigue the reader. Look at how long it takes for A. Gary to get into the "scientific" material of his essay in his establishing paragraph, and look at the extent to which he allows his prose to wax romantic in order to create an appropriate point of view about the information to come:

LEAD: A snowy silence has begun to grip Yel-
               lowstone, stirring the huge herds of
               bison and elk to move toward the
               rivers and steamy thermal basins of
               America's premier national park. There
               the primal warmth of the planet spouts
               and bubbles forth to melt the snow and
               moderate the chill of the long Wyoming
               winter on the Earth's skin.

               Soon there will be hundreds of bi-
               son gathered around the hot springs

and geysers, and there will be thousands of elk—far more than normal, for
the last seven winters have been com-
paratively kind to the 16,000 animals
in Yellowstone's northern elk range.
The lame and weak have been spared
weather of truly lethal force; the
very old and the very young have not
been tested by sustained cold or by
forbidding layers of ice-crusted snow
between them and their meager food
sources.

A killing winter is overdue. Inevitably, by the end of this season or
another soon to come, exhaustion and
starvation will ravage the elk, their
carcasses a springtime blessing to
hungry bears and other scavengers but
a grim greeting to the new season's
tourists, a spectacle of death seemingly inappropriate to this preserver
of wildness and beauty.

BILLBOARD: It is not poor park management,
though, that has set up the coming
die-off, not someone's error of elk
husbandry. It is the opposite: a de-
liberate park policy of park scientists and administrators to keep hands
off, to let nature take its course and
exact its price.

Two paragraphs later:

Today after a decade of research,
National Park Service biologist Dou-
glas B. Houston has concluded that the

> grazing lands of the elk never were in
> danger; that most of the range deteri-
> oration his predecessors saw was
> traceable not to elk but men and,
> ironically, the high-minded effort to
> fight forest fires. Houston has also
> found that the population of the
> northern herd is dependably regulated
> by changing fertility rates, food sup-
> ply, and Wyoming's relentless
> winter.[48]

This is rather dramatic. It creates a kind of suspense, with the payoff coming in a dramatic twist: "It is not poor park management . . . It is the opposite. . . ." Another more direct author, for instance, one concerned about maintaining the right tone for a college course essay, might have written it this way:

LEAD: Scientists and administrators of Yel-
             lowstone park have embarked on a new
             policy of "laissez-faire management"
             of animal populations based on results
             of research by National Park Service
             biologist Douglas B. Houston on elks
             in Yellowstone National Park.

BILLBOARD: Houston's work shows that most of the
             range deterioration his predecessors
             saw was traceable not to elk but men
             and, ironically, their high-minded ef-
             fort to fight forest fires. From now
             on, they are going to let nature take
             its course.

This is a perfectly serviceable lead and billboard. In comparing it with the original, many of you would be tempted on first glance to favor it. However, the first version accomplishes some things that the second does not. First, it emphasizes the essential and underlying goals of the research—to preserve nature and its values—which in some sense *is*

more important than the scientific methods involved. It evokes a specific scene on a winter's day in Yellowstone and weaves it into an account of the natural migratory patterns of a herd of elk. By doing so, the
author of the first subtly captures the sympathy that humans naturally
feel for the elk, the impulse to protect them from die-offs. We get to
sympathize with the perspective of the park managers and administrators who tried to manage herd populations through more artificial
means and, unwittingly did damage to the ultimate health of the herd.
In other words, the evocative lead actually helps us understand the play
between two scientific paradigms, an old one of animal husbandry and
management, and the newer laissez-faire paradigm which a scientist's
research has validated. In sum, the essay in general can employ subtlety
that a formal research article cannot afford.

Finally, here's a **personal lead,** relying on the direct involvement
of the author, and the first person point of view, which many students—and scientists—assume is out of bounds for their professional
communications. Yet, I would welcome a paper that began this way as
a submission for my course:

One sunny morning in the middle of November, 1982,
David J. Helfand, an astronomer colleague at
Columbia University, came into my office to tell
me a remarkable story. He had just returned from a
business trip to the Arecibo radio-telescope ob-
servatory in Puerto Rico. While he was there he
learned that Donald C. Blacker of the University
of California at Berkeley and his collaborators
had discovered a 1.558-millisecond radio pulsar in
the constellation Vulpecula. That would make the
radio pulsar, whose official name is 1937 + 214,
the fastest one known.[49]

Exits or Closings

Writers as well as lovers know that partings are difficult. One of the
most challenging parts of writing an essay is finding a graceful way to
exit the stage. Many journalists, even magazine journalists, are trained
in the newspaper tradition: they try hard to conserve column inches
or space. They tend to focus on the material in the front end. They

learn to structure an article like an inverted pyramid, weighting every-thing at the top (beginning) and ignoring things at the end, rather than like a story which usually has a strong beginning, a heavy middle, and a satisfying end.

By contrast, students writing research papers or essays may be tempted to go in the opposite direction and reach for some sweeping generalization that will cap off their paper, perhaps in one last-ditch effort to impress the reader. As a result, endings—like partings—are often awkward.

However, telling a story certainly means paying as much attention to the last words as to the title and lead paragraphs. There are many tactics that you can employ in ending your article, story, or paper. Listed below are several tactics that one expert science writer, James Gleick, used in different chapters of his book, *Chaos: Making a New Science.*[50] Of course they are not exhaustive, but they give a good sense of the range of endings you can use to conclude an essay about science.

Summarize

But unlike most physicists, Marcus eventually learned Lorenz's lesson, that a deterministic sys-tem can produce much more than just periodic be-havior. He knew to look for wild disorder, and he knew that islands of structure could appear within the disorder. . . . He could work within an emerg-ing discipline that was creating its own tradition of using the computer as an experimental tool. And he was willing to think of himself as a new kind of scientist: not primarily an astronomer, not a fluid dynamicist, not an applied mathematician, but a specialist in chaos.[51]

Broaden the Scope

As Mandelbrot himself acknowledged, his program described better than it explained. He could list elements of nature along with their fractal dimensions—seacoasts, river networks, tree barks, galaxies—and scientists could use those numbers to make predictions. But physicists wanted to know more. They wanted to know why. There were forms in nature—not visible forms, but shapes embedded in the fabric of motion—waiting to be revealed.[52]

Set a Dramatic Mood or Scene

This one is worthy of a short story about Sam Spade:

"Somehow the wondrous promise of the earth is that there are things beautiful in it, things wondrous and alluring, and by virtue of your trade you want to understand them." He put the cigarette down. Smoke rose from the ashtray, first in a thin column and then (with a nod to universality) in broken tendrils that swirled upwards to the ceiling.[53]

Choose a Pithy, Sweeping, or Visionary Quotation

"I have not spoken of the esthetic appeal of strange attractors. These systems of curves, these clouds of points suggest sometimes fireworks or galaxies, sometimes strange and disquieting vegetal proliferations. A realm lies there of forms to explore, and harmonies to discover."[54]

And just for good measure, this is the conclusion of an entirely different magazine essay:

Perhaps the missionary image he holds of himself is closest to the truth. This is what Gajdusek wrote in his journal on 10 July 1960, aboard a Pan American Boeing 707: "To bring this age of cosmology, atomic and nuclear structure, information theory in human communication and in the interpre-

tation of biological continuity, in touch with its
roots as they are still evident in so-called
'primitive' cultures, is my mission. . . . To bring
man in his diverse cultural experiments far removed . . . is all I can strive for . . . that I
shall do with the zealousness of a foolish, comic,
inspired, ridiculous—yet passionate—pediatric
apostle."[55]

THEMES AND TOPICS FOR SCIENCE ESSAYS AND TERM PAPERS

Simple definition: Explain what a certain phenomenon, theory, model, or hypothesis is. Give illuminating examples.

Simple exposition: Explain the state of knowledge about this phenomenon, theory, or model. Explain what a certain discipline is or what a certain research project does.

Simple analysis: Analyze how and why a certain aspect of science works. This may involve translating some scientific analysis, or it may involve analyzing one of the cultural, economic/political, social, human, personal, or intellectual aspects of sciences.

Dramatic exposition: Explain competing theories or views of a scientific idea.

History: How did this aspect of science develop?

Progress: Compare and contrast the changing views on a certain aspect of science from the past to the present.

The wonder of nature: Present a new and somewhat amazing discovery in science that opens up imaginative vistas, gives us a glimpse of the future, or simply leaves us fascinated.

Science and you: Describe a scientific discovery and how, when it becomes part of the marketplace, it will have an impact on _____ (e.g., your health, the environment, the economy, the way you communicate, learn, play, work, . . .)

Trends: Describe a trend in scientific research or applications toward concentrating on a certain avenue or method or phenomenon.

Vanguard, new visions, speculations, or works-in-progress: Discuss a promising new venture at the forefront of scientific experimentation and technology.

Interview: Give an account (or a transcript) of your interview with a scientist.

Profile/Biography: Show how the subtle interaction of biography and science worked in the case of some interesting, famous, or influential individual. Tell the story of an individual and his/her career of accomplishments in science.

Autobiography. Tell how you experienced science during your career.

Need to know: Present new knowledge that readers should have both for its intrinsic interest and so they can be informed citizens.

Special interest: Provide information that readers, as informed citizens or members of a special group, need to know about some fact, theory, discovery, or application.

Speculation: State your belief that a given hypothesis is true. Explain the hypothesis and its consequences if it is true. In articles like this it is important to present opposing viewpoints.

Contexts for understanding: Describe the consequences and contexts for understanding some new scientific fact or theory.

Evocations and personal visions: Present a personal view of how an aspect of science resonates in your imagination. From science we can forge new metaphors and new modes of understanding, expanding our minds and our horizons.

Isaac Newton provides us with one of the finest examples of such an evocation. In this passage from his *Opticks,* Newton meditates on unanswered questions in the study of nature, which was in his age called "Natural Philosophy." Newton poses these questions somewhat rhetorically, since his purpose is not really to list areas for future research, although many of the questions he posed are still being researched today. Rather, his purpose is to move from the sense of order he has discovered in studying light to a larger cosmological and metaphysical vision he has of order in the universe generally, an order which for him proceeds from a Divine Intelligence.

The main business of natural philosophy is to argue from phaenomena without feigning hypotheses, and to deduce causes from effects, till we come to the very first cause, which certainly is not mechanical; and not only to unfold the mechanism of the world, but chiefly to resolve these and such like questions. What is there in places almost empty of matter, without dense matter between them? Whence is it that Nature doth nothing in vain; and whence arises all that order and beauty which we see in the world? To what end are comets, and whence is it that planets move all one and the same way in orbs concentric, while comets move all manner of ways in orbs very eccentric, and what hinders the fix'd stars from falling upon one another? How came the bodies of animals to be contrived with such art, and for what end were their several parts? Was the eye contrived without skill in opticks, and the ear without knowledge of sounds? How do the motions of the body follow from the will, and whence is the instinct in animals? . . . And these things being rightly dispatch'd, does it not appear from phenomena that there is a being incorporeal, living, intelligent, omnipresent, who in infinite space, as it were in his sensory, sees the things themselves intimately, and thoroughly perceives them, and comprehends them wholly by their immediate

```
presence to himself: Of which things the im-
ages only carried through the organs of sense
into our little sensorium, are there seen and
beheld by that which in us perceives and
thinks. And tho' every true step made in this
philosophy brings us not immediately to the
knowledge of the first Cause, yet it brings
us nearer to it, and on that account is to be
highly valued.⁵⁶
```

Science in its earlier forms in the seventeenth and eighteenth centuries did not make the genre distinctions we do today between rigorous scientific reportage of experiments and more general observations. Newton here has ended a chain of observations and induction with a passage intended to share his vision. It tells a rather complete story. Furthermore, Newton's vision itself is of a sort we are not likely to see in a contemporary science journal, let alone one a modern scientist is likely to talk about in a professional forum. Newton moves freely between cosmology and metaphysics because he sees an intimate connection between the order of a small niche of the universe—the nature of light and whether or not it propagates through a medium—and the order of the whole. His imagination is tuned to unraveling narrower questions until they entail ultimate ones. This excerpt also shows that some of the great essayists can be scientists talking about science outside the venue of a rigorous research report.

Meditation or self-expression—The literary (pure) essay: Here the style of the prose itself, rather than the information communicated by that prose, is in the forefront, though it doesn't overshadow that information. This type of essay is a literary act of self-expression and evocation as much as it is an exposition of knowledge. Or to put it another way, it merges literary or esthetic approaches to knowledge with the scientific approach. Even as it explores a highly subjective state, it exposes a kind of knowledge that cannot be obtained through the normal operation of scientific discipline or even via the usual news reports or magazine articles on science.

Your motives for writing this essay may be varied: to express some fervent belief or strong emotion; to evoke an emotion or state of mind; to attempt to capture in words a mighty vision or insight; to share an esthetic or even irrational appreciation of science; to use the act of writing—especially the power of metaphor and imagery—to work out speculations, half-formed intimations, and intuitions. You may write intimately, as in the following excerpt from *The Star Throwers* by Loren Eiseley. Eiseley draws out the subtleties in his own perception, creating imaginative resonances between the subject and the reader through words.

When I was a young man engaged in fossil hunting in the Nebraska badlands I was frequently reminded that the ravines, washes and gullies over which we wandered resembled the fissures in a giant exposed brain. The human brain contains the fossil memories of its past—buried but not extinguished moments—just as this more formidable replica contained deep in its inner stratigraphic convolutions earth's past in the shape of horned titanotheres and stalking, dirk-toothed cats. Man's memory erodes away in the short space of a lifetime. Jutting from the coils of the earth's brain over which I clambered were the buried remnants, the changing history, of the entire age of mammals—millions of years of vanished daylight with their accompanying traces of volcanic outbursts and upheavals. It may well be asked why this analogy of earth's memory should so preoccupy the mind of a scientist as to have affected his entire outlook upon nature and upon his kinship with—even his concern for—the plant and the animal world about him.[57]

The answer Eiseley pursues lies in "the feeling of awe, of dread of the holy" playing on nature, which characterizes the work of a number of naturalists and physicists even to the present day.

THE STYLE OF SCIENCE ESSAYS

You have already gotten a good sense of the language of science essays by reading the journalistic examples in the previous section. However, it is helpful to look systematically at some of the stylistic tools in language that are especially useful in describing scientific concepts.

Many inexperienced writers think that descriptive writing means using general or abstract adjectives enthusiastically.

X: This was one of the most terrific and fantastic explosions in the sky that humans had ever witnessed ever since the dawn of history itself. It must have been terrifying, wild, and magnificent.

In fact, however, a clear presentation of the *details* of a subject, especially **details that excite the senses,** will create vividness more quickly and effectively than any hyperbolic (exaggerated) adjective. Try to perform this mental exercise: pretend that you are seeing, hearing, smelling, tasting and/or touching the thing you are describing for the first time. Better yet, imagine that you are the first one from your planet ever to have encountered this phenomenon or idea.

Suddenly, a speck of light appeared in that quadrant of the night sky where no light had appeared before, just to the west of Orion's belt. It was a small red star. But what extraterrestrial haze had cleared to make it suddenly visible? No haze at all. Rather, we were witnessing the birth of a supernova, a brief, searing light signaling at the same time the birth of a new stellar beast and the extinction of an older, anonymous one. Then, just as the naked eye became adjusted to this new light and the brain accustomed to its presence, the supernova started to change colors and grow. The light pooled now, shifting from red to blue, unfolding from its own center, rippling outward in a slowly developing burst. Although it was silent,

```
it was impossible not to imagine a sound as space-
time itself ripped with the explosion of this
tempest.
```

Establish a Point of View

Another effective way to make your writing vivid is by establishing a **point of view.** The most convenient point of view for a science re-port, of course, is that of the scientist. Here, James Gleick adopts the point of view of one of the leading scientists responsible for discover-ies. This is a tactic—the third person intimate—that we usually find in novels, yet Gleick often uses this tactic in his popular books about sci-ence.

```
When inspiration came, it was in the form of a
picture, a mental image of two small wavy forms
and one big one. That was all—a bright, sharp im-
age etched in his [Feigenbaum's] mind, no more,
perhaps, than the visible top of a vast iceberg of
mental processing that had taken place below the
waterline of consciousness. It had to do with
scaling, and it gave Feigenbaum the path he
needed.[58]
```

If you are a scientist or are involved in the story, you can use the first person (*I saw this, I did that*). In general, though, the most use-ful point of view is the neutral third person narrator who simply por-trays and arranges the facts.

```
A new study suggests that ozone pollution at lev-
els generally considered safe can double a per-
son's sensitivity to allergens that cause asthma
attacks.
```

```
The research, reported in the July 27 issue of the
British journal Lancet, is the most recent in a
string of studies suggesting that ozone pollution
even at currently acceptable levels is a threat to
human health.[59]
```

Use Analogies

An analogy is a comparison between two things that brings out similarities or creates striking images in the reader's mind. A **formal analogy** creates a mental model of similarities in which specific properties of a more familiar object are compared to those of a less familiar object in order to make the latter more comprehensible to your audience or to show proportions between the two objects. "The antlers of a buck are like the tusks of an elephant." Proportionate analogies create mental models or structures of resemblances. They are very close to being actual models.

We can therefore regard the spectrum of light from an atom as similar to the pattern of sound from a musical instrument. Each instrument produces a characteristic sound, and just as the timbre of a violin differs markedly from that of a drum or clarinet, so the colour mixture of light from a hydrogen atom is characteristically distinct from the spectrum of a carbon or uranium atom. In both cases, there is a deep association between the internal vibrations (oscillating membranes, undulating electron waves) and the external waves (sound, light).[60]

Because analogies tend to be both vivid and illuminating, analogies are extremely useful tools whenever you need to explain new information, as in teaching or in science exposition.

Literary analogies leave a strong impression or image in the reader's mind and add a vivid touch to your prose. Consider the following examples:

If as Schrödinger conjectured, the attributes of measuring devices were fuzzy to the extent of a few quanta, this fuzziness would be utterly undetectable, like a firefly in the glare of the sun.[61]

The essence of non-locality is unmediated action-at-a-distance. A non-local interaction jumps from body A to body B without touching anything in-between. Voodoo injury is an example of a non-local interaction. When a voodoo practitioner sticks a pin in her doll, the distant target is (supposedly) instantly wounded, although nothing actually travels from doll to victim. Believers in voodoo claim that an action <u>here</u> causes an effect <u>there</u>; that's all there is to it. Without benefit of mediation, a non-local interaction effortlessly flashes across the void.[62]

[T]he markings on the pampa of Nazca bear no resemblance to a single astronomy text, even a complicated one. Seen from the air, the plain looks more like an unerased blackboard at the end of a busy day of class, cluttered with overlapping but unrelated signs.[63]

Use Metaphors, But Exercise Caution

A **metaphor** is a way of carrying knowledge or meaning from one object or realm into another by equating two unlike things or ideas. Metaphors often lack the precision of analogies, but they are more fundamentally powerful and imagistic. Metaphors can capture essential and powerful truths in ways no other verbal expression can:

Man is a wolf.

The cancerous glial cell is an imperialist.

One of the features of a metaphor is *surprise:* because you don't expect "man" to be equated with "wolf," it makes you shift mental gears. Another power of metaphor is *extensiveness:* a metaphor can imply a whole world of resemblances, only some of which are actually explored or explained by the author. The rest is left up to the reader's imagination:

A "creature" consisting only of ones and zeros has emerged from its computer womb and is causing a scientific sensation: Without human guidance it reproduces, undergoes spontaneous genetic changes, passes them on to offspring and evolves whole new

```
species whose interactions mimic those of real bi-
ological evolution and ecology.⁶⁴
```

There are several intertwined metaphors here which combine to paint a picture of an underlying, coherent image—a **conceit** or extensive metaphor in which a computer-generated model is equated to a living being. Note the care with which the author uses his metaphors. The first metaphor is in the word "creature"—as in "living thing"— and the author carefully puts it in scare quotes. Scare quotes are those marks used not when the word is new or quoted, but when the word's interpretation is not exactly meant to be literal. The second metaphor equates a computer with a "womb." Note also that the metaphor does not require a stretch. The purpose of the computer experiment was to model life and evolutionary processes itself:

```
The creature, actually a coded set of eighty in-
structions written in a special "machine language"
understood by the operating cores of computers, is
the work of Thomas S. Ray, a plant biologist at
the University of Delaware, who became a computer
expert to study the underlying dynamics of life.⁶⁴
```

SOME CAUTIONARY WORDS ABOUT TELLING SCIENCE AS A STORY

There are several cautions to keep in mind when you write about science. The temptation to stretch and fill in missing blanks is strong when you are concerned with telling a story. Here are some guidelines to help you resist this temptation:

CHECKLIST #23

GENERAL GUIDELINES FOR WRITING ESSAYS ABOUT SCIENCE

☐ Be careful to preserve the integrity of the scientific information.

☐ Be especially careful not to report interpretations as conclusions or mistake speculations for conclusions.

☐ Report the data accurately.

☐ Note carefully and respect the conditions which your primary sources used to modify or restrict their conclusions and claims.

☐ While adding or changing the context for understanding an investigation, data, or theory, try to preserve the sense of the original context.

☐ Strike a balance between telling the story and exciting the imagination, on one hand, and giving the straight scientific dope on the other hand.

☐ Use descriptive language and details.

17

Revising and Editing

"Wisdom consists of knowing when to avoid perfection."

Horowitz's Rule[65]

Now that you have written your first draft of a paper, whether a formal scientific report or a magazine article, where do you go from here? Your work is hardly ready for submission to an instructor in a course or to a journal. Editing is essential to the writing process. There's an old saying in the writing business: *All good writing is rewriting.*

Knowing how to write well and anticipating strategies for rewriting could save you steps in the long run. In this chapter, I suggest a three-step approach I call "deep editing." It is really quite simple and, I believe, more sensible than simply following a list of do's and don'ts. It is based on how we as readers tend to treat language itself. As is true of much of the other advice in this book, success in deep editing first requires a shift in attitudes toward writing.

THE REAL WRITING IS IN THE REWRITING

I don't know any writer who gets it right the first time. Certainly no professional writer I know submits anything right out of the printer or typewriter. The first step to good writing is recognizing that writing really succeeds only when you *rewrite* it, often with more than two or three drafts. By implication, this means that a good writer must become his or her own editor. And again, by implication, this means that you must be able to recognize bad writing and fix it.

Editing and rewriting are the keys to good writing. Scientists are prone to submit unrevised writing perhaps more than other professionals. It's not hard to understand why. The eagerness to be the first to publish results always puts pressure on getting those reports out quickly. Most scientists are naturally torn between writing and getting back to the "real work" in the lab or the field to continue experiments and observations. And because of more and more specialized science curricula in college, you may have fewer opportunities to develop the sensitivity to language you need to recognize mistakes and correct them.

But there is another, more subtle reason that science reporting often goes unrevised: many technical and scientific writers tend to view writing as transparent. Words, like mathematical formulas, should be unambiguous. A common attitude is "Everyone who is smart enough will understand what I mean."

Editors are practiced in grammar, spelling, punctuation, and word usage. They know the tricks of the trade that come from long experience in turning sentences around and extracting clear expressions from muddied prose. Even before learning these editorial skills, you should begin by acquiring a positive attitude toward editing and revising by acknowledging that getting it right usually means more profound and essential revisions than fixing the spelling, punctuation, and grammar in the first draft.

AN EXERCISE IN EDITING

Many students think editing prose is like fixing a car: you merely *take out bad things and replace them with good ones—and then it's fixed!* This can work to a point, in some cases. But for the most part, real editing and rewriting means more than just fixing mistakes. Language is too slippery, offers too many alternatives, to ever allow us to be sure we have hit on *the* perfect formulation of an idea in words. And the right way to say something depends on what that something is. Even Vladimir Horowitz, the great violinist noted for his perfection of form as well as musical expressiveness, counseled that *"wisdom consists of knowing when to avoid perfection."*

For instance, take excerpt (1) below, which is actually grammatically correct and, for scientific prose, quite normal. But it is really quite graceless:

(1) The grafted-cell neurotransmitter phenotypic
expression was studied in two samples of immunoreactivity catecholamine pathway enzyme staining:

TH, the rate-limiting enzyme, and phenylethanolamine N-methyltransferase (PNMT). The data under
these circumstances do not necessarily indicate
whether the enzymatic action was blocked by
the immunosuppressants. Three possible explanations for the results might potentially be afforded:. . .

Working with (1) you would expand the noun strings into verbs
and nouns, which helps to show their proper relationships:

X: The grafted-cell neurotransmitter phenotypic
expression was studied

would convert to

The neurotransmitter phenotypic expression in
grafted cells was studied

But then you could go further:

The expression of neurotransmitter phenotypes in
grafted cells was studied

or further:

The way grafted cells express their neurotransmitter phenotypes was studied

or even further (though you don't want to go overboard):

The way grafted cells express the phenotypes of
their neurotransmitter was studied

Then you could eliminate the passive voice:

We studied the way grafted cells express the phenotypes of their neurotransmitter. . . .

Now compare the two sentences, the one directly above and the first
sentence in excerpt (1).

Similarly, look at another phrase from excerpt (1):

X: the enzymatic action was blocked by the immunosuppressants.

can be edited by making the passive voice active:

YES: `immunosuppressants blocked the enzymatic ac-`
`tion.`

The next clause:

X: `Three possible explanations for the results`
   `might potentially be afforded`

needs an actor in active voice. So we supply one:

`Current theory can potentially afford three possi-`
`ble explanations`

Then, take out the squirrelly language "can afford":

`Current theory affords three possible explanations`

Simplify the fancy "affords" to the simple "offers":

`Current theory offers three possible explanations`

To combine the revised phrase with the sentence preceeding it, you would add one of the transitional words—although—to show logical, temporal relations between ideas:

`Although the data under these circumstances do not`
`necessarily indicate whether the enzymatic action`
`was blocked by the immunosuppressants`

Combine the thoughts from two simple sentences into one larger, more coherent and mature statement:

`Although the data under these circumstances do not`
`necessarily indicate whether the enzymatic action`
`was blocked by the immunosuppressants, current`
`theory offers three possible explanations.`

Take out some more squirrelly language ("necessarily"):

`Although the data under these circumstances do not`
`indicate whether the enzymatic action was blocked`
`by the immunosuppressants, current theory offers`
`three possible explanations`

And we have produced a finished—but not perfect—product:

(2) We studied the way grafted cells express the
phenotypes of their neurotransmitter in two samples of catecholamine pathway enzymes that we
stained for immunoreactivity: TH, the rate-limiting enzyme, and phenylethanolamine N-methyltransferase (PNMT). Although the data do not indicate
whether the enzymatic immunosuppressants blocked
the enzymatic action, current theory offers three
possible explanations

There's not a single editor who would be likely to blink twice at
this passage (2), and most authors should be content if they had wres-
tled their material into this shape. But to prove Horowitz's Rule, consider the following alternative (3), which goes to another level of editing.

(3) This experiment studied the way grafted cells
express the phenotypes of their neurotransmitter
in two samples of catecholamine pathway enzymes
stained for immunoreactivity. The first was TH,
the rate-limiting enzyme, and the second,
phenylethanolamine N-methyltransferase (PNMT).
Results did not indicate whether the enzymatic immunosuppressants blocked the enzymatic action.
However, current theory offers three possible explanations

Is (3) better or worse than (2)? On what basis did you form your
judgment?

EDITING MEANS MORE THAN
FIXING ERRORS

Prose isn't like a car. Taking bad things out and replacing them with
good things doesn't always make a passage go. Though they can help,
those sorts of changes tend to be merely cosmetic. Rather, real editing
means knowing where the bad stuff came from in the first place and

cutting it off at the source. It also means knowing that *the best style is when the form of the sentence matches the ideas it is meant to transmit.* The best expression is not a programmed algorithm of grammar, but the result of an interaction between an author's ideas and words, and those words and the expectations and abilities of the audience.

Bad writing tends to derive not from grammatical and mechanical errors alone, but from misperceptions about what language should be doing. We will explore these misperceptions and then discuss ways to change them in Chapter 19. Some writers simply don't feel comfortable enough with how writing should sound. Other writers write to impress. They like the sound of complex, obscure, overly conditional, and passive prose. They believe it makes them sound smarter than they are. But I think most *poor science* writing can be explained by the disease hypothesis of bad professional prose: Bad writing is hereditary and communicable.

Imagine an unpracticed author reading an excerpt like (1) above. The unpracticed author (UA) will pick up on the bunch of nouns acting together ("grafted-cell neurotransmitter phenotypic expression"), the passive voice ("was studied," "was blocked," "might potentially be afforded"), and the long—though justifiably so—technical terms ("phenylethanolamine N-methyltransferase"). Then, because he has not understood the reasons for these verbal maneuvers, the UA can unfortunately end up sounding like this when he goes to write his own first scientific article:

```
(4) As it has been seen from the aforementioned,
under certain circumstances it may be the case
that the prioritization of the research methodolo-
gies by the experimental designer to utilize ana-
lytical techniques on the phenylethanolamine N-
methyltransferase (PNMT) sample via employment of
titration columns should precede the utilization
of electron-spectroscopic analyses via employment
of the beta-diffraction spectroscopy equipment,
which is the procedure that was performed in this
instance, yielding the data indicated in the fig-
ure accompanying, which as mentioned above, leaves
only three possible interpretations open to the
observer.
```

You can understand why the UA wrote (4). He probably read hundreds of passages like (1) in scientific articles, picked up on the features that actually make it work as (marginal) science writing, and simply misapplied it. As my grandfather used to say, "Those who don't know, do too much." Start deleting words and phrases that are puffed up or redundant and there will be nothing left. But imagine you are responsible for editing these paragraphs; perhaps you wrote them yourself. How do you begin?

SIX STEPS TO DEEP EDITING

I often have to look at someone else's work that looks like (4). Even more painfully, I often have to deal with my own examples of this sort of stuff. Rather than working with really terrible sentences, I try an alternative tack. I step away from the sentence both mentally and physically: I get out of my chair, stop staring at the computer screen, and sit on the couch. Even better would be to lock the offending sentence or passage in the drawer for a day or two, or refuse to call it up on the screen. Most of us write at the last possible moment, which means that we don't have time to do anything but bang away at our own prose, sitting glued to the monitor.

Did you even notice that you stop hearing the humming of a fluorescent light after being in the room with it for long enough, or you stop seeing a dot on a page if you stare at it directly for long enough? These are examples of the cognitive principle of "adaptation." The brain simply stops registering a stimulus if it is presented persistently enough. In the same vein, if you repeat a simple word to yourself over and over again, after a time it can seem like a nonsense syllable. After looking at the same words for a while, you can't see or hear them anymore, much less look at them with a critical eye. The same effect applies when you edit your prose. If you are too close to it, it has become too familiar. Obviously, the cure is to:

1. **Make the words new to you again.** There are several ways to accomplish this. You can put time between writing and editing the same passage by setting the manuscript aside and refusing to look at it for a certain period. The more time the better—at least 24 hours, so your memory of the words has time to move from short-term into long-term storage. If you

can't get time, get *space*. Change rooms, postures, anything to give yourself a new view of the words.

2. **Derive the key thought of what you want to say.** Try to *reimagine what you were trying to say in the first place*. I try to visualize the intention of the sentence, if it's at all possible. Generally there is some core idea lurking behind all the verbiage, a picture of something doing something. The third step is to put it into different words.

3. **Explain that kernel to a nonexpert, using language as simple as possible.** In some cases, I think of explaining it to a friend who is smart but completely unscientific. Teachers know that this is one of the hidden values of teaching: in trying to communicate complex ideas, facts, and relationships to the uninformed, you simplify and purify them in your own mind.

After performing steps 1–3 on excerpt (4) from page 205, this is the kernel intention and restatement I got:

```
(5) In these circumstances, we used titra-
tion columns before the beta-diffraction
spectroscope on the phenylethanolamine N-
methyltransferase (PNMT) sample. We can in-
terpret the data this method yields in three
ways:. . .
```

In sum, deep editing relies on three basic steps, each of which is a psychological or mental trick. The end result is prose that says—or comes closer to saying—what you intend to communicate. On top of these three steps, if there is any bad writing left, go on to step 4.

4. **Take out the bad things and replace them with good ones.**

Finally, you have to know when to stop: "Wisdom consists of knowing when to avoid perfection." Perhaps two other old sayings also apply as corollaries to Horowitz's Rule:

5. **If it ain't broke, don't fix it,** and

6. **Quit while you're ahead!**

In the following chapters, we will look at why good scientific thinking can lead to bad science writing habits and ways to break those habits. You can use these suggestions to edit your work after you've written the first draft. However, it is simpler to understand the basis for good writing first and put those ideas into practice the first time around. On the other hand, it is unrealistic to expect you'll get it even close to right in the first draft. Remember that the real craft of writing is in the editing.

18

A Scientific Approach to Style

Writing about science is a subset of all writing. To do it well, you have to master the basic skills of literacy, of grammatical knowledge, and of the mechanics of syntax, punctuation, and spelling. Nothing will lose your audience's confidence in your authority quicker than misspelling a word or writing ungrammatically. This book assumes that you do, indeed, have command of these skills, or at least know where to get information about them.

Beyond the basic requirements that you are knowledgable about English, however, science writing poses special challenges. First, as hinted at in Chapter 2, decades of poor practices have passed from generation to generation until they have acquired the force of habit, if not law. Second, certain tendencies in proper scientific thinking carry over to writing as poor stylistic practices. For instance, you may be tempted to prefer things over actions, and therefore to write with lots of nouns rather than verbs, because you may think doing so is more precise or concrete. Similarly, it is tempting to suppress the human actor, to use the passive voice instead of first person (I, we), because you may think it is more objective and modest.

This chapter takes a scientific approach to writing sentences and explains how to cure the stylistic problems we explored in Chapter 17. We will look at what makes a sentence work, not only grammatically but in terms of how your readers process information in the sentence. Then, based on this understanding, we will look at what sentence formations and stylistic tactics make your prose most effective.

HOW DO SENTENCES WORK?

Grammar is the set of rules for writing correctly. *Syntax* is the set of choices you make in relating clauses, phrases, and parts of speech. A sentence can have perfectly correct grammar but lousy syntax. And indeed, when science writing goes wrong it is usually because of syntactical errors not grammatical ones.

The real question for any writer grappling with syntax is, "What do readers expect of a sentence?" Studies of how people read have confirmed what linguists have suspected for a long time. There is, in English anyway, a pattern for delivering information in the sentence that is more effective than other patterns because readers not only expect the sentence to fall into that pattern, their brain works better to process it that way.[66]

The simplest way to describe these expectations is to look at the basic sentence:

Subject	Verb	Object
John	threw	the ball.

The subject = thing whose story the sentence tells *[John]*.

The verb = action the subject performs *[threw]*.

The object = thing on which the subject acts *[the ball]*.

Readers of English expect that information will come to them in this form. Readers expect the subject to come at the beginning of the sentence or at least be the first noun they encounter in the sentence, and the verb and object to follow in that order. So although we can decipher the following sentences, they make reading more difficult and can lead to ambiguity:

X: The ball to Susan did John throw.

X: Throw the ball John did.

X: Susan was thrown the ball by John.

Another primary insight into communication in sentences is that readers look for connections between ideas. It is easier for readers to find the connections if they are at the beginning of a new idea than within the idea itself: sentences that use transitional terms in the front end or combine clauses with conjunctions like *and, but,* and *so* are easier than sentences that bury ideas in nested clauses. In short, the structure of an effective sentence generally follows a few simple principles:

CHECKLIST #24

SIMPLE GUIDELINES FOR STRUCTURING SENTENCES

☐ The subject and the verb should occur as close together as possible.

☐ Information that links an idea to the previous one or gives a context for understanding the idea should come first in the sentence or clause.

☐ "Revealing," new, and/or important information should be placed in the last part of the sentence. Save the best for last!

☐ Communicate the action of a sentence in an active verb. Avoid passive verbs and weak "linking" verbs like "is," "was," and "has."

☐ Communicate the action of a sentence and relationships among things in an active verb rather than through nouns and nouns acting as adjectives. Use verbs to avoid noun strings and nominalization.

☐ Don't get cheap with words: it's inefficient.

☐ Ideas that are strung together with conjunctions and transitional words that show their relations (like boxcars) are easier to understand than ideas nested inside each other (like Russian dolls).

Avoid Orphaned Verbs

The subject and the verb should occur as close together as possible. As soon as your readers figure out what the subject of a sentence is, they expect the action to come quickly. They are eager to know what it is that the subject did or what makes it so important.

X: The third moon of Samedon, Hephaestus, named after the Greek god of blacksmithing, and known to be primarily composed of iron, revolving every three days about the larger planet and discovered in the 23rd century by the Mertsager Exploration Mission launched from Luna, has one-third Earth's gravity.

The sentence is kind of like a suspenseful roller coaster ride. Yet, in the end, it's annoying. Why? Because the subject, "The third moon of Samedon," is separted from its verb, "has," by almost forty words! It would have been better if the author had put the subject and the verb together:

```
The third moon of Samedon, Hephaestus, has one-
third Earth's gravity.
```

This now forces the author to adopt some other good strategies—cures for the problem of orphaned verbs, discussed below.

Atomize

To return the verb to its parent subject, construct other, smaller sentences out of the phrases and clauses that separated them:

```
Hephaestus is the third moon of Samedon.

It is named after the Greek God of black-
    smithing.

It is composed primarily of iron.

It is appropriately named as a result.

It revolves around Samedon every three days.

It has one-third Earth's gravity.

The Mertsager Exploration Mission discovered it
    in the 23rd century.

Mertsager was launched from Luna.
```

However, this should only be the first step in reconstructing your prose. Notice that four of the six sentences now rely on forms of the weak verb "to be" (*is*).

Rebuild and Recombine

The next step is to rebuild by recombining the little sentences of the S-V-O structure into a larger sentence so they flow better. If possible, use linking terms to connect sentences:

```
Hephaestus, the third moon of Samedon, is named
after the Greek God of blacksmithing because it is
```

composed primarily of iron. It revolves around
Samedon every three days. It was originally dis-
covered in the 23rd century by the Mertsager
Exploration Mission, which was launched from Luna.
Its gravity equals one-third Earth's.

Links, Contexts, and/or the Subject of a Sentence Should Come First

Especially in science, the connections between ideas are important.
Readers of English expect the phrase that links two sentences logically or contextually to begin the second sentence. They also expect
the sentence to begin with the general information that "locates" the
ideas in a sentence or that links the information to come with prior
information.

Hence, readers like to have transitional words and phrases at the
beginning of sentences (see the listing below) or at the beginning of
clauses within the same sentence.

X: The conclusion that pterodactyls did not fly
is falsifiable, therefore, as a result of
this previous data.

YES: Therefore, as a result of this data, the
conclusion that pterodactyls did not fly is
falsifiable.

X: We excluded this variable from our second
calculations, for reasons explain.

YES: As explained above, we excluded this variable from our second calculations.

Use Transitional Words to Help the Flow of Ideas

Use these words and phrases at the beginning of your sentences to indicate the relationship among ideas and to help move the reader
along.

To provide an example:	*To compare:*	*To summarize:*
for example	also	in other words
for instance	in the same manner	in short

To provide an example:

to illustrate the point
specifically
that is

To compare:

similarly
likewise
in the same vein
in comparison to

To summarize:

in summary
in conclusion
finally
that is

To contrast:

but
however
yet
nonetheless
in contrast to
nevertheless
still
even though
on the contrary
although
despite
in opposition to

To indicate temporal relationships:

before
earlier
during
now
simultaneously
meanwhile
at the same time
when
while
later
following
then
immediately
    thereafter
after
afterwards
suddenly
subsequently
once again

To indicate logical relationships:

so
if
or
therefore
consequently
as a result
obviously
clearly
if and only if
it follows that
logically
since
because
nonetheless
by implication

To indicate spatial relationships:

below
above
beneath

To show sequence:

and
also
besides

To add conditions:

apparently
seemingly
perhaps

To indicate spatial relationships:	*To show sequence:*	*To add conditions:*
beyond	further	only when
nearby	furthermore	if and only if
at hand	additionally	it might be
across	moreover	possibly
behind	next	under these
throughout	too	circumstances
nowhere	also	in these cases
everywhere	first, second, third . . .	under these conditions
	finally	in the case of

New and/or Important Information Should Be Placed in the Last Part of the Sentence

Until you stop to think about it, it may be hard to believe that even this modest part of your prose, the sentence, has a sort of drama in it: You get broad considerations or connections out of the way, then you give the exposition of the thing you're talking about, then comes the action, and then . . . the payoff! New information or new actors are introduced. It is saving the best for last that puts a sort of punch or zing in sentences. For instance, compare these pairs of sentences:

X: Handicapped people ought not to be seriously considered as subjects for these experiments.

YES: Of course, no one would seriously suggest that we conduct these experiments on handicapped people.

X: It should not be thought that the entire discipline would grind to a halt if these procedures were not followed, or that a flood of inaccurate data would ensue.

YES: Even if researchers continue to ignore these procedures, most data will still be accurate and the discipline will hardly grind to a halt.

The latter sentence in each case puts the emphasis where it has the greatest effect: even our inner voice tends to inflect those last words: *handicapped people; grind to a halt.*

Of course you would quickly go crazy trying to evaluate what is the newest or most important bits of information in *all* your sentences and then trying to arrange them so they *always* appear last, but when you want to add some extra vigor to your statements, save the best for last.

Using Forms of the Verb "to be" Makes Weak Links

Using "is," "are" and other forms of the "to be" verb simply denotes an equation between two words. It is stronger to make the second word in the equation into an adjective.

X: The saturation of the liquid by solutes <u>is</u> inevitable.

YES: The solutes inevitably <u>saturate</u> the liquid.

X: The following steps <u>are</u> the directions:. . .

YES: <u>Follow</u> these directions:. . .

X: Crushing C_{60} <u>is</u> an easy way to produce diamonds.

Yes: To produce diamonds easily, <u>crush</u> C_{60}.

Use Active Voice and Avoid Passive Voice

Scientists tend to assume that impersonal prose is somehow more objective and therefore more scientific. This results in the passive voice. Passive voice arises when a writer puts the thing acted on (*object*) in the position of the actor (*subject*). In almost all cases, this requires that the writer use a form of the verb "to be" to assist (as an *auxiliary*) the unnatural transformation.

Passive voice deserves a much longer and more elaborate treatment because it is one of the most universal, persistent, and damaging habits of scientific writing. I call passive voice unnatural because *the world is intrinsically active;* it is made up of phenomena, things, and people—nouns—performing actions—verbs—on other things or people—objects (See Figure 18.1).

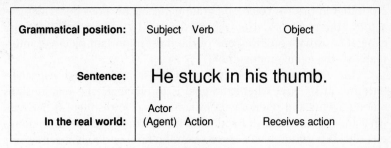

FIGURE 18.1
Grammar of the Active Voice

Note that in active voice, the grammatical positions match events in the real world.

```
Peter Piper picked a peck of pickled peppers.

The dish ran away with the spoon.

He stuck in his thumb.

He pulled out a plum.

He said, "Oh what a good boy am I!"
```

In passive voice, *the thing receiving the action* is put in the grammatical position usually reserved for *the thing doing the action*. The result is a mismatch between the grammar of the sentence and the world the sentence should describe (See Figure 18.2).

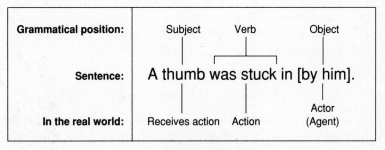

FIGURE 18.2
Grammar of the Passive Voice

Note that in passive voice, the grammatical actor does not match the actor in the real world; the verb gets longer by adding "was," and you can get away with omitting one of the most important pieces of information—the agent—altogether.

This mismatch becomes especially tempting, and especially harmful, in science, where the goal is to elucidate the relationships among agents and phenomena in nature and to distinguish between what the human actor did and what the instrumentation or phenomena did. It is certainly *not* more scientific (and certainly it seems less natural) to say

> **X:** A peck of pickled peppers was picked [by Peter Piper].
>
> **X:** A spoon was run away with [by the dish].
>
> **X:** A thumb was stuck in.
>
> **X:** A plum was pulled out.
>
> **X:** "Oh, what a good boy am I!" was said [by him].[67]

Two additional bad things happen to the prose as a result of using passive voice:

1. The verb becomes longer, because it needs help from a "to be" form to twist itself into passive;

2. You can now hide the agent entirely and still preserve the grammatical correctness of the sentence. That's what makes the passive voice so useful in politics—the speaker can disguise or omit mentioning the name of the person responsible for an action:

   X: Mistakes were made.

   X: Civilian buildings were unintentionally bombed.

Then why does passive voice persist as the peculiar disease of science writing, despite decades of warnings and advice from textbooks, teachers, and journal editors to avoid it?

The diagnosis is pretty simple, but the cure has been difficult.

Passive voice arises from several factors. The first is a natural modesty in most academic enterprises: boasting, self-adulation, arrogant claims, putting the ego forward, and the notion of seeking personal gain go against the grain of academic ethics. As a result, most academics and researchers naturally tend to shun the word "I."

The second source of the passive voice in science writing comes from the confusion between the personal pronoun (I) and subjectivity. Scientists know that it is wrong to introduce opinion into factual scientific reportage and opinion or bias arise from having a personal point of view. This is tacit in every scientific enterprise and teachers drum it into young scientists. But as a result, many scientists quite naturally and fundamentally—but incorrectly!—believe that *mentioning a human agent somehow automatically introduces subjectivity* into what is supposed to be the purely objective discourse of science writing. In other words the affection for passive voice arises from a taking a rule that should apply only to certain local or specific instances and globalizing to include a whole grammatical form. For instance, it is certainly subjective to say

```
I think . . .

I believe . . .

We supposed that . . .

Nezlick imagines . . .
```

But are the following any more appropriate or less subjective?

```
X: It had been thought that . . .

X: It had been believed that . . .

X: It is supposed that . . .

X: It has been suggested (Nezlick, 1991)
   that . . .
```

Subjectivity is introduced by the act of stating an opinion, whether it is yours or someone else's. Disguising subjectivity in the passive voice compounds it rather than eliminating it since passive voice makes it harder to tell who is expressing an opinion. If you really pay attention to the phrases above, you are left with questions: Who thought that. . . ? Who believes that. . . ? Who supposes that. . . ?

And is it inappropriate to say the following?

```
We took reagent A and mixed it with the cata-
    lyst.
```

```
In three cases we isolated naturally occurring
    peptides.
```

Is it inappropriate to describe a speculation in the concluding portions of a research report in the following manner?

```
As a result of these data, we concluded
    that . . .
```

As opposed to

```
As a result of these data, it can be concluded
    that. . .
```

The answer in all these cases is no, it is not inappropriate.

However, the problem is quite difficult to root out in science writing— and indeed most academic writing. Passive voice becomes habitual very quickly. It sets up a grammatical pattern that becomes hard to break. Like riding a bicycle downhill, it achieves a momentum of its own.

The first parts of most science papers are supposed to include a statement of the problem and a discussion of hypotheses, along with a review of literature. All of these naturally require reference either to the author's beliefs or the results and opinions expressed by others in written reports. Consequently, it is here that the author first is tempted to use passive voice to avoid referring to other human agents:

X: It was hypothesized that . . .

X: We suggest that . . .

X: We hypothesize that . . .

X: We designed the following experiment to test the hypothesis that . . .

Note that in the following case, the solution in literature citations is to focus on the *nature of the results or contribution in the active voice,* thereby eliminating the need to include the human agent(s)—the author of the article cited—at all.

X: Expression vectors developed from several viruses have been shown to express reporter genes in mammalian cells in vitro (17).

X: Several viruses express reporter genes in mammalian cells in vitro (17).

However, once you mount the passive voice bicycle, it's hard to get off again. The passive voice patterns spills over into the methods and materials section, and even into the conclusions section where, in both cases, it can do damage. In the M & M section, you can easily introduce ambiguity by trying to avoid the human actor or by generally putting the mechanical agent (the piece of apparatus or chemical or measuring device) in the objective case.

X: As can be seen from the data presented in Figure 1. . . .

Here are other phrases in the passive voice that recur in many science reports and articles. Try to weed them out of your writing.

X: As has been previously remarked . . .

X: It has been previously established that . . .

X: The intention has been to create new procedures whereby this hypothesis can be tested.

X: It was thought to be of interest to compare the macrocharacteristics of . . .

X: Based on these data, the following model can be proposed . . .

X: The solution of this problem is treated by this study.

X: It was found that . . .

X: These [phenomena] were viewed . . .

X: . . . were studied . . .

X: It was observed that . . .

X: A computer model has been developed that
    simulates the . . .

You can see that a good deal of the motivation in these sentences to use passive voice comes from a desire to avoid mentioning the human actor or personalizing the author. Yet this only creates an "aura" of objectivity without actually adding objectivity to your writing.

Use Verbs; Avoid Nominalization and Noun Strings

Things are a lot easier to pin down than *actions, processes,* and *events.* Adam and Eve in the Garden of Eden were told to name the animals, not the processes of nature. This hereditary bias toward "thingness" (in our culture, anyway) lures many students into thinking that somehow nouns are "truer" than verbs. As a result, their prose tends to focus excessively on things instead of actions and people, and so tends to ignore verbs in favor of nouns, or even to convert verbs to noun-like words.

X: Following termination of activation of soil
    sampling mode, the process resolution was
    achieved.

BETTER: To conclude the process, we sampled the
    soil.

Some linguists attribute this practice to Germanic influence, which tends to pile up and combine nouns in one part of a sentence and let descriptions and actions hang themselves where they please.

The following sentence is afflicted with two noun strings. Can you identify them?

X: R2 continuity intensive modulation is effec-
    tuated by inorganic molecular infolding.

You can fix them—"R2 continuity intensive modulation" and "inorganic molecular infolding"—by figuring out which nouns describe things and which nouns describe relationships between things. You can convert the latter into verbs or adverbs.

YES: When inorganic molecules fold in on themselves, they change R2 continuity inten-
sively.

To make matters worse, much scientific prose converts good, punchy, serviceable verbs into nouns anyway, just in case:

X: Direct observations of the correlation of
activities led to conclusions about the in-
stigation of these processes.

BETTER: By directly observing how these activities correlate, we drew conclusions about
what had instigated them.

The grammarians word for this is *nominalization.* Avoid it. Again, the best cure is to rewrite the sentence using a verb that describes the relationship between the nouns in your sentence.

GETTING CHEAP WITH WORDS IS INEFFICIENT

One of the most prevalent problems among scientist-authors is that their instinct for efficiency carries over into the use of words, resulting in a kind of cheapness or parsimony. In other words, *when it comes to writing, many scientists get cheap with words.* They naively assume that words and paper are precious commodities and that fewer words use less paper and so are better. Even very good style manuals "probe" how much more effective one practice is than another (such as active versus passive voice or using verbs rather than nominals) by comparing how many more words the bad style requires. This encourages you to assume that in matters of style, less is always better. The result is a generation of scientists who try to "engineer" or "rationalize" their prose to obtain maximum economy by applying a rule of parsimony. The prose they produce, however, is anything but efficient:

Application of comparative very long baseline in-
terferometry yields little significant vertical
ratio two-measurement offset results.

While we all like conciseness of expression and clarity, these two ideals often have little to do with how many words you use. To take a very simple example, read these two sentences:

```
(1) Cells enzymatically harvested from luminal
surfaces of selected grafts permit, under circum-
stances detailed by us in previous research, more
successful treatment, to be applied with other
general approaches, explained below.
```

```
(2) Under these circumstances, which we detailed
in previous research, the cells that were enzymat-
ically harvested from the luminal surfaces of the
selected grafts will permit a more successful
treatment that is to be applied with other general
approaches, which we explain below.
```

There is no doubt that (1) is comprehensible *to most readers* as it stands and it uses fewer words. But it is *not* more efficient than (2). Sentence (2) is easier to read. An article built of sentences like (2), although it will require more words, in the long run will probably be simpler and quicker to read. Those little words grease the wheels of prose.

This has been proven by mostly failed or impoverished attempts to get a computer to translate between languages. Out of this research has emerged sound advice as well as empirically persuasive evidence about how to make sentences easier to understand.

- **Put in the articles** *(a, the)*.

```
X: Run data through analysis program by pick-
ing random sample from sets used in study.
YES: Run the data through the analysis pro-
gram by picking a random sample from the sets
used in the study.
```

- **Put in the relative pronouns** *(which, that, who, what)*.

X: We accomplished it by a technique proven effective.
YES: We accomplished it by a technique that has proven effective.
X: Our results suggest epithelial cells work.
YES: Our results suggest that epithelial cells work.

- **Don't try to pack too many ideas into one sentence.**

- **Use transitional words liberally.**

In short, it is most economical to use as many words and sentences as necessary to make yourself as clear as possible to the most people.

DON'T BURY IMPORTANT POINTS IN SUBORDINATE CLAUSES OR SUB-SUBORDINATE CLAUSES

A *subordinate clause* is a thought inserted into the main thought of the sentence. A *sub-subordinate clause* is a thought inserted into a subordinate clause. Much of scientific prose can get tangled with thoughts inside thoughts—like those Russian dolls that have smaller versions nested inside each other. The following example is grammatically correct, but it is awkward and difficult to decipher.

X: After the conclusion of data gathering from the application of Method 1, which revealed to us that the concentrations always fall below 0.4 µl/l—**when theory predicts they should remain constant**—we proceeded to apply Method 2.

To correct nested clauses, first unpack the sentences into separate actions and thoughts.

We applied Method 2 after concluding our data gathering from Method 1.

Method 1 showed us that the concentrations always fall below 0.4 µl/l.

Theory predicts that the concentrations should remain constant.

Then keep them as separate sentences and/or recombine them with linking words—transitional phrases conjunctions (*and, or, if, but so,);* and coordinating conjunctions (*however, yet, although, because, thus, therefore, whereas, etc.*). This makes your thoughts read in a more orderly fashion, in a way the mind is more prepared to receive them: like boxcars in a train, one after another.

YES: Method 1 revealed that concentrations always fall below 0.4 µl/l, <u>whereas</u> theory predicts they should remain constant. When we finished gathering data from Method 1, we applied Method 2.

YES: Theory predicts that concentrations will remain constant. However, Method 1 revealed that they always fall below 0.4 µl/l. As a result, we proceeded to apply Method 2.

PERHAPS: Since Method 1 revealed that concentrations always fall below 0.4 µl/l, <u>and</u> theory predicts they should remain constant, we applied Method 2 after we finished gathering data from Method 1.

Note that the solution here is to break the clauses in the subordinate positions into their own sentences or string them together in one sentence. This means stringing your thoughts like boxcars using conjunctions and coordinating conjunctions rather than nesting thoughts inside each other in phrases stacked like Russian dolls.

FINAL WORDS ABOUT SCIENTIFIC STYLE

So much has been written and said about the need for clarity and precision in science writing, that I would not presume to give you the final words about them myself. Instead, let me borrow from the wisdom of the ages:

> *"Bad scientific writing involves more than stylistic inelegance: it is often the outward and visible form of an inward confusion of thought."*
>
> —*F. Pete Woodford, "Sounder Thinking Through Clearer Writing,"*[68]

> *"The language of truth is simple."*
>
> —*Seneca (the Younger)*

> *"Craft needs clothes but truth loves to go naked."*
>
> —*Thomas Fuller,* Gnomologia *(1658)*

19

How and When to Define Your Terms

"[W]ords stand in the way and resist the change. . . . [T]he high and formal discussions of learned men end oftentimes in disputes about words and names; with which . . . it would be more prudent to begin, and so by means of definitions reduce them to order. Yet even definitions cannot cure this evil . . . since the definitions themselves consists of words, and those words beget others."

—*Sir Francis Bacon,* The New Organon, *Book I, (1620)*

One of the most common problems in writing about science is knowing which terms require definition and to what level those terms need to be defined. The problem of knowing when to define a term is an extension of the problem of knowing your audience. Highly technical terms that don't need to be defined for an audience of experts will need to be defined for anyone who is less expert. Terms which are in doubt in one field may be quite well understood in another. And you can't always be sure everyone in your audience is as familiar with a term as you think they ought to be.

When I ask my students why they didn't define a technical term, they often give several thoughtful reasons:

- They believe that most of their audience is already familiar with the term and are surprised to find out they may not be.

- They are afraid that by defining a term that is familiar to some of their audience, they will be insulting them.

• They are afraid that by defining a term that is obvious to their audience they will seem unsure or novice-like, since only a newcomer would need to define a term like that.

Weighing against this however is a generalization that might help you think through the problem: *When in doubt, define.* When you doubt that your expert audience understands a term in precisely the way you do, define it. When you doubt that *everyone* in your audience understands a term, define it. When you doubt that everyone in your audience is as expert as you, define the term. When you know there is disagreement over definition of a term, define it. Imagine another student who is reading your work for a more general research report and who may be relatively new to the field. Think about a researcher in a related field who may not be familiar with the term as it is defined in your discipline. And remember that your first job is to communicate.

In the end, it costs very little to define and not doing so may be expensive. Furthermore, there is a profit to be made. When you define a term that is familiar to most (but perhaps not all) members of your audience, you are at least reaffirming a common ground and erecting familiar markers so that you can proceed with your story, like the storyteller who begins "Once upon a time. . . " even though everyone knows the story is going to begin that way. There is nothing wrong with repeating common information in introductory or context-setting parts of a report. On the other hand, you must also be reasonable. Otherwise you could spend your entire time defining all your terms to the nth degree. You have to develop a feel for which terms are safe to pass and which terms require elaboration.

HOW TO DEFINE TERMS

There are many ways to define terms. The first is the simplest: Devote a sentence to stating the term and giving its definition (following the basic form "Term X is predicate Y."). (**Note:** In all the following examples of definitions, I have underlined the term being defined. However, in the originals, none of these terms were underlined. I advise my students to italicize, underline, or place in quotes a term or phrase when it is being used as a word for the first time in their papers. However, this is a matter of taste and not a convention or rule.)

A <u>Cepheid variable</u> is a relatively young star,
several times more massive than the sun, whose luminosity changes in a periodic way, brightening
and then dimming more slowly.

However, don't pack too much of the definition into one sentence.
Spread it out across as many sentences as you need to define the term
to the proper depth:

It pulsates because the force of gravity acting on
the atmosphere of the star is not quite balanced
by the pressure of hot gases from the interior of
the star.[69]

Another simple method is to call attention to the fact that you are
using a new term by using such phrases as "is said to be _____" or
"is called _____" or "is termed _____."

The nerve cell is said to be <u>depolarized</u> if its
resting potential becomes more positive and <u>hyper-
polarized</u> if it becomes more negative.[70]

There is also a counterintuitive phenomenon . . .
called <u>antichaos:</u> some very disordered systems
spontaneously "crystallize" into a high degree of
order.[71]

A third method is simply to put a defining phrase in parentheses
after the new term:

When the workers transplanted a piece of embryonic
rat hippocampus into the gap in the fimbria, the
<u>cholinergic</u> (acetylcholine-releasing) fibers grew
through the graft and into the host hippocampus.[72]

In some instances, it is ideal to explain the concept first before
giving the term used to define it:

There is a whole family of fossils remarkable for
their flat, soft bodies found primarily in the
Ediacara Hills of South Australia. These are
called the <u>Edicarian fauna.</u>[73]

```
In many DNA and RNA viruses, including those that
cause the common cold and polio, the virus repli-
cates by inducing the cell to copy the viral ge-
netic material and make viral proteins. A multi-
tude of new virus particles take shape, and the
infected cell bursts, releasing the protein. This
process of bursting the cell is called lysing, and
the viruses that use the process cause what are
therefore called lytic infections.⁷⁴
```

There are a couple of good rules of thumb to follow when you define terms:

- Always define a term where you first introduce it. Keep your
  definition as close to the first occurrence of the term as possible.

- Don't use one new or mysterious term in the definition of another.

The definition of *cholinergic* (above) requires that the reader
know what *acetylcholine* is, which in this instance is a safe bet, but it
might have been risky for another audience. On the other hand, in
the sciences, almost any term or idea can be defined to virtually any
depth. You can extend the vista of a definition almost infinitely simply
by asking "Why?" or "What?" or "How?" like a persistent four-year-
old. The Nobel Prize–winning physicist Richard Feynman, in his collection of lectures on introductory physics, discusses this temptation
to define a concept *ad infinitum*, even when it is as apparently simple
as the concept of motion:

> We have now seen two examples of motion, adequately described with
> very simple ideas, no subtleties. However, there *are* subtleties—several
> of them. In the first place, what do we mean by *time* and *space*? It turns
> out that these deep philosophical questions have to be analyzed very
> carefully in physics, and this is not easy to do. The theory of relativity
> shows that our ideas of space and time are not as simple as one might
> think at first sight. However, for our present purposes, for the accuracy
> that we need at first, we need not be very careful about defining things
> precisely. Perhaps you say, "That's a terrible thing—I learned that in sci-
> ence we have to define *everything* precisely." We cannot define *any-
> thing* precisely! If we attempt to, we get into that paralysis of thought
> that comes to philosophers, who sit opposite each other, one saying to

the other, "You don't know what you're talking about!" The second one says, "What do you mean by *know?* What do you mean by *talking?* What do you mean by *you?*" and so on. In order to be able to talk constructively, we just have to agree that we are talking about roughly the same sort of thing. You know just as much about time as we need for the present, but remember that there are some subtleties that have to be discussed; we shall discuss them later.[75]

For instance here is an excerpt from a paper discussing Leik Myrabo's model for a laser-powered intercontinental spaceship:

From the station, the beam will hit concentrating mirrors on the outside of the capsule and focus, now super-hot, on the bottom of the craft. The beam will react with the atmosphere around the bottom and create a plasma-producing shockwave, thrusting the craft forward.

Lasers are beams of concentrated light. The term is an acronym for light amplification by the stimulated emission of radiation. Laser light does not disperse like light from a conventional source, e.g., a light bulb or the sun. Where a conventional lightbeam that is 1/2-inch in diameter at its source will be about 100 yards diffuse after a mile, a laser lightbeam might be only 3/4-inch in diameter after traveling a mile. This property makes lasers ideal for transferring energy, since so little waste occurs from diffusion.

Still need amplification?

Lasers work by powerfully exciting atoms of a light-amplifying substance such as rubies, gases, or liquids which release the light in a coherent beam.

Yeah, but how?

Lasers are produced by stimulating the emission of energy from one quantum—or bundled—source.

```
Typically, a strong energy pulse is sent through a
substance with free electrons which are excited to
a higher quantum state. When all the electrons re-
turn to their natural quantum state, they emit
photons in bundles or coherent packets.
```

And of course, the chain of defining does not end here. What is a *photon?* What is *energy?* What is a *quantum state?*

A NOTE ON JARGON

If you read a complicated, thickly worded science article, it may be hard to believe that language is just as precious to the scientist as it is to the poet, but it is, though the results may be jarringly different. Most scientific prose sounds like babble to outsiders. As a result, you have probably been commanded by a misguided English teacher somewhere along the line to *avoid jargon.*

This advice is useless! One writer's jargon is another's technical nomenclature. Furthermore, jargon is efficient and fun. Being able to use jargon is a sign of membership in a group. It's your group's slang, your secret lingo. Jargon helps you conduct your business swiftly without a lot of definitions. Jargon is even an expression of bonding, of camaraderie. Technical language is highly refined to refer to things and actions that are very specific and have no other name, things you would have to draw a picture of to explain if you didn't have a word for them, such as:

```
3-[(1,3-dihydro-1,3-dioxo-H-isoindol-2-yl)oxy]-3-
oxopropanoic acid
```

Sometimes, like a picture, one good technical term is worth a thousand words.

*The real trouble in using jargon doesn't come from what you say but **when** you say it and **to whom.*** Just as it is impolite to purposefully allude to a private matter between you and a friend when there is a third party present, it is impolite to use jargon ostentatiously, knowing it will leave some of your readers in the dark. By doing so, you are in effect erecting a barrier between those who are "in the know" and those who aren't. You are tacitly telling some readers they don't belong. It's rude. Therefore you must know your audience so that you have a good sense of what the range in their vocabulary is likely to be.

If you know that your audience doesn't understand a term and you use it anyway, or if you choose a complex expression over a simpler, more familiar word, then you might be motivated by a desire to impress someone else with your knowledge. It's easy for all of us to fall into this trap. But the simplest way to impress someone is to get the facts to them in a clear, orderly, and persuasive fashion.

The Perils of Assuming Your Audience Is "In the Know"

My favorite story about defining scientific terms is the one about a professor who asked a student to help him set up a microphone for a guest speaker. The student, Jeff, was having difficulty screwing the microphone head to the body. The professor said, "Turn it clockwise, Jeff, clockwise."

"What did you say?" Jeff asked.

"I said, screw it in clockwise."

It was obvious from the look on his face that Jeff was unfamiliar with the term. The professor asked, "Don't you know what clockwise means?"

Jeff just shook his head.

"Well, Jeff," said the professor, lapsing into his best professorial tone. "How does a clock move?"

Jeff thought for a minute and then brightened.

"Like this!" And he flicked his ten fingers on and off like blinking lights.

The final message about defining terms is clear: it is not easy to know when your audience has the same experience as you. When in doubt, define your terms.

20

How to Use Numbers, Symbols, Units, Formulas, and Equations

Numbers are part of the language of science. A whole series of protocols have evolved for using them. In what follows, the word "numeral" refers to Arabic numbers (*1,2,3,...*) unless otherwise specified. The word "name" refers to the word spelled out (*one, two, three ...*). The word "measure" refers to units denoting a dimension of space, time, mass, energy, information, or some other measurable aspect.

NUMBERS

- **When the number does not denote a measure or dimension, use the *name* for numbers between zero and ten (except when the number describes a mathematical operation), and the *numeral* for all others, (except when it is the first word of a sentence).**

```
three dogs
32 cats
three-quarters of the population
120 people
raised to the power of 2
3 orders of magnitude greater
he added 6 to the result
```

One hundred and twenty people attended the
conference but 63 decided to leave.

- **You can use numerals to name an item, an experiment, or a sample.**

In experiment 12 we gathered sample 14 in
Building 7.

- **You can use the names of very large numbers in combination with numerals, but in that instance use the name of the measure or dimension.**

16 billion
146 thousand years
2.4 million liters

- **Form the plural of a number by adding 's.**

All the 100's were lined up in the output.
None of the 2's finished the race.

- **Decimals are preferred to fractions. If the fraction falls between −1 and 1, use a zero before the decimal.**

| **X:** | 1/2 | 12 1/4 | −.314 |
| **YES:** | 0.5 | 12.25 | −0.314 |

- **When using the names of fractions, hyphenate.**

seven-eighths
twenty-two-twenty-fifths

- **To write a sequence of consecutive numbers or a range of values, use a hyphen between the first and last numerals in the series. Use the entire last number.**

X: pages 327-56
YES: pages 327-356

YES: from 6-8
YES: The numbers 1-99

Mathematical Operators

• **Leave a space before and after mathematical operators.**

X: 2×17 = 34
YES: 3 + 4 = 7

• **Do not leave a space between the positive, negative, or the plus-or-minus sign and the number.**

YES: +327.6 is greater than +327
YES: 3140 yr (±10)
YES: −0.5
YES: −log 17

MEASURES AND DIMENSIONS

• **When you are noting an amount of a measure, generally use the numeral separated by a space from the name of the measure, which you can abbreviate.**

• **Do not use a period after the abbreviation of the measure.**

• **In the instances of $ or %, do not use a space between the number and the sign.**

X: twelve and six-tenths hr
X: twelve and six-tenths hours
X: 12.6 hours
X: forty-two kg. or 42 kg. or 42kg
YES: 12.6 hr
YES: 42 kg
YES: 17 mB
YES: 0.23%
YES: $120.00
YES: 99 m/sec^2

YES: 2 log 27

• Use numerals for years and decades, but don't abbreviate them.

X: '70s
X: '92
X: the seventies
YES: 2000 B.C.
YES: the 1930s

• Use numerals with A.M. and P.M. or B.C. and A.D.

7:42 a.m.   1066 A.D.

NUMBERING LISTS AND ITEMS

• To form a numbered list within a paragraph, use numerals within parentheses.

They had three objections: (1) there weren't
enough data; (2) the data were inaccurate;
(3) the interpretations were based on poor
statistical models.

• To form a numbered list in list format, use numerals followed by a period:

1. fishing
2. tennis
3. aerobics

EQUATIONS AND FORMULAS

• Write equations and formulas on their own lines and number them consecutively with a numeral in parentheses at the right margin.

- **Do not use punctuation after the formula.** The following are the third and fourth equations in a paper:

$$3x^2 - 4y^2 + 12z^2 = f(n) \qquad (3)$$

$$3x + 14y + 12z = f(m) \qquad (4)$$

- **In the body of the text you would then refer to the equation or formula by its number in parentheses.**

```
As the equation for this curve (3) shows,...
Using (3) we would apply ...
```

- **If you don't have access to a typewriter or computer with the symbols fonts (mostly Greek letters), handletter them neatly.**

FINAL WORDS ABOUT MATHEMATICS AND SCIENCE WRITING

So much of scientific knowledge is couched in terms of mathematics and numbers because there is such a strong sense in science that quantifying our observations of nature make them both more concrete and easier to manipulate and evaluate. As Eugene Wigner has said, mathematics has an almost "unreasonable effectiveness" in describing nature, so much so that it is hard not to believe that mathematics is the very language of the universe itself.

This is an old idea in science. We can trace it back to the Pythagoreans, the Greek geometers of the fifth century B.C. Perhaps Galileo summarized it best in his essay, *Knowledge* (1623):

> Philosophy is written in this grand book—I mean the universe—which stands continually open to our gaze, but it cannot be understood unless one first learns to comprehend the language and interpret the characters in which it is written. It is written in the language of mathematics. . . . Without these, one is wandering about the universe in a dark labyrinth.

21

Conclusion

One World—Science and Writing

One of the most unfortunate byproducts of the modern university system is the pigeonholing of writing into a separate discipline. Except in rare instances, students have to look in very different parts of the catalog and perhaps even go to different buildings on campus in order to do science *and* to learn about writing. As a result, it is easy to come to the mistaken conclusion that the two have little to do with each other and involve very different ways of viewing the universe; that writing belongs over there in the older humanities section of the university (or universe), along with philosophy and arts.

At the same time, our culture implies, through television documentaries, magazines, schools, movies, and novels, that science takes place behind some laboratory door, high atop an ivory tower, in the secret recesses of a well-guarded corporate building, far afield under the ocean, in space, or at the business end of a mysterious instrument. Once in a while, a sheaf of papers covered with formulas and complex diagrams written in a barely-comprehensible jargon gets generated by this activity. But of course, this sort of writing has nothing to do with the kind of writing that goes on *over there* on the other side of campus.

Yet if you look at how science shapes our daily lives, and at the many forms scientific activity takes, then you see that science and culture are inseparable. Science is not only the objective activity of gathering data in the laboratory and building theories from logical processes. As science grows, it will continue to be influenced by social and cultural forces and will itself continue to be an influential cultural and social force. It is virtually inconceivable, for instance, that the theory of evolution could have been discovered and phrased just that way by anyone other than a learned European man of the nineteenth century. And it is similarly inconceivable to imagine our own era of intellectual life without Darwin's theory.

In order to be both an effective writer and an effective scientist, it is important to see precisely how and why writing contributes to the larger goals of science. How does writing help science go forward? To what extent do science and writing resemble each other? To what extent is science a social and cultural activity? To what extent is science subject to the forces of cultural influence, personality, politics, fashion, and language?

SCIENCE IS NOT ONLY
A RATIONAL ACTIVITY

Many scientists when they write try to make their writing as rational and logical as other procedures in science. However, while writing is orderly, it not strictly logical. That's why computers have such difficulty understanding natural language. When students assume that they must write with the same rationality that they use in applying the scientific method, their writing begins to sound a little like it was generated by a computer. But to take the point even further, it is possible that science itself is not as rational as all that.

In this century we have come to learn that science does not necessarily accumulate truths and facts in a sure and progressive fashion toward a total picture, slowly filling in some paint-by-numbers picture of the universe. Rather, science is fluid. It is always contingent, always open to revision, always growing organically, sometimes in fits and starts. For long times, a strong theory can rule scientific views, only to be debunked by a surprising new insight or discovery.

The great philosopher of science Karl Popper described the twentieth-century condition of science this way:

> Science is not a system of certain, or well-established statements, nor is it a system which steadily advances toward a state of finality. . . . The demand for scientific objectivity makes it inevitable that every scientific statement must remain *tentative forever*. It may indeed be corroborated, but every corroboration is relative to other statements which, again, are tentative. Only in our subjective experiences of conviction, in our subjective faith, can we be "absolutely" certain.[76]

This is only fitting, since science has also learned that nature itself is not a system of causality. Nature is not a "certainty machine." This century's discoveries in quantum physics, relativity, and cosmology have also disclosed a nature that doesn't work to suit our common-sense notions of time, space, and certainty.[77] Our human experience of time, space, energy, and information at the macroscopic level are local phenomena, and our experience here does not account for reality elsewhere at more exotic places: near black holes, in subatomic spaces, at very high speeds, and in the first instants of creation. At the subatomic level, reality as we know it apparently does not exist at all. Some quantum physicists despair of whether there is anything much sensible we can say about it even if it does.[78]

In fact, in this century we have learned that the closer we look at nature, the more we fulfill Lord Kelvin's dictum: *Not only is nature stranger than we think it is, it is stranger than anything we* <u>*can*</u> *think.* One of the most mysterious phenomena in nature is the human mind itself. The closer we look at it, the more complex and baffling it becomes. Questions like "How does thinking work?" and "What is consciousness?" continue to elude any simple mechanical explanations.

When you first stumble on these views of science, perhaps in a physics course, you may find them strange and unsettling. But if you think of writing as an activity that negotiates the boundary between the logical and the irrational, the known and the mysterious, then it brings science back home as a very personal and human activity, as well as underscoring the importance of writing.

SCIENCE ALWAYS INVOLVES A POINT OF VIEW

A simple exercise brings this point home. Read the list of subjects below and cross off those that don't belong under the heading SCIENCE:

stars, comets, galaxies, atoms and molecules, fossils, dinosaurs, microbes, viruses, bacteria, genes, feelings, love, pheromones, drugs, chemicals, plastic, MTV, music, sound, fluid dynamics, perception, thinking, the mind, theories, nerves, jogging, fitness, aerobics, physiology, anaerobic bacteria, chrysanthemums, botany, Richard Nixon, politics, political science, *The Cosby Show,* television, signal processing, integrated electronics, pizza, diet, "The Mona Lisa," oil, paint, color, beauty.

By now you have probably guessed the point: *No particular subject or thing is scientific per se.* Rather, *science is a way of looking at the world.* It is a point of view and an activity devoted to pursuing that point of view. While we have strong intuitions about what does and does not constitute correct "scientific activity," it is hard to generalize. Studies of ESP and UFOs are usually excommunicated from "legitimate" scientific discussions, conferences, and journals even if the scientists who study them follow all the proper methods and use proper scientific language. Pizza in itself is not scientific, but neither are molecules or stars. But examining pizza from a certain context—say from the point of view of how humans metabolize carbohydrates, fats, and proteins together—qualifies it as a bona fide scientific phenomenon.

Disseminating what you've discovered about these phenomena in a certain fashion—writing authoritative research reports about them—gives a perspective on pizza or stars or molecules: a scientific narrative.

Science doesn't really exist anywhere in particular. It comes from individual authors adopting a certain point of view that has been prescribed by their discipline. These authors tell the story of what they've seen from that point of view, and tell it in such a way that everyone will understand that they are telling a proper science story and not some other kind of tale.

When you are writing a laboratory or research report or even an essay for a college course, it is easy to lose sight of the fact that you are choosing how to tell a story. Yet, even within the narrow range of options that may be open to you in a course assignment, your writing is still the art of choice.

Scientists might very well learn something from the way journalists provide a framework or context for the science they report. Many journalistic habits of style, certain grammatical forms, have a grace and clarity that would help scientific reports even in formal journal articles:

- the first person pronoun;

- shorter sentences;

- active voice;

- a sense of the drama in a scientific project;

- stating things in simplest possible terms.

These are all habits you should practice when writing the formal scientific paper. Most editors think more of these practices would be better. Based on what we know about the shape of science as a cultural activity, more would be *appropriate,* too.

THERE IS NO SCIENCE WITHOUT SOMEONE TELLING ITS STORY

In this century, insights about science have led to new visions of the relation between science and how we communicate it. Yet, strangely, views of science *writing* have lagged behind. In essence, a nineteenth-century stylistic paradigm has been governing twentieth-century science writing. To bring the practice of scientific writing into the twentieth century, we need to acknowledge the consequences of these revelations for writing about science.

First and foremost, we can now broaden our view of what constitutes the proper writing of science. You need not be a practicing scientist reporting lab results to be a coauthor of the story of science. As a result of these new views of science we also know that the scientist does not merely blueprint the machine. The job of the scientist as an intelligent observer is not simply to map some universal architecture completely, since that seems to be impossible. Rather, the scientist's highest calling is to tell a grand and coherent narrative of nature, a convincing portrait that explains the details and predicts the future behaviors of phenomena. By describing phenomena in their most precise and detailed minutiae, the scientist helps to fill out this grand narrative, turning nature into discourse.

The quantum situation provides a good analogy. Quantum physics has taught us that the photon exists as a wave and as a particle, and that the position and momentum of the photon cannot both be known in advance. The best you can do is to describe the photon as a probability wave, described by Schrödinger's equations. However, when you make an observation of the particle, you essentially freeze the Schrödinger wave, forcing the photon to choose its condition. This is called "collapsing the Schrödinger wave." Your observation, in a literal sense, has created the reality you observe. While this does not describe what literally happens at the macroscopic level or any level above the quantum one, it does provide us with a sort of parable about the relationship between the scientific observer and the phenomena he or she observes. Scientific activity and its communication are so bound up in each other that you cannot distinguish one from the other. In many senses, *the story of science does not exist until you tell it.*

Were nature a machine and science a perfect system for mapping it, then science writing would be a matter of simply interviewing nature and transcribing the answers. Language would be transparent. Every word would have an obvious meaning and there would be no ambiguity, as it is in a machine code for computer programming.

From the earliest days of the first professional association of scientists, The Royal Society (founded in 1657), scientists (they called themselves "natural philosophers" then) have been seeking a pure and formal language of nature that would express the unadorned truth without embellishment, metaphor, or ambiguity. This search has so far failed. There is no such thing as *the* language of truth with which we can tell *the* story of science. Until we find one, all we have are different sets of conventions that govern different kinds of stories, an array of alternatives from which we must choose when we want to write about science.

Yet, in practice, what most scientists think they are doing is describing what they find. Like umpires, they are "calling them as they see them." They feel confident in this, and rightly so, because they are viewing nature through a finely-ground lens of the scientific method, which is a tried-and-true means for getting at data about natural phenomena.

Nonetheless, when it comes to disseminating the results of research and how you got them, you have to choose how best to order and present those facts. Should you call a press conference or give an interview? Should you wait for the next convention of your associates and call a poster session—an impromptu meeting to announce a new breakthrough? Should you write a formal article for the journal of your subdiscipline? Should you leak a rumor over electronic mail or in a casual conversation? Should you let the university news and communications office issue a carefully-contrived blurb to the media? These are very similar to the choices a creative writer makes when he or she is captured by an inspiring image but has to choose whether to present it as a poem, play, short story, screenplay, essay, or novel.

From a functional point of view, the scientific fact does not exist until it is communicated in a scientific context. In short, the scientist is in the position of a different kind of umpire, one who says, "They ain't nothing until I call them."

THE HISTORY AND FUTURE
OF SCIENCE WRITING

When we learn how to write about science, we tend to view the rules and formats as engraved in stone, *laws of writing about science* that are as immutable as the *laws of physics.* It *is* true that the principles of writing about science tend to change very slowly because they have their basis in the nature of scientific reasoning and discourse itself. Nonetheless, they do change, even as science itself changes.

The scientific article is an invention of the seventeenth century, and it has slowly evolved and is still evolving. To appreciate this we need only look at what the first and authoritative science journal of the first scientific society, *The Philosophical Transactions of the Royal Society of London,* published in its pages through its first century or so (1665–1800). Here is how one scholar describes what he found there:

> Despite the folk belief that science rests on the experiment and scientific communication revolves around the experimental report, only a small part of the volumes examined up to 1800 were devoted to reporting on experiments. Both in terms of the percentage of total articles and percentage of pages, experimental articles accounted for only between 5 and 20 percent of each volume through volume 80. Only in volume 90, opening the nineteenth century, did the percentages substantively rise to 39% of the articles and 38% of the pages. . . . Until 1800, however, it is clear that experiments were only one of the many types of information to be transmitted. . . . The bulk of the articles and pages were devoted to observations and reports of natural events, ranging from remarkable fetuses and earthquakes through astronomical sightings, anatomical dissections and microscopical observations, while passing through reports of human accomplishments such as interviews with the prodigy Mozart and travelogues of journeys to China and Japan. Technological advances and medical cures were also frequently reported. . . . [In short], the

business of scientists did not seem to be restricted to experimenting or even theorizing, which received even less space than experiments.[78]

Actually, if we examine the important general scientific journals of today—such as *Nature* or *Science*—or the journals that also report transactions of a scientific society, we are likely to find a somewhat similar mix—though in different proportions—of "general interest" reportage and strict scientific experimental or theoretical reports.

In short, there is no need to feel that the form of the scientific article is so regulated that you cannot experiment with it, or that there isn't any room for you to take some chances. Both the nature of scientific reportage and science itself continually evolve.

SCIENCE TELLS MANY DIFFERENT STORIES

On my desk is the 13 July 1990 issue of *Science,* chosen at random from a pile by my desk. In leafing through the pages I find the following sorts of entries:

Introductory Sections:

Editorial on "Conflict of Interest"

Letters to the Editor

News and Comment (Includes an interesting article about "damage control" in the Hubble Telescope fiasco and mostly political, government-related issues, although this may be a product of *Science*'s location in Washington, D.C.)

Research News
Two-page entries (Some whimsical and eye-catching titles: "X Marks the Spot," "New Scissors for Cutting Chromosomes.")

Formal Sections:

"Articles" approx. seven pages each (e.g., "Comparing Brains")

"Research Articles" approx. seven pages each (e.g., "Soluble Human Complement Receptor Type 1: In Vivo Inhibitor of Complement Suppressing Post-Ischemic Myocardial Inflammation and Necrosis")

"*Reports*" *two-three pages each* (e.g., "Hind Limbs of Eocene
   Basilosaurus: Evidence of Feet in Whales" and "Identification of
   Small Clusters of Divergent Amino Acids that Mediate the Opposing
   Effects of *ras* and *Krev-1*")

End Sections:

Book Reviews

Products and Materials blurbs
Classified Ads

Along the way there is a lot of **advertising,** mostly of scientific equipment.

For the purpose of proving the point about the multiple stories of science, the most pertinent section is "Letters to the Editor." Here we see all that noisy, political, human interaction: the grand passions and small dramas, the turf wars and jealousies and indignities that play out on the stage of scientific research. For the most part, the interchanges are defensive. The writers, all of them practicing scientists, are staking claim to something and guarding it: an interpretation, a report of who made a discovery first, a reputation. Some letters answer other letters. Some try to correct impressions left by articles published in previous issues. The impression is of an ongoing dialogue, a noisy forum.

For instance, one scientist writes:

```
The News & Comment article of A concerning state-
ments made by me was misleading. I never meant to
discredit any scientist. . . .
```

Another writes:

```
I'm afraid B only compounds the problems in his
article on X with his reply to C, who was under-
standably upset that B neglected to mention the
experimental discoverers of Y.
```

Quite by chance, but not surprisingly, the first letter in this issue includes some comments about the relationship between science journalism and science:

Unfortunately, *E* demonstrates another major problem facing scientists involved in research related
to well-publicized regulatory issues: the propen-
sity of the press to make sweeping generalizations
and the frequent inability of the journalists to
go beyond superficialities in reporting science
related to complex regulatory issues.

These letters are not symptoms of the modern decline of science. We could find similar exchanges, defenses, and claims—border wars and skirmishes—in the correspondence sections of scientific journals that are centuries old. They are an inevitable, and probably a crucial, aspect of the vitality of science. Good writing is indispensable to all of them. To some of them, like letters to the editor of a learned journal, knowing how to write forcefully in defense of a position is the foremost skill.

THE SCIENTIST COAUTHORS
THE SCRIPT OF SCIENCE

In this new view of science, writing about science becomes an active and crucial part of the ongoing negotiation of the truth, not merely a recording of data. It's how you put the data together, how you narrate the story, as much as the data themselves, that matter. The only eternal aspect of science is its mutability. The truth itself is ephemeral, shifting as the story of nature grows, alters, and undergoes revision and editing, and as our own perspective on the human role in nature matures.

After all, it is dangerous to our health on this planet to continue to act as if our species of featherless bipeds is somehow placed above and apart from nature, passive spectators or controlling commanders. One of the fine legacies of twentieth-century science is that it has laid to rest the notion that nature is here for our proprietary use alone. Science, and scientists, have made clear that our fate and the fate of the larger cosmos are intimately intertwined. In this spirit, the scientist-writer is engaged in a noble and ennobling venture, expressing the humanity of science, the unity of the tale-teller and the tale that is told.

Appendix A:

Avoiding Sexist Language

Sexist language hurts everyone. Describing all scientists as male by referring to the generic type as "he" or using "man" or "mankind" to mean all of humanity at the very least implies that women are not included. To write:

```
The scientist is above all else a man of reason.
```

is to communicate a message about the exclusive sex of scientists.

The table below, taken from the *Publication Manual of the American Psychological Association*[80] may help you if you are looking for quick alternatives:

Instead of . . .	*Use . . .*
man, mankind	people, humanity, human beings, humankind, human species
man's achievements	human achievements, achievements of the human species
the average man	the average person, people in general
to man the helm, man a project	to pilot, staff a project, hire personnel, employ staff
man-machine interface	user-system interface, human-machine interface
manpower	work force, personnel, workers, human resources

But avoiding sexist language is not easy. There are no simple mechanical fixes to the problem of gendered language. Our language is designed by deep structure and by habit to have gender associations. Every word has a nuance and introduces a subtle flavor into a sentence, so there is no such thing as a neutral or "harmless" change. For

instance, in a zealous effort to avoid sexism, you may find that you repeat the phrase "he or she" or "she and he" over and over, rendering
your prose toneless and deadening. In short, it is virtually impossible
to revise a sentence without distorting the original meaning.

I am about to lead you on a relatively extensive study of this problem in language. Along the way, I hope you will learn quite a bit about
language apart from the issue of sexism itself. The problem at hand
shows how social and even political questions play out in the individual words you choose. Furthermore, learning the strategies for mentally editing your sentences even as you write them the first time provides a good model for how to think about sentence structure
generally. Finally, while it may be difficult to revise a sentence without distorting the original *meaning*, you may find you've gotten it
closer to the original *intention*.

The following list of suggestions relies heavily on work and advice
already presented by scholars who have studied the problem inten-
sively. For more information and a more complete discussion of the
problem, consult Frank and Treichler's *Language, Gender and
Professional Writing: Theoretical Approaches and Guidelines for
Nonsexist Usage*.[81] I have taken many of their points of advice in the
discussion below.

- **Change singular noun phrases and pronouns to plurals.**
  This is often the most painless way to avoid male "generic" pronouns in writing, but it can sometimes create less elegant-
  seeming sentences, since it takes the focus away from an individual actor and instead substitutes a group. The result can be
  less dramatic, though subtly so. In the following example, the
  first editing seems to suffer no damage, but the second does
  suffer a change from the specific image of a single scientist to
  the more confusing image of multiple scientists working in
  multiple labs.

  X: The biochemist must learn how the chromatograph works before he designs the methods
  section.

  OK: Biochemists must learn how the chromatograph works before they design the methods
  section.

X: When he works alone in his lab, the scientist often must struggle with uncooperative
equipment.

PERHAPS: When they work alone in their labs,
scientists must often struggle with uncooperative equipment.

Changing from singular to plural can also introduce ambiguity because the singular is often used to distinguish between two possible
antecedents, as in the following sentence:

ORIGINAL: An astronomer who collaborates with
remote data-processing sites may find that
his work is actually made more complex.

POOR CHANGE: Astronomers who collaborate with
remote data-processing sites may find that
their work is actually made more complex.

Does "their" refer to astronomers or to remote data-processing sites?

- Shift from third person pronoun (he, she, they) to the first person (I, we) or the second person (you).

X: An anthropologist often finds she is
caught between cultures.

YES: As anthropologists, we often find we are
caught between cultures.

X: As an anthropologist, you will often find
you are caught between cultures.

This can also make your prose more personal, which is not necessarily
a bad thing. However, in some instances, using the first- or second-
person pronoun is inappropriate. Furthermore, many journal editors
might find it strange, although there is nothing intrinsically wrong
with it.

- **Use "he or she" or "she or he" occasionally.**

- **Alternate masculine and feminine pronouns in appropriate contexts.**

- **Use the generic "she" where the antecedent is clearly female.**

- **Use true generics in place of "man":** "humankind," "human beings," "women and men," "people," "humanity."

- **In titles, use the title as the person to whom it belongs would use it.** Do not decide that you will change someone's title to Chairwoman or Chairperson or Chair or Ms. if they announce themselves in correspondence or in person some other way.

- **Avoid expressions you dislike.** Don't write in any way you don't want to. Writing is self-expression. If for reasons of preference, political ideology, sense, or tone you wish to use any word, do so. Don't let any group, editor, rule, or convention change the way you want to write or use words. That's the essence of owning your work and a basic principle of free speech. But also understand that there may be a cost attached to your choices, since other people are likely to take your words as seriously as you do and may disagree with your choices.

- **Respect others' preferences.** "When members of a group specify how they wish to be designated, take their arguments seriously and, if possible, respect their preferences. If a particular usage irritates you, try to find a reasonable alternative."[81]

Less Desirable Solutions to Sexist Language

The following alternatives to sexist language create other stylistic or even grammatical problems of their own.

- **Mix a plural pronoun with a singular subject noun to avoid specifying "he" or "she."**

```
A gastroenterologist studies the digestive
tract; they are not responsible for disorders
of the cardiovascular system.
```

"A gastroenterologist" is singular. Using "they," the plural pronoun, causes a disagreement in number.

- **Use alternative-gender forms requiring slashes or parentheses: s/he, he/she, his/her, hers/his, her/him, he(she), (s)he.**

- **Use "he or she" or "she or he".**

  X: He isn't a true archaeologist if he doesn't perform field work.

  OK: He or she is not a true archaeologist if he or she doesn't perform field work.

But the best way to handle this is to rewrite the sentence—e.g., "A true archaeologist must perform field work"—and avoid the whole mess.

- **Use passive voice to avoid the problem of defining an actor or agent.**

  X: In order for the astronomer to gauge fluctuations in pulsars, he will look for the slightest perturbations in signals across a broad spectrum.

  YES: In order to gauge fluctuations in pulsars, perturbations in signals across a broad spectrum will be examined by astronomers.

- **Use "who" (the indefinite pronoun) instead of "he" or "she."** This requires that you also change the sentence around to include an adjective or noun clause.

  X: If he understands chromatography, the biochemist will have an easier time setting up his experiment.

  YES: Biochemists who understand chromatography will have an easier time setting up the experiment.

- **Use "one" instead of "she" or "he."**

  X: If he understands chromatography, the biochemist will have an easier time setting up the experiment.

  PERHAPS: If one understands chromatography, one will have an easier time setting up the experiment.

As you can see, this often leads to awkward phrasings, since once you choose the "one" form, you cannot grammatically switch to he, she, you, or I.

- **Use, in order from most preferred to least preferred: "anyone," "those of us," "no one," or "readers."**

  X: When she understands the chromatograph, she will have an easier time setting up the experiment.

  YES: Anyone who understands the chromatograph will have an easier time setting up the experiment.

  PERHAPS: Those of us who understand the chromatograph have an easier time setting up the experiment.

  AWKWARD BUT ACCEPTABLE: No one who understands the chromatograph has a hard time setting up the experiment.

  AVOID IF POSSIBLE: Readers who understand the chromatograph will have an easier time setting up the experiment.

- **Depersonalize your sentence entirely by changing verbs into noun phrases.**

  Understanding chromatography insures an easier experimental setup.

The problem of sexism in language is interesting on several counts. In learning how to deal with it as a writer, you learn to analyze your language at a new level of specificity. It reminds you of the social and human aspects of writing and of questions of unbiased discourse that go hand in hand with the best qualities of scientific thought.

Appendix B:

Style Guides, Articles, Manuals, and Books on Writing about Science

Disciplinary Style Guides

American Psychological Association, *Publication Manual*, Third Edition. Washington, DC: APA, 1983.

Council of Biology Editors, *CBE Style Manual*, Fifth Edition. Betheseda, MD: CBE, 1983. Available from American Institute of Biological Sciences, 1401 Wilson Blvd., Arlington, VA 22209.

American Chemical Society, *The ACS Style Guide: A Manual for Authors and Editors.* Washington, DC: ACS, 1986. Available from ACS, 1155 Sixteenth St., N.W., Washington, D.C. 20036.

American Institute of Physics, *Style Manual,* Fourth Edition. New York: AIP, 1990. Available from AIP, 335 East 45th Street, New York, NY 10017.

American Mathematical Society, *A Manual for Authors of Mathematical Reports.* Providence, RI: AMS, 1973. Available from AMS, P.O. Box 1571, Annex Station, Providence, RI 02901.

American National Standards Institute Publications

The American National Standards Institute is dedicated to developing standards in all arenas of scientific practice. Their many publications, including the ones listed below, are available by writing to them at 1430 Broadway, New York, NY 10018.

American National Standard for the Preparation of Scientific Papers for Written or Oral Presentation. ANSI z39.16-1979. 1989.

The American National Standard for Writing Abstracts. ANSI z39.14-1979.

American National Standard Mathematical Signs and Symbols for Use in Physical Sciences and Technology. ANSI Y10.20a-1975.

American National Standard Letter Symbols for Units Used in Science and Technology. ANSI Y10.19-1969.

General Style Guides

Barclay, W., M. T. Southgate, and R. T. Mayo. *Manual for Authors and Editors: Editorial Style.* Los Altos: Lange Medical Publications/American Medical Association, 1981.

Barrass, R. *Scientists Must Write: A Guide to Better Writing for Scientists, Engineers and Students.* London: Chapman & Hall, 1978.

Bates, J. D. *Writing with Precision: How to Write So That You Cannot Possibly Be Misunderstood.* Washington, DC: Acropolis Books, 1980.

Bernstein, T. M. *The Careful Writer.* New York: Atheneum, 1966.

Collinson, R. *Abstracts and Abstracting Services.* Santa Barbara, CA: ABC Clio, Inc., 1971.

Cook, C. K. *Line by Line: How to Edit Your Own Writing.* Boston: Houghton Mifflin Company, 1985.

Cremmins, E. T. *The Art of Abstracting.* Philadelphia: ISI Press, 1982.

Day, R. A. *How to Write and Publish a Scientific Paper.* Phoenix, NY: Oryx Press, 1988.

DeBakey, L. *The Scientific Journal: Editorial Policies and Practices.* St. Louis: Mosby, 1976.

Fredette, J. M. *Handbook of Magazine Article Writing.* Cincinatti: Writers Digest Books, 1988.

Frank, F. W. and Paula A. Treichler. *Language, Gender and Professional Writing: Theoretical Approaches and Guidelines for Nonsexist Usage.* New York: The Modern Language Association, 1989.

Huth, E. J. *How to Write and Publish Papers in the Medical Sciences.* Philadelphia: ISI Press, 1982.

Jones, W. P. and M. L. K. Jones *Writing Scientific Papers and Reports.* DuBuque: Wm C. Brown Publishers, 1981.

Kevles, B. *Basic Magazine Writing.* Cincinatti: Writers Digest Books, 1987.

King, L. *Why Not Say It Clearly? A Guide to Scientific Writing.* Boston: Little Brown and Company, 1978.

Lanham, R. *Style: An Anti-Textbook.* New Haven and London: Yale UP, 1974.

Meyer, M. *The Little, Brown Guide to Writing Research Papers.* 3rd ed. New York: HarperCollins, 1994.

Maimon, F. W. *Writing in the Arts and Sciences.* Boston: Little, Brown, 1981.

Michaelson, H. B. *How to Write and Publish Engineering Papers and Reports.* Philadelphia: ISI Press, 1982.

O'Connor, S. and F. P. Woodford. *Writing Scientific Papers in English: An ELSE-Ciba Foundation Guide for Authors.* Amsterdam: Elsevier Exacerpta Medica, 1977.

Preston, Daryl W. and Eric R. Dietz. *The Art of Experimental Physics,* with software by R. H. Good. New York: Wiley, 1991.

Riggs, J. C. *Bibliography on the Preparation and Presentation of Documents Containing Scientific or Technical Information.* Paris: UNESCO, 1978.

Schoenfeld, R. *The Chemist's English.* VCH Verlagsgesellschaft mbH, Weinheim, FRG, 1986.

The Royal Society of London, *General Notes on the Presentation of Research Papers.* London: The Society, 1974.

Trelease, S. F. and E. S. Yule. *Preparation of Scientific and Technical Papers.* Baltimore: The Williams and Wilkins Company, 1930.

University of Chicago Press, *The Chicago Manual of Style,* 14th ed. Chicago: University of Chicago Press, 1993.

Woodford, F. P. *Scientific Writing for Graduate Students: A Manual on the Teaching of Scientific Writing.* NY: Rockefeller University Press, 1968.

Zinsser, W. *On Writing Well.* 2nd ed. NY: Harper & Row, 1980.

Research about Science Writing

Borman, S. C. "Communication Accuracy in Magazine Science Reporting." *Journalism Quarterly* (summer 1978): 345–6.

Bostian, L. "How Active, Passive and Nominal Styles Affect Readability of Science Writing." *Journalism Quarterly* 60 (1983): 635–40.

Bostian, L. "Comprehension of Styles of Science Writing." *Journalism Quarterly* 61 (1984): 676–8.

Gopen, G. and J. Swan. "The Science of Science Writing." *The American Scientist.* 78 (November–December 1990): 550–8.

Halloran, S. M. and A. B. Bradford. "Figures of Speech in the Rhetoric of Science and Technology." In *Essays on Classical Rhetoric and Modern Discourse,* edited by R. J. Connors, Lisa S. Ede, and Andrea A. Lunsford, 179–92 Carbondale: Southern Illinois University Press, 1984.

Prelli, L. J. *A Rhetoric of Science: Inventing Scientific Discourse.* Columbia: University of South Carolina Press, 1989.

Appendix C:

Science and Engineering Dictionaries and Encyclopedias

Alger, M. S. *Polymer Science Dictionary*. London; New York: Elsevier Applied Science, 1989.

Asimov, I. *Asimov's Biographical Encyclopedia of Science and Technology*. [The lives and achievements of 1510 great scientists from ancient times to the present chronologically arranged], 2nd rev. ed. Garden City, NY: Doubleday, 1982.

Barnhart, R. K. , Steinmetz, eds. *Hammond Barnhart Dictionary of Science*. Maplewood, NJ: Hammond, 1986.

Besancon, Robert M., ed. *Encyclopedia of Physics,* 3rd edition. New York: Van Nostrand, Rheinhold, 1985.

Bever, Michael B. *Encyclopedia of Materials Science and Engineering*. Oxford: Pergamon Press; Cambridge, MS: MIT Press, 1986.

Brook, R. J. *Concise Encyclopedia of Advanced Ceramic Materials*. Pergamon Books, 1991.

Bynum, W. F., E. J. Browne, R. Porter, eds. *Dictionary of the History of Science*. Princeton, NJ: Princeton University Press, 1981.

Carr, Donald D. NormanHerz, eds. *Encyclopedia of Materials Science and Engineering*. Cambridge, MS: MIT Press, 1989.

Cahn, R. W. and Michael B. Bever, eds. *Encyclopedia of Materials Science and Engineering*. New York: Pergamon Press, 1988.

Collocott, T. C., *Chambers Dictionary of Science and Technology*. New York, Barnes & Noble, 1978.

Cooke, Nelson ed. *Electronics and Nucleonics Dictionary* [Terms used in television, radio, medical electronics, industrial electronics, space electronics, military electronics, avionics, radar, nuclear science, and nuclear engineering.] 3d ed. New York, McGraw-Hill, 1966.

Debus, Allen G., *Marquis-Who's Who, in Science: Notable Scientists from Antiquity to the Present.* Chicago, Marquis-Who's Who, 1968.

A *Dictionary of Scientific Terms: The Foundations of Science.* Boston, Ginn, 1966.

Durbin, P. T. *Dictionary of Concepts in the Philosophy of Science.* New York: Greenwood Press, 1988.

Ecker, R. L. *Dictionary of Science & Creationism.* Buffalo, NY: Prometheus Books, 1990.

Fairbridge, R. W. and C. W. Finkl, eds. *The Encyclopedia of Soil Science.* New York: Van Nostrand, Rheinhold, 1979.

Fairbridge, R. W. and David Jablonski, eds. *The Encyclopedia of Paleontology.* New York: Van Nostrand, Rheinhold, 1979.

Goudie, Andrew, ed. *Encyclopediac Dictionary of Physicial Geography.* New York: Basil Blacwell, 1985.

Illingworth, V. *Dictionary of Computing.* 3rd ed. Oxford and New York: Oxford University Press, 1990.

International Encyclopedia of Chemical Science. Princeton, NJ: Van Nostrand, 1964.

Ito, Kiyosi, ed. *Encyclopediac Dictionary of Mathematics.* Cambridge, MA: MIT Press, 1987.

Kent, Allen and James G. Williams eds. *Encyclopedia of Computer Science and Technology*, vol. 24. Marcel Dekker, 1991.

Law, M. H., *Guide to Information Resource Dictionary System Aapplications General Concepts and Strategic Systems Planning.* Gaithersburg, MD: Information Systems Engineering Division, Institute for Computer Sciences and Technology, National Bureau of Standards, 1988.

Lerner, Rita and George L. Trigg, eds. *Encyclopedia of Physics.* Reading, MA: Addison-Wesley, 1981.

Mark, H. F. and Jacqueline I. Kroschwitz, eds. *Encyclopedia of Polymer Science and Technology*, 2nd Ed. New York: Wiley, 1985.

Marks, R. W. *The New Physics and Chemistry Dictionary and Handbook.* New York: Bantam, 1976.

Merton, R. K. and D. L. Sills, eds. *International Encyclopedia of the Social Sciences*. New York: Macmillan, 1991.

Meyers, R. A. *Encyclopedia of Physical Science and Technology*. Orlando: Academic Press, 1987.

McGraw-Hill Encyclopedia of Astronomy. New York, McGraw-Hill, 1983.

McGraw-Hill Encyclopedia of Chemistry. New York: McGraw-Hill, 1983.

McGraw-Hill Encyclopedia of Electronics and Computing. New York: McGraw-Hill, 1983.

McGrraw-Hill Encyclopedia of Energy. New York: McGraw-Hill, 1981.

McGraw-Hill Encyclopedia of Engineering, 5th ed. New York: McGraw-Hill, 1983.

McGraw-Hill Encyclopedia of Environmental Science. New York: McGraw-Hill, 1980.

McGraw-Hill Encyclopedia of Geological Science. New York: McGraw-Hill, 1978.

McGraw-Hill Encyclopedia of Oceanographic and Atmospheric Sciences. New York: McGraw-Hill, 1980.

McGraw-Hill Encyclopedia of Physics. New York: McGraw-Hill, 1983.

McGraw-Hill Encyclopedia of Science and Technology. New York: McGraw-Hill, 1987.

Newman, J. R. *The Harper Encyclopedia of Science*. New York: Harper & Row, 1967.

Nierenberg, W. A., *Encyclopedia of Earth System Science*. San Diego: Academic Press, 1991.

O'Bannon, L. S. *Dictionary of Ceramic Science and Engineering*. New York: Plenum Press, 1984.

Ogilvie, M. B. *Women in Science: Antiquity Through the Nineteenth Century* Cambridge, MA.: MIT Press, 1986. [Biographical dictionary with annotated bibliography.]

Pugh, E. *Pugh's Dictionary of Acronyms and Abbreviations in Management, Technology and Information Science*. Phoenix, AZ: Oryx Press, 1981.

Ralston, A. and E. D. Reilly, eds. *Encyclopedia of Computer Science and Engineering*, 2nd Ed. New York: Van Nostrand, Reinhold, 1983.

Ramalingom, T. *Dictionary of Instrument Science*. New York: Wiley, 1982.

Pfafflin, J. R. and E. N. Ziegler, eds. *Encyclopedia of Environmental Science and Engineering.* New York: Gordon and Breach, 1976.

Ralston, A., and C. L. Meek, eds. *Encyclopedia of Computer Science.* New York: Petrocelli/Charter, 1976.

Speck, G. E. and B. Jaffe, eds. *A Dictionary of Science Terms: The Science Reader's Companion.* New York, Hawthorn Books (1965).

Usher, G. A. *A Dictionary of Botany, Including Terms Used in Biochemistry, Soil Science and Statistics.* Princeton, NJ: Van Nostrand (1966).

Uvarov, E. B., D. R. Chapman, and A. Isaacs, *The Penguin Dictionary of Science,* 5th ed. London: Allen Lane, 1979.

Van Nostrand's Scientific Encyclopedia, 3d ed. Princeton, NJ: Van Nostrand, 1983. [Aeronautics, astronomy, botany, chemical engineering, chemistry, civil engineering, electrical engineering, electronics, geology, guided missiles, mathematics, mechanical engineering, medicine, metallurgy, meteorology, mineralogy, navigation, nuclear science & engineering, photography, physics, radio and television, statistics, zoology.]

Walker, P. M. B. *Chambers Science and Technology Dictionary.* New York: Cambridge University Press, 1988.

Wolman, B. B. *Dictionary of Behavioral Science.* New York: Van Nostrand, Reinhold, 1973.

Yule, J-D.. *Phaidon Concise Encyclopedia of Science and Technology.* New York: Facts on File, 1978.

Endnotes

1. D. Ansley. "The New World," *Discover* (September 1990): 60–69.
2. Richard Lanham, *Style: An Anti-Textbook.* (New Haven and London: Yale UP, 1974), 19.
3. F. Peter Woodford, "Sounder Thinking Through Clearer Writing," *Science 156* 3776 (12 May 1967): 743–45. Copyright 1967 by the AAAS.
4. Michael B. Green, "Superstrings," *Scientific American* (September 1986): 48–73.
5. Eric Partridge, *Usage and Abusage: A Guide to Good English,* 6th revised ed. (London: Hamish Hamilton, 1965), 357.
6. *Reimagining the World: A Critique of the New Age, Science, and Popular Culture* (Bear & Company, 1991).
7. This laboratory demonstration is based loosely on one described in R. Alexander and D. Sparlin, *Physics Laboratory Manual,* p. 19. My thanks to Professor Tom "Doc" Shannon at Rensselaer Polytechnic Institute for calling it to my attention.
8. D. W. Preston and E. R. Dietz, *The Art of Experimental Physics.* With software by R. H. Good. (New York: Wiley, 1991), 7–8.
9. Sam F. Trelease and Emma Sarepta Yule, *Preparation of Scientific and Technical Papers* (Baltimore: The Williams and Wilkins Company, 1930).
10. B. R. Nag and S. Mukhopadhyay, *J. of Physics: Condensed Matter 3* (May 1991):3757–65.
11. The American National Standards Institute, Inc. *The American National Standard for Writing Abstracts,* ANSI z39. 14-1979 (New York: 1979).
12. R. L. Collinson, *Abstracts and Abstracting Services* (Santa Barbara: ABC Clio, Inc., 1971).
13. Adapted from Apostolos P. Georgopoulos, et al., "Mental Rotation of the Neuronal Population Vector," *Science 243* (13 January 1989): 234–36. Copyright 1989 by the AAAS.
14. Based on William C. Davis, *Scientific American 256,* no. 5 (May 1987): 72.
15. E. Kunze, "Observations of Shear and Vertical Stability From a Neutrally Buoyant Float," *J. of Geophysical Research,* 95 (15 October 1990): C10, 18, 127–18, 142.
16. K. Fujita, P. Lazarovici, and G. Guroff, "Regulation of the Differentiation of PC12 Phenochromocytoma Cells," *Environmental Health Perspective 80* (1989): 127–42.

17. N. Kapuleas, "Complete Constant Mean Curvature Surfaces in Euclidean Three-Space," *Annals of Mathematics 131* (1990): 239–330.

18. Based on D. W. Deamer, "Role of Amphilic Compounds in the Evolution of Membrane. Structure on the Early Earth," *Origins of Life 17* (1986): 3–25. Reprinted by permission of Kluwer Academic Publishers.

19. Victor E. Viola and Grant J. Mathews, "The Cosmic Synthesis of Lithium, Beryllium and Boron," *Scientific American*, (May 1987).

20. Based on Daniel Jean Stanley, Tery A. Nelson, and Robert Stuckenrath, "Recent Sedimentation of the New Jersey Slope and Rise," *Science 226*, no. 4671 (12 October 1984): 125–33.

21. Based on B. Giese and E. Kührt, "Theoretical Interpretation of Infrared Measurements at Deimos in the Framework of Crater Radiation," *ICARUS 88*: 372–79.

22. Harry F. Noller and Carl R. Woese, "Secondary Structure of 16S Ribosomal RNA," *Science 212*, no. 4493 (24 April 1981): 403. Copyright 1981 by the AAAS.

23. Claudio Rebbi, "A Lattice Theory of Quark Confinement," *Scientific American* (February, 1983). Reprinted by permission of Kluwer Academic Publishers.

24. Based on Paul R. Young and H. C. Huang, "Iodide Reduction of Sulfilimines: Evidence of a Minor Role for Catalysis by Hydrogen Bonding in the Decomposition of Sulfurane Intermediates," *J. Am Chemical Society 109* (1987): 1810–13.

25. P. Molina, P. M. Fresneda, and P. Almendros, "Iminophosphorane-Mediated Synthesis of Fused Carbazoles," *Tetrahedron 47*, no. 24 (Pergamon Press, 1991): 4181.

26. G. B. Huffnagle, J. L. Yates, and M. F. Lipscomb, "Immunity to a Pulmonary Cryptococcus Neoformans Infection Requires both CD4+ and CD8+ T Cells," *J. Experimental Medicine* (The Rockefeller University Press) *173* (April 1991): 793–94.

27. Based on C. Kottmeier, "Winter Observations of the Atmosphere Over Antarctic Sea Ice," *J. of Geophysical Research 95*, no. D10 (September 20 1990):16,551–560.

28. Based on M. N. Reguiero, P. Monceau, and J-L. Hodeau, "Crushing Carbon 60 to Diamond at Room Temperature," *Nature 355* (16 Jan 1992):238.

29. Based on D. Green, et al., "The Strange Periodic Comet Machholz," *Science 247* (2 Mar 1990):1063. Copyright 1990 by the AAAS.

30. *Ibid.*, 1065.

31. Based on an illustration in Barbara E. Brown and John C. Ogden, "Coral Bleaching," *Scientific American* (January 1993). Reprinted by permission of Kluwer Academic Publishers.

32. Alan Burdick, "Faithful Witness: The Empirical Method Intrudes on Medieval Medicine," *The Sciences* (January/February 1990): 34.

33. R. M. Pirsig, *Zen and the Art of Motorcycle Maintenance*. (New York: William Morrow & Company, 1974).

34. G. Gale, "The Anthropic Principle," *Scientific American* (December 1981). Reprinted by permission of Kluwer Academic Publishers.

35. Norman H. Sleep et al., "Annihilation of Ecosystems by Large Asteroid Impacts on the Early Earth," *Nature 3242* (9 November 1989): 141.

36. This is an edited excerpt from Francis L. W. Ratnieks and P. Kirk Visscher, "Worker Policing in the Honeybee," *Nature 342* (14 December 1989): 796–97.

37. Derek York, "The Earliest History of the Earth," *Scientific American* (January 1993).

38. *Ibid.*

39. Based on Ursula Neissert, "How Many Genes to Start With? A Computer Simulation About the Origins of Life," *Origins of Life 17* (1987): 155–69.

40. Based on David J. Wald et al., "Rupture Model of the 1989 Loma Preita Earthquake from the Inversion of Strong-Motion and Broadband Teleseismic Data," *Bulletin of the Seismological Society of America 81*, no. 5 (Oct 1991): 1540–72.

41. Based on W. L. Garrison, et al., "Data Systems Requirements for Geographical Research," *Scientific Experiments for Manned Orbital Flight 4* (1965): 139–52.

42. Based on G. Hahn and M. E. Bailey, "Rapid Dynamical Evolution of a Giant Comet Chiron," *Nature 348* (8 November 1990): 132–36.

43. Derek York, "The Earliest History of the Earth," *Scientific American* (January 1993).

44. Neissert, op. cit.

45. Based on Jacob E. Trombka, et al., "The Study of Basic Physical/Biological Phenomena Under Zero-G Conditions in Earth Orbital Spacecraft," *Scientific Experiments for Manned Orbital Flight 4* (1965): 261–71.

46. J. S. Walker and C. S. Vause, "Reappearing Phases," *Scientific American* (May 1987).

47. Alwyn C. Scott, "The Solitary Wave," *The Sciences* (March/April 1990): 28–29.

48. Gary, "Where Nature Takes Its Course," *Science 83* (November 1983): 44–55.

49. Jacob Shaham, "The Oldest Pulsars in the Universe," *Scientific American* (February 1987). Reprinted by permission of Kluwer Academic Publishers.

50. James Gleick, *Chaos: The Making of a New Science* (New York: Viking, 1985).

51. *Ibid.*, 56.

52. *Ibid.*, 118.

53. *Ibid.*, 187.

54. *Ibid.,* 153.

55. Roger Bingham, "Outrageous Ardor," *Science 81* (September 1981): 55–61.

56. I have modernized spelling and punctuation in some places. Sir Isaac Newton, *Opticks* 2nd English edition, (1717).

57. Excerpted from *The Star Thrower* by Loren Eiseley (NY: Random House, 1978). Copyright© 1978 by the Estate of Loren C. Eiseley, Mabel L. Eiseley, Executrix.

58. Gleick, *Chaos: The Making of a New Science,* 175.

59. "Link Between Asthma and 'Safe' Ozone Levels Is Studied," *New York Times.* (6 August 1991): C-3.

60. Paul Davies, *Other Worlds: Space, Superspace, and the Quantum Universe* (New York: Touchstone/Simon and Schuster, 1980).

61. Nick Herbert, *Quantum Reality: Beyond the New Physics* (Garden City: Anchor Press/Doubleday, 1985).

62. *Ibid.,* 212–13.

63. Anthony E. Aveni and Helaine Silverman, "Between the Lines: Reading the Nazca Markings as Rituals Writ Large," *The Sciences* (July/August 1991): 39.

64. Malcolm W. Browne, "Computer Imitates Life—Perhaps Too Well," *New York Times,* (27 August 1991).

65. Quoted in John Peers, *1001 Logical Laws* (New York: Gordon Bennett, 1979), 41.

66. Much of the following discussion is based on work reported by G. Gopen, and J. A. Swan, in "The Science of Science Writing," *Journalism Quarterly 78* (November–December 1990): 550–58.

67. I am indebted to Dr. David Carson, my colleague at Rensselaer Polytechnic Institute, for showing me this striking method for teaching the perils of passive voice.

68. *Science* 156, no. 3776 (12 May 1967): 745.

69. Wendy L. Freedman, "The Expansion Rate and Size of the Universe," *Scientific American 267,* no. 5 (November 1992): 54.

70. Based on Tomaso Poggio and Christof Koch, "Synapses That Compute Motion," *Scientific American 256,* no. 5 (May 1987): 48

71. Stuart A. Kauffman, "Antichaos and Adaptation," *Scientific American 265,* no. 2 (August 1991): 78.

72. Alan Fine, "Transplantation in the Central Nervous System," *Scientific American 253,* no. 2 (August 1986): 55.

73. Based on Mark A. S. McMenamin, "The Emergence of Animals," *Scientific American 256,* no. 4 (April 1987): 95.

74. Based on Martin S. Hirsch and Joan C. Kaplan, "Antiviral Therapy," *Scientific American* (April 1987). Reprinted by permission of Kluwer Academic Publishers.

75. Richard P. Feynman, Robert B. Leighton, and Matthew Sands, *The Feynman Lectures on Physics* (Reading: Addison-Wesley Publishing Company, 1977).

76. Karl Popper, *The Logic of Scientific Discovery* (New York: Basic Books, 1964).

77. See R. I. G. Hughes, "Quantum Logic," *Scientific American* (October 1981): 202–13.

78. For a fine discussion of the impact of quantum physics on our view of reality, see Nick Herbert, *Quantum Reality: Beyond the New Physics* (Garden City: Anchor Press/Doubleday, 1985), and Paul Davies, *Other Worlds: Space, Superspace, and the Quantum Universe* (New York: Touchstone/Simon and Schuster, 1980).

79. C. Bazerman, "Reporting the Experiment: The Changing Account of Scientific Doings in the Philosophical Transactions of the Royal Society, 1665–1800." Privately circulated paper. 1983.

80. Third Edition. (Washington DC 1983): 45.

81. W. Frank and P. A. Treichler, *Language, Gender and Professional Writing: Theoretical Approaches and Guidelines for Nonsexist Usage.* (New York: Modern Language Association, 1989).

82. *Ibid.*, 198.

Index

Abbreviations, in literature listings, 120
Abstracts, 75–84
    descriptive abstracts, 83–84
    functions of, 75, 76–77
    indicative abstracts, 81–83
    informative abstracts, 79–81
    lab report, 54
    listing of scientific abstracts, 256–261
    placement of, 76
    time for writing of, 75–76
    writing guidelines, 77–79
ACS Style Guide, The, 116
Active voice, 217, 221
    use in research paper, 126–127
Analogy, 196–197
    formal analogy, 196
    literary analogy, 196
Animals in study, in methods and materials section, 125
Apparatus
    description of, 29–32
    drawings of, 31–32, 58
    in methods and materials section, 123–124, 125, 127
Appendices, lab report, 61–62
Argument, forms of, 151–152
Articles (*a, the*), 224
Audience
    defining, 5–6
    needs of, 6–7

for research paper, 69–70
Authority, of other scientists, 152
Author names, in literature listing, 117

Bar graphs, 138, 144
Be verbs, 216
Biased language, examples of, 157–158
Bibliography, 115–120
    abbreviations in, 120
    author names, 117
    books with editors, 118
    book titles, 118
    chapters in edited volumes, 118–119
    dissertations, 119
    government publications, 119
    journal titles, 118
    lab report, 59–60
    order of citation, 116–117
    reports, 119
    titles of papers, 117–118
    unpublished material, 119–120
Biology, style manual for, 116
Book titles, in literature listing, 118

CBE Style Manual, 116
Chapters of books, in literature listing, 118–119

Charts, 141, 145–146

Chemicals, in methods and materials section, 124–125

Chemistry, style manual for, 116

Citations. *See* Literature citations

Clauses, 225–226
  nested clauses, avoiding, 225–226
  subordinate clause, 225
  sub-subordinate clause, 225

Computer
  versus lab notebook, 35–37
  use as lab notebook, 38

Computer flowcharts, 146–147

Conceit, 198

Conclusion of essay, 186–189
  to set dramatic mood, 188
  summary, 187–188
  with visionary quotation, 188–189

Conclusion of research paper, 164–173
  comparison to others in field, 167–168
  to define unanswered questions, 168–169
  directions for future research in, 170
  lab report, 58–59
  research paper, 68–69
  to restrict/expand results, 165–167, 171
  statement of, 164–165

Conditional language, in writing about science, 14–17, 166

Conjunctions
  coordinating conjunctions, 226
  transitional phrase conjunctions, 226

Contextualization, in introduction, 87–88

Coordinating conjunctions, 226

Data analysis
  in lab notebook, 37–39

in results section, 133–134

Data interpretation
  in lab notebook, 43–46
  lab report, 57–58
  research paper, 68

Data presentation, in results section, 132–133

Data sheets, preparation of, 33–35

Decimals, 236

Deduction, 153–154

Definition, as scientific topic, 92

Definition of terms, 228–234
  glossary of lab report, 60–61
  importance of, 228–229, 234
  in introduction, 88, 89
  method for, 229–233
  research paper, 68

Descriptive abstracts, 83–84

Descriptiveness, and writing about science, 13–14

Details, in essays, 194

Dictionaries, scientific, 265–268

Dimensions, numbers in, 237–238

Dissertations, in literature listing, 119

Dramatic lead, 182–183

Drawing conclusions
  in lab notebook, 47
  in lab report, 57

Drawings, 141, 147–148
  of apparatus, 31–32
  in lab notebook, 39–43
  lab report, 58
  in methods and materials section, 125

Edited books, in literature listing, 118

Editing, 201–208
  deep editing, steps in, 206–207
  examples of, 202–204
  nature of, 204–206

Encyclopedias, scientific, 265–268

Equations, format for, 238–239
Error calculations, in lab notebook, 46
Essays, 180–198
    analogies, 196–197
    conceit, 198
    conclusions, 186–189
    details, 194
    leads, 181–186
    literary essay, 192–193
    metaphors, 197–198
    point of view, 195–196
    topics for, 189–193
Evidence, arrangement of, 151
Executive summary
    elements of, 83–84
    lab report, 54
Explanations, in introduction, 87, 88–89
Expository lead, 181–182

Flowcharts, 141, 146–147
Formal analogy, 196
Formulas, format for, 238–239
Future research, recommendations for, 170–171

Glossary, lab report, 60–61
Government publications, in literature listing, 119
Graphs, 141, 144–145
    bar graphs, 138, 144
    in lab notebook, 39–43
    line graphs, 145, 146
    scatter graphs, 144–145

Hazards, in methods and materials section, 127
Hypotheses/models/theories (HMT), 104–111
    evaluation of, 104–105
    placement in research paper, 109–110
    wording of, 105–109
Hypothesis
    ex post facto, 103
    formulation of, 101–102
    nature of, 101
    relationship to research problem, 102–103
    statement, lab report, 56
    testing, and data interpretation, 44, 45–46
    in title, 71–72

Indefinite pronouns, 254
Indexes, general, 256
Indicative abstracts, 81–83
Induction, 152–153
Informative abstracts, 79–81
Interpretation of results, 150–163
    coordination of presentation of data with, 158–163
    deduction in, 153–154
    forms of argument in, 151–152
    induction in, 152–153
    logical language in, 156
    most certain to least certain order in, 154–155
    order of presentation, 152
Introduction of lab report, 55–56
Introduction of research report, 85–97
    broad approach in, 85–86
    to contextualize, 87–88
    to define, 88, 89
    as explanation, 87, 88–89
    functions of, 85
    narrow approach in, 86
    and topic of paper, 92–94
    writing checklist for, 97
Introductory remarks, research paper, 68
Introductory sentences. *See* Leads

Jargon, situations for use of, 233–234

Journal titles, in literature listing, 118

Lab notebook, 21–47
  assembly of apparatus, description of, 29–32
  bound notebook for, 25–26
  versus computer, 35–37, 38
  data analysis, 37–39
  data interpretation, 43–46
  data sheets, 33–34
  drawing conclusions, 47
  error calculations, 46
  functions of, 23–24
  guidelines for recording data, 34–35
  ink, use of, 26
  introducing experiment, 27
  compared to lab report, 49–50
  materials, description of, 27–29
  method/procedure of experiment, 32–33
  parts of, 25
  style for, 26
  tables/graphs, 39–43
Lab report
  abstract, 54
  appendices, 61–62
  bibliography, 59–60
  conclusion, 58–59
  data interpretation, 57–58
  drawings, 58
  executive summary, 54
  glossary, 60–61
  hypothesis statement, 56
  introduction, 55–56
  compared to lab notebook, 49–50
  letter of transmittal, 50–51, 52
  literature review, 57
  methods section, 57
  table of contents, 54–55

  title/cover page, 51, 53–54
Leads, 181–186
  dramatic lead, 182–183
  expository lead, 181–182
  oblique lead, 183–186
  personal lead, 186
Letter of transmittal, lab report, 50–51, 52
Line graphs, 145, 146
Lists, numbers in, 238
Literary analogy, 196
Literary essay, 192–193
Literature citations, 112–120
  bibliography, 115–120
  style manuals for protocols, 116–117
  in text citations, 113–115
Literature review, lab report, 57
Literature search, research paper, 68
Logical relations, words/phrases for, 156, 166

Manual for Authors of Mathematical Reports, A, 116
Materials, description in lab notebook, 27–29
Mathematical operations, format for, 237
Mathematics, style manual for, 116
Measures, numbers in, 237–238
Metaphors, 197–198
Methods and materials section, 121–130
  components of, 121–122
  method, nature of, 122–123
  writing guidelines, 123–130
Methods section
  lab notebook, 32–33
  lab report, 57
Models. See also Hypotheses/models/theories (HMT)
  nature of, 100–101

Nominalization, 222–223
Numbers, 235–239
    decimals, 236
    equations, 238–239
    formulas, 238–239
    fractions, 236
    large numbers, 236
    in lists, 238
    for mathematical operations, 237
    measures/dimensions, 237–238
    numeral for, rule for use of, 235
    plurals, 236
    range of numbers, 237
    for time periods, 238
    words for, rule for use of, 235

Object of sentence, 210, 216
Oblique lead, 183–186
Outline
    components of, 8
    for research paper, 63–64
    for term papers, 175–176

Paper titles, in literature listing,
    117–118
Passive voice, 216–220, 254
    example of use of, 125–126
    in scientific writing, 12–13
Peer review, 69
Personal lead, 186
Persuasion, 152
Photographs, 138
    best use of, 141
    in lab report, 58
Physics, style manual for, 116
Pie chart, 138
Plurals, numbers, 236
Point of view
    essays, 195–196
    and science, 243–244
    term papers, 179
Prewriting, 65, 66, 91–93

    to define problem, 91–93
    to formulate hypothesis, 101–103
Procedure, in methods and materi-
    als section, 128–129
Publication Manual, APA, 116

Qualitative information
    in data interpretation, 44–45
    in results section, 131–132
Quotations, in conclusion of essay,
    188–189

Relative pronouns, 224–225
Reports, in literature listing, 119
Research paper
    abstracts, 75–84
    audience for, 69–70
    conclusions, 68–69
    data interpretation, 68
    definition of terms, 68
    and hypotheses/models/theories
        (HMT), 104–111
    interpretation of results, 150–163
    introduction, 85–97
    introductory remarks, 68
    literature citations, 112–120
    literature search, 68
    methods and materials section,
        121–130
    newness of topic, 95–97
    outline, 63–64
    parts of, 67
    preparation to writing, 65, 66
    results, 131–134
    scope of, 65, 67
    style of, 65
    subject of, 67
    title, 71–74
    topic. *See* Research problem
Research problem
    defining problem, 91–93
    newness of, 91, 95–97

prewriting on, 91–93
relating topic to theory, 93–94
types of problems in science,
    92–93
Research report
conclusions, 164–173
visual material, 136–149
Results, 131–134. *See also* Interpre-
    tation of results
writing guidelines, 131–134
Review, of research papers, 69
Revising. *See also* Editing
importance of, 200–201
order of information, 97

Scatter graphs, 144–145
Sentences
active and passive voice, 216–222
basic parts of, 210
clauses, 225–226
placement of new information in,
    215–216
subject-verb-object structure,
    211–213
syntax guidelines, 211
transitional words/phrases,
    213–215
use of words, 223–225
Sexist language, 250–255
alternatives to masculine terms,
    250–253
and grammatical issues, 253–255
Social sciences, style manual for,
    116
Statistical methods, in data interpre-
    tation, 43–44
Style
conservative, 18–19
journalistic, 19–20
of research paper, 65
Style Manual, AIP, 116
Style manuals
general, 263–264

for sciences, 116, 262–263
Subjects, in methods and materials
    section, 124
Subject of sentence, 210, 216
Subordinate clause, 225
Sub-subordinate clause, 225
Summary, conclusion of essay,
    187–188
Symbols, fonts or hand lettered, 239
Syntax, guidelines for, 211

Table of contents, lab report, 54–55
Tables, 141, 142–143
guidelines for composition of,
    142
in lab notebook, 40, 43
parts of, 143
Term papers, 174–180
components of, 175
narrowing topic, 179
nature of material in, 176–177
point of view, 179
researching topic, 178–179
topics for, 178, 189–193
writing guidelines, 180
Theories. *See also* Hypotheses/mod-
    els/theories (HMT)
nature of, 99–100
relating topic to current theory,
    92, 93–94
Time periods, numbers for, 238
Title, 71–74
elements to avoid, 73–74
elements of, 71–73
Title/cover page, lab report, 51,
    53–54
Titles of works, bibliographic cita-
    tion of, 117–118
Tone, of research papers, 69–70
Topic
for term papers, 178–179,
    189–193
See also Research problem

Transitional words/phrases, 213–215
　　to add conditions, 214–215
　　for comparing and contrasting,
　　　213–214
　　for example, 213–214
　　for logical relationships, 214
　　to show sequence, 214–215
　　for summarizing, 213–214
　　for temporal relationships, 214

Uncertainties, in conclusions,
　　168–169
Unpublished material, in literature
　　listing, 119–120

Verbs, 210
　　be verbs, 216
　　nominalization, 222–223
　　and sentence structure, 211–213
　　strong verbs, 216
　　in title, 72–73
Visual material, 136–149
　　charts, 141, 145–146
　　computer flowcharts, 141,
　　　146–147
　　drawings, 141, 147–148

functions of, 136, 148–149
graphs, 141, 144–145
protocols for use of, 137
to simplify information, 139–140
tables, 141, 142–143
Voice, 216–222, 217
　　active voice, 126–127, 221
　　passive voice, 12–13, 125–126,
　　　216–220, 254

Writing about science, 241–249
　　audience for, 5–7
　　communication flow in, 23
　　complexity of, 11–12
　　conditional language in, 14–17
　　conservative style in, 18–19
　　as creative endeavor, 3–4
　　and descriptiveness, 13–14
　　and goals of writing, 6
　　history of, 246–247
　　idols of, 11
　　passive voice in, 12–13
　　presentation of new in, 90–91,
　　　95–97
　　reporting mode for, 19–20
　　scope of topics in, 247–249